THE COMPLETE MASTER CHEFS

ARABELLA BOXER

PAT CHAPMAN

CLARE CONNERY

JILL DUPLEIX

PAUL GAYLER

VALENTINA HARRIS

ELINOR KLIVANS

AGLAIA KREMEZI

KAREN LEE

ROWLEY LEIGH

ALASTAIR LITTLE

BRUNO LOUBET

RICHARD OLNEY

JACKI PASSMORE

GORDON RAMSAY

PAUL AND JEANNE RANKIN

MICHEL ROUX

JANEEN SARLIN

MICHELE SCICOLONE

YAN-KIT SO

RICK STEIN

ROGER VERGÉ

CAROLE WALTER

ANTONY WORRALL THOMPSON

THE COMPLETE MASTER CHEFS

240 recipes from the world's top chefs and cookery writers

PHOTOGRAPHY BY SIMON WHEELER

TED SMART

First published in 1997 by
George Weidenfeld & Nicolson
The Orion Publishing Group
Orion House
5 Upper St Martin's lane
WC2H 9EA

This edition produced for
The Book People Ltd
Catteshall Manor, Catteshall Lane
Godalming, Surrey, GU7 1UU

ISBN: 0 297 82234 9

Designed by Paul Cooper Design and The Senate
Edited by Anne Johnson
Photographs by Simon Wheeler
Food styling by Joy Davies
Index by Hilary Bird

contents

ARABELLA BOXER is half-Scottish, half-American. She lived in the north of Scotland as a child, but moved to London after the Second World War, and spent summer holidays with her American grandparents in Maine. She lived in New York, Paris and Rome before settling in London after her marriage to Mark Boxer, the cartoonist and editor. She was food writer and, latterly, food editor of English *Vogue* for 18 years. She has published ten books, and has won both André Simon and Glenfiddich Awards for food writing. She is currently Vice President of the Guild of Food Writers.

PAT CHAPMAN's passion for curry was virtually inherited, his ancestors having been in India for 200 years. He founded the world-renowned Curry Club in Surrey in 1982 and it was not long before he set up a national network of curry restaurant reporters, which led to his regular publishing of the highly successful *Good Curry Restaurant Guide*. Pat frequently broadcasts on television and radio, and holds regular cookery courses. He is a consultant chef to a number of UK Indian restaurants and he has appeared as a guest chef for Hilton Hotels and Selfridges Restaurant in London, as well as at the celebrated Taj Mahal Intercontinental hotel in Bombay. Pat has written 18 books, which have sold approaching 1 million copies, including such best sellers as *The Curry Club 250 Favourite Curries and Accompaniments*, *The Balti Curry Cookbook*, *Curry Club Indian Restaurant Cookbook* and *Quick and Easy Curries* for BBC Books. His repertoire also includes successful books on Thai, Chinese, Bangladeshi and Middle Eastern cookery.

CLARE CONNERY is one of Ireland's leading food experts: author, journalist, broadcaster, chef and restaurateur. She has owned her own cookery school, restaurant and delicatessen, and as food correspondent for BBC Northern Ireland for 15 years, she wrote and presented many food programmes, including six series of *Cook with Clare*. She is the author of a number of books, including *In An Irish Country Kitchen*, *The Salad Book*, *Quick and Easy Salads*, *Store Cupboard Cookery* and *The Irish Cook Book*. Clare currently runs a food consultancy and catering company from bases in Belfast and London.

JILL DUPLEIX is one of Australia's leading cookery writers. She is the author of seven cookbooks, including *New Food*, which won the Australian Publishers Award for best-designed book of 1994, and *Allegro al dente*, a collection of pasta recipes accompanied by a CD of some of the world's best-loved opera arias. She is also the food editor of *The Sydney Morning Herald* and *Elle Australia*, and is a popular food commentator on radio and television. She lives on the edge of the Pacific Ocean in Sydney, where she draws inspiration from the tangy, tropical tastes of the foods of the Pacific Rim.

PAUL GAYLER was one of the first chefs in Britain to craft truly innovative dishes for vegetarians, for which he built an enviable reputation while he was head chef at Inigo Jones restaurant in Covent Garden. After 23 years dedicated to the kitchens of some of the most respected restaurants in London, he is now executive chef at The Lanesborough Hotel at Hyde Park Corner. His cooking for The Conservatory restaurant there combines classical disciplines with Oriental overtones. His first book, *Virtually Vegetarian*, was published in 1995 and his second, *Great Value Gourmet*, in 1996. He has appeared on HTV's *Green Grow the Dishes* series and also on BBC-TV's *Hot Chefs*.

VALENTINA HARRIS grew up in Rome, where she gained diplomas in teaching and cooking at the Scuola di Alta Cucina Cordon Bleu School. She moved to London in 1976. In 1984 Valentina published her first cookery book, *Perfect Pasta*, which has since been translated into six languages. She has written a further 12 books, including *Recipes from an Italian Farmhouse* (1989), *Valentina's Complete Italian Cookery Course* (1992) and *Valentina's Italian Regional Cookery*, which accompanied a BBC-TV series of the same name. Valentina regularly appears on television and radio, and contributes articles on various aspects of Italian cuisine to many newspapers and magazines. She is in great demand at food events and has given innumerable cookery demonstrations throughout Europe, in Australia, New Zealand, America and Japan.

ELINOR KLIVANS has won numerous awards for her baking. A native Floridian and graduate of the University of Florida with an honours degree in English and education, she has studied under many noted chefs, both at La Varenne cookery school in Paris and at the International Pastry Arts Center under Albert Kumin (formerly pastry chef at the Four Seasons restaurant in New York and at the White House). Her many roles have included those of cookery teacher, demonstration cook and bakery consultant, and for 12 years she worked as a dessert chef at Peter Ott's restaurant in Camden, Maine. Her articles have been published in several magazines, including *Bon Appétit*, and she has appeared on television and radio shows across the United States. Elinor's book *Bake and Freeze Desserts*, published in 1994, was nominated for a Julia Child Award for first cookbook. She is currently working on *Bake and Freeze Chocolate Desserts*.

AGLAIA KREMEZI is a journalist and photographer with a regular column in the Athens Sunday newspaper *Kyriakatiki Eleftherotypia*. She also contributes to the *Los Angeles Times*. Born in Athens, she has always been passionate about cooking and collects cookbooks and recipes from all over the world. She has studied the history of Greek and Mediterranean food in detail and has taken part in conferences on food in several countries. Her book, *The Foods of Greece*, published in the USA in 1993, won a Julia Child Award for first cookbook. A compilation of her food columns, *Recipes and Stories* (1993), became a best-seller in Greece and was followed by a second collection entitled *Garlic, Honey and Mandrake*. She has written two other cookbooks in English: *Mediterranean Pantry* (1994) and *Mediterranean Hot* (1996).

KAREN LEE is well known in the United States as an author, caterer and teacher, appearing frequently on national and local radio and television shows. She has owned and operated her own cooking school in New York City since 1972, and is noted as a top caterer by the *Zagat Guide*, *New York Magazine* and *New York Times*. She has written three books on Chinese cooking, and her latest book, *The Occasional Vegetarian*, is now in its third printing.

ROWLEY LEIGH was born in Manchester in 1950. He lived in various parts of the UK as a child, including five years in Northern Ireland. He read English at Cambridge University but left without a degree. He then tried country life and farming for a few years before coming to London in 1976. Falling into cooking because he needed a job in a hurry, he spent eighteen months at Joe Allen's in Covent Garden before going to work for Roux restaurants in 1979. He was a cook at Le Gavroche, a pâtissier, a meat buyer and finally head chef at Le Poulbot for three years. Rowley Leigh opened Kensington Place in London's Notting Hill with Nick Smallwood and Simon Slater in 1987 and is still there. In 1995 he became a columnist on *The Guardian*.

ALASTAIR LITTLE taught himself to cook and opened his own eponymous restaurant in London's Soho in 1985. His second restaurant, Alastair Little Lancaster Road, opened early in 1996 in Notting Hill. In the summer he also runs La Cacciata cookery school in Orvieto, Italy. He has co-authored two books with Richard Whittington: *Keep It Simple*, which won the Glenfiddich Food Book of the Year Award in 1994, and *Food of the Sun* (1995). They also contribute a column to the *Daily Mail* on Saturdays. Alastair Little has made a number of television appearances: on BBC-TV's *The Good Food Show* and *Ready Steady Cook*, among others.

BRUNO LOUBET was born in the Bordeaux region of southwestern France. After working in restaurants in Brussels and Paris, Bruno came to London and worked for Pierre Koffman at La Tante Claire, before becoming head chef at a restaurant called Gastronome One, where he was awarded the title Young Chef of the Year 1985 by The Good Food Guide. After a spell with Raymond Blanc at Le Manoir Aux Quat'Saisons near Oxford, Bruno returned to London, to the Four Seasons at the Inn on the Park Hotel, where within one year he had earned his first Michelin star at the age of 29. He also found time to complete his first book, *Cuisine Courante*. In 1992 Bruno opened Bistrot Bruno in London's Soho, which was named Restaurant of the Year 1994 by *The Times*. With the opening of his new restaurant, L'Odéon, in late 1995, he has appeared in *Vogue*, *Harper's & Queen* and numerous other magazines and newspapers. Bruno has also published a second book of recipes, *Bistrot Bruno: Cooking From L'Odéon*.

RICHARD OLNEY was born in Iowa and studied at the University of Iowa and at Brooklyn Museum Art School. He has lived in France since 1951, and moved to Provence in 1961. He writes about food and wine for magazines in America and Britain, and between 1963 and 1980 he was a regular contributor to *Cuisine et Vins de France* and *La Revue du Vin de France*. He was the consultant editor of the 27-volume Time-Life series, *The Good Cook*, and is the author of many books, including *The French Menu Cookbook*, *Simple French Food*, *Yquem*, *Ten Vineyard Lunches*, *Romanée-Conti*, *Provence The Beautiful Cookbook* and *Lulu's Provençal Table*.

JACKI PASSMORE is the author of over 20 Asian cookbooks, including the award-winning *Asia the Beautiful Cookbook* and *The Encyclopedia of Asian Food and Cooking*. For 12 years she worked as a food writer in Hong Kong, travelling extensively to study the cuisines of Asia. She now lives in Brisbane, Australia, where she continues her career as a food writer and restaurant consultant, and runs her cooking school, Jacki Passmore Cooks.

GORDON RAMSAY began his career in cooking by working for Marco Pierre White and at Le Gavroche in London before spending two and a half years in Paris, under Guy Savoy and Joel Robuchon. At the age of 26 he returned to London to open his own restaurant, Aubergine, in October 1993. His light, subtle and sophisticated cooking earned him his first Michelin star in 1995. He has appeared on a number of TV programmes, including BBC2's *Food and Drink*, and his book, *A Passion for Flavour*, was published in September 1996.

PAUL AND JEANNE RANKIN have travelled together through Asia, experiencing at first hand many of the cuisines which make extensive use of chillies and spices. They learned the classical culinary skills at Le Gavroche in London, and then worked in a number of restaurants in Canada and the USA. In 1989 they returned to Northern Ireland, Paul's birthplace, and opened their own restaurant, Roscoff, in Belfast; it became the first restaurant in Northern Ireland to be awarded a Michelin star, in 1991. Their 15-part TV series, *Gourmet Ireland*, was shown throughout Ireland and the UK in 1994, and has also been screened in the USA and Canada, Australia, New Zealand, Hong Kong and Japan. There have since been two more series, accompanied by the books *Gourmet Ireland 1* and *2*. Their first collection of spicy recipes, *Hot Food Cool Jazz*, was published in 1994. They have also appeared on *Ready Steady Cook* for BBC 2 and *Curious Cooks* for BBC Radio 4.

MICHEL ROUX's delicious desserts have made him famous throughout the world. He began his career as a pastry chef apprentice at the Pâtisserie Loyal in Paris, and then worked for the British Embassy in Paris and for Mlle Cecile de Rothschild. With his brother Albert, he opened Le Gavroche in London in 1967. The Waterside Inn at Bray in Berkshire opened in 1972 and since then has consistently won many major international gastronomy awards. Michel Roux was awarded Meilleur Ouvrier de France en Pâtisserie in 1976 and received the Chevalier de l'Ordre National du Mérite in 1986 and the Chevalier de l'Ordre des Arts et des Lettres in 1990. With Albert, he has written several books, including *New Classic Cuisine* (1983), *Roux Brothers on Pâtisserie* (1986), *At Home with the Roux Brothers* (1988), which accompanied a BBC television series, *French Country Cooking* (1989) and *Cooking for Two* (1991). He published *Desserts – A Lifelong Passion* in 1994.

JANEEN SARLIN is the owner and president of Cooking with Class, a New York City catering company and cooking school established in 1975. She is a syndicated food columnist, gives lectures and teaches cooking classes across the United States and produces a weekly radio programme, *The Seasonal Chef*. Janeen is a member of the International Association of Culinary Professionals, The American Institute of Wine and Food, The James Beard Foundation, Les Dames d'Escoffier, The New York Woman's Culinary Alliance and The International Association of Women Chefs. Raised on a dairy farm in Minnesota, she learned the basic traditions and secrets of roasting from her grandmother and mother. Janeen is the author of *Lunches To Go* (1984) and *Food From An American Farm* (1991).

MICHELE SCICOLONE is a writer who specializes in food, wine and travel. Her latest book, *La Dolce Vita*, is a collection of recipes for 'life's sweet pleasures', Italian desserts. It was nominated as Best Dessert Book of 1994 by the International Association of Cooking Professionals. Her previous book, *The Antipasto Table*, was nominated as Best Italian Cookbook of 1991 by the James Beard Foundation. Michele is also the author of two books on fish cookery. Michele writes for *The New York Times*, *Gourmet*, *Food & Wine* and *Eating Well* magazines and is a contributing editor to *Wine Enthusiast* magazine and the *Berlitz Travellers' Guide to Northern Italy*. She teaches cooking at schools around the United States and has appeared on national television on CBS *Morning Show*, *Good Morning America* and *The Home Show* as well as many local television and radio programmes.

YAN-KIT SO was born in China and grew up in Hong Kong. She settled in London in the early 1970s, and has also lived in the United States, India and France. She has given demonstrations at The Women's Institute and taught at notable cookery schools such as Leith's School of Food and Wine and the Cordon Bleu Cookery School in London. Yan-kit So has written a handful of books on Chinese food and culture, including *Wok Cookbook* (1985), *Classic Food of China* (1992) and *Yan-Kit's Classic Chinese Cookbook* (1984), which won the two premier British awards for cookbooks: the Glenfiddich Food Book of the Year and the André Simon Award.

RICK STEIN and his wife Jill opened The Seafood Restaurant at Padstow, Cornwall, in 1975, as a small, harbourside bistro selling locally caught fresh fish. In the past 20 years it has become one of the best-known restaurants in the UK, with an international reputation; it has won awards from all the major food guides. Rick Stein's first cookery book, *English Seafood Cookery*, was the Glenfiddich Food Book of the Year in 1989. He writes occasional pieces for national newspapers, among them *The Sunday Times*, the *Independent on Sunday* and the *Independent*. Rick Stein's BBC-TV series *Taste of the Sea* was one of 1995's most successful television cookery programmes. Nominated for a number of awards, it won the Glenfiddich Television Programme of the Year Award. It was accompanied by a book of the same name, which was chosen as the André Simon Food Book of 1995.

ROGER VERGÉ has become synonymous with the food and sunshine of Provence, where he opened his Restaurant du Moulin de Mougins in 1969. His first book, *Ma Cuisine du Soleil* (1978), was translated into English as *Cuisine of the Sun*, and Cuisine du Soleil is the name of his cooking school in Mougins. He is also the author of *Entertaining in the French Style* (1986) and *Roger Vergé's Vegetables* (1994). Roger Vergé was awarded the lifelong title Meilleur Ouvrier de France in 1972 and became a Chevalier de la Légion d'Honneur in 1987.

CAROLE WALTER studied patisserie and the culinary arts with notable chefs in France, Austria, Italy and Denmark. She is a charter member of the International Association of Culinary Professionals and past president of the New York Association of Cooking Teachers. A teacher, writer and consultant, she has frequently appeared on American television. She is the author of a number of books, including *Great Cakes*, which won the Best Baking Book of 1992 award from The James Beard Foundation.

ANTONY WORRALL THOMPSON first made his mark on the London restaurant scene in 1981 when he opened Ménage à Trois in Knightsbridge. Reflecting the vogue of the time for small helpings of beautifully presented food, Ménage à Trois served only starters and puddings; it led to Antony's first book, *The Small and Beautiful Cookbook*. He is now the creative force behind a number of London's top restaurants, among them dell'Ugo, Bistrot 190, The Atrium, Palio and Drones. He has written several more books, including *Modern Bistrot Cookery*, *30-Minute Menus*, based on his column in *The Sunday Times*, and *Supernosh*, written with Malcolm Gluck, in which light, modern food is matched with easily available wines. In 1987 he was awarded the 'chef's Oscar' – Meilleur Ouvrier de Grande Bretagne (MOGB) – one of only five chefs to have merited this lifelong title. Familiar to viewers of BBC-TV's *Ready Steady Cook*, he has also appeared on *Food and Drink* and *Hot Chefs*, among others.

soups

Valentina Harris

BAKED FENNEL SOUP

6 LARGE FENNEL BULBS, OR 8 SMALLER ONES, WASHED
    AND CUT INTO THIN SECTIONS, DISCARDING THE
    HARD EXTERIOR PARTS
100 G/3½ OZ UNSALTED BUTTER
SALT AND FRESHLY GROUND BLACK PEPPER
200 G/7 OZ FRESH, SOFT CHEESE (BEL PAESE,
    CAMEMBERT, BRIE), SLICED
9 SLICES OF CIABATTA BREAD, CUBED
2 TABLESPOONS FRESHLY GRATED PARMESAN CHEESE

SERVES 4

Preheat the oven to 160°C/325°F/Gas Mark 3.

Boil the fennel in enough salted water to cover, until tender. Drain, reserving the liquid. Thoroughly butter a large ovenproof dish and arrange half the fennel in the dish. Season lightly, then scatter half the cheese over the fennel.

Fry the cubes of bread in half the remaining butter, until golden. Sprinkle half the fried bread cubes over the fennel and cheese. Top with another layer of fennel, salt and pepper, cheese and bread cubes. Pour the reserved liquid over the top. Leave to settle for a few minutes, then sprinkle with the Parmesan and dot with the remaining butter. Bake for about 35 minutes. Serve piping hot.

I like to follow this soup with a platter of different kinds of salami served with two or three types of bread, and then a tray of oven-baked apples.

Arabella Boxer

CABBAGE SOUP WITH CROÛTES

600 ML/1 PINT CHICKEN STOCK (PAGE 374)
675 G/1½ LB CABBAGE (WEIGHED AFTER TRIMMING),
   THICKLY SLICED
40 G/1½ OZ BUTTER
1 TABLESPOON SUNFLOWER OIL
2 ONIONS, CHOPPED
1 LARGE POTATO, SLICED
SEA SALT AND BLACK PEPPER
300 ML/½ PINT MILK

GARNISH

6 SLICES OF DAY-OLD COUNTRY BREAD, ABOUT
   1 CM/½ INCH THICK, HALVED IF LARGE
25 G/1 OZ BUTTER

SERVES 6

Put the stock into a large saucepan, add the cabbage, bring to the boil, then simmer for 6 minutes. Drain, reserving the stock.

In a clean pan, heat the butter and oil and fry the onion gently for 10 minutes. Add the sliced potato and cook for a further 3 minutes. Pour on the hot cabbage stock and simmer for 25 minutes.

Add the cooked cabbage and 600 ml/1 pint water. Bring back to the boil and simmer for 10 minutes. Season to taste with salt and pepper.

Leave to cool for 5 minutes, then lift out about 325 g/12 oz of the cooked cabbage. Process or chop this cabbage and keep warm. Pour the rest of the soup into a liquidizer or food processor and blend with the milk. Reheat and adjust the seasoning to taste.

To serve, toast the bread and spread lightly with butter. Pile the chopped cabbage on the croûtes, allowing about 2 tablespoons for each one. Serve the soup hot, in broad soup plates or bowls, with a croûte in each.

Arabella Boxer

GRILLED AUBERGINE SOUP
with peppers and tomatoes

1 LARGE AUBERGINE

2 RED PEPPERS

3 TABLESPOONS SUNFLOWER OIL

1 BUNCH OF SPRING ONIONS, SLICED

3 BEEFSTEAK TOMATOES, SKINNED AND CUT INTO
  QUARTERS

500 ML/16 FL OZ CHICKEN STOCK (PAGE 374)

2 TABLESPOONS FRESH ORANGE JUICE

2 TABLESPOONS FRESH LIME JUICE

SEA SALT AND BLACK PEPPER

1½ TABLESPOONS CHOPPED FRESH CORIANDER

SERVES 6

Grill the aubergine and peppers under a hot grill, turning frequently, until the peppers are charred evenly all over, about 12 minutes. Remove the peppers, leaving the aubergine under the grill for a further 12–15 minutes or until soft when squeezed.

Leave the peppers and aubergines until they are cool enough to handle. Skin the peppers, discarding the interior membrane and seeds, and chop roughly. Cut the aubergine in half lengthways, scoop out the flesh with a spoon and chop roughly.

Heat the oil in a small frying pan and cook the sliced spring onions for 3 minutes.

Put the tomatoes into a liquidizer or food processor and process to a rough pulp. Add the chopped peppers and aubergine and process again. Add the spring onions, chicken stock, orange and lime juice, salt and pepper and process once more. Chill for at least 1 hour.

Serve sprinkled with coriander.

Arabella Boxer

CORN SOUP
with cherry tomatoes

4 EARS OF SWEETCORN, OR 400 G/14 OZ FROZEN
   SWEETCORN KERNELS
1 LITRE/1¾ PINTS CHICKEN STOCK (PAGE 374)
25 G/1 OZ BUTTER
1 TABLESPOON SUNFLOWER OIL
2 BUNCHES OF SPRING ONIONS, WHITE PARTS ONLY,
   SLICED
SEA SALT AND BLACK PEPPER
¼ TEASPOON DRIED CHILLI FLAKES (OPTIONAL)

GARNISH

6 CHERRY TOMATOES, CUT INTO 3–4 THICK SLICES
1 TABLESPOON OLIVE OIL

SERVES 6

Slice the kernels off the ears of corn, using a small sharp knife. Bring the stock to the boil and set aside.

Heat the butter and oil in a large saucepan over low heat and cook the sliced spring onions for 3 minutes, then add the corn kernels. Cook gently for 3 minutes, then pour on the hot stock, adding salt, pepper and chilli flakes to taste. Bring to the boil, then simmer gently, half covered, for 15 minutes, or 10 minutes if using frozen corn.

Leave to cool slightly, then purée in a liquidizer or food processor. Return to the pan to reheat; adjust the seasoning to taste.

Brush the cherry tomato slices with olive oil and quickly brown in a nonstick pan over high heat. Pour the soup into individual bowls and serve hot, garnished with the tomato slices.

Alternatively, omit the chilli flakes when cooking the soup and omit the tomato garnish; instead add a spoonful of cold salsa fresca (page 375) to each bowl of hot soup.

Antony Worrall Thompson

PROVENÇAL FISH SOUP

Paul & Jeanne Rankin

HOT AND SOUR PRAWN SOUP

(Tom Yam Gung)

6 TABLESPOONS GOOD OLIVE OIL
2 LEEKS, FINELY SLICED
4 GARLIC CLOVES, FINELY CHOPPED
4 LARGE RIPE TOMATOES, CHOPPED
1 CARROT, FINELY SLICED
3 STALKS OF FENNEL
1 STICK OF CELERY, SLICED
2 SPRIGS OF THYME
1.5 KG/3 LB FISH (GRONDIN, GURNARD, RASCASSE, JOHN DORY OR OTHER NON-OILY FISH)
GOOD PINCH OF SAFFRON
SALT AND GROUND BLACK PEPPER
2 TABLESPOONS PERNOD (OPTIONAL)
4 TABLESPOONS DOUBLE CREAM (OPTIONAL)

TO SERVE
SLICES OF BAGUETTE, TOASTED
ROUILLE (PAGE 375)

SERVES 6

Heat the olive oil in a large saucepan. Add the leeks, garlic, tomatoes, carrot, fennel, celery and thyme and cook until all the vegetables have softened.

Chop the fish, discarding the eyes and gills, and add to the vegetables. Let them brown very lightly, then add 2.8 litres/5 pints water. Bring to the boil and add the saffron. Reduce the heat and simmer for 30 minutes.

Strain the soup through a fine sieve into a clean saucepan. Pass the vegetable and fish residue through a vegetable mill and add the resulting purée to the soup.

Taste and adjust the seasoning and stir in the Pernod and cream if you wish.

Serve with toasted baguette slices spread with rouille.

16 RAW PRAWNS, IN THEIR SHELLS
1 LEMON GRASS STALK, SLIT LENGTHWAYS
8 THIN SLICES OF FRESH GINGER
1 FISH STOCK CUBE OR 1 TOM YAM BROTH CUBE
2 FRESH RED CHILLIES, SEEDED AND CUT IN HALF
2 KAFFIR LIME LEAVES, OR 4 STRIPS OF LIME PEEL
1 TOMATO, CUT INTO WEDGES
2 TABLESPOONS THAI FISH SAUCE
SALT AND PEPPER
SMALL BUNCH OF CORIANDER
2–3 LIMES

SERVES 4

Place the prawns in a saucepan with 1.5 litres/2½ pints water. Add the lemon grass, ginger and stock cube. Bring to the boil and simmer for 1 minute. Remove and shell the prawns.

Return the prawn shells to the stock with the chillies and lime leaves or peel. Simmer for 5–6 minutes, then strain the stock into a clean saucepan. Retrieve the chillies and lime leaves (discard the peel and lemon grass) and return to the strained stock.

Add the tomato to the stock and simmer for 2–3 minutes.

Season the soup with fish sauce, salt and pepper. Add the coriander leaves, squeeze in the juice of two limes and drop in the lime skins. You are aiming for a taste that is hot and sour with a distinct citrus flavour. Adjust the flavour to your taste with additional lime juice or a pinch of salt.

Return the prawns to the soup to heat through, then serve at once.

LENTIL BROTH
with crispy duck skin

25 G/1 OZ BUTTER

2 TABLESPOONS OLIVE OIL

1 LEEK, THINLY SLICED

1 SMALL CARROT, SLICED

1 SMALL STICK OF CELERY, SLICED

225 G/8 OZ PUY LENTILS, WASHED AND DRAINED

BROTH

½ DUCK

1 LEEK, HALVED

1 CARROT, HALVED

1 STICK OF CELERY, HALVED

1 BAY LEAF

150 ML/¼ PINT DRY WHITE WINE

1 LITRE/1¾ PINTS CHICKEN STOCK (PAGE 374)

SEA SALT AND BLACK PEPPER

SERVES 6

Begin making the broth the day before you want to serve it. Cut the breast meat off the duck; detach the skin and set aside. Put the carcass into a saucepan with the broth ingredients. Bring to the boil and simmer for 2½ hours. Strain, cool and chill overnight.

The next day, remove all fat from the surface and reheat the broth. Heat the butter and oil in a large saucepan and cook the sliced leek for 2 minutes. Add the carrot and celery and cook for 2 minutes. Add the drained lentils, stir for 1 minute, then pour on the hot broth and simmer for 20 minutes. Adjust the seasoning to taste, add the whole duck breast and poach gently for 15 minutes.

Meanwhile, remove most of the fat from the duck skin; cut the skin into strips. Fry gently in a nonstick pan for about 4 minutes or until they have become crisp and golden brown. Drain on paper towels.

Cut the poached duck breast into dice. Serve the soup hot, with some of the diced breast in each bowl, sprinkled with the crisp skin.

Alastair Little

FARO
(Mixed bean and barley soup)

250 G/9 OZ BARLEY, SOAKED IN PLENTY OF LIGHTLY
  SALTED WATER FOR SEVERAL HOURS
1 x 400 G/14 OZ CAN OF BORLOTTI BEANS
1 x 400 G/14 OZ CAN OF CANNELLINI BEANS
1 x 400 G/14 OZ CAN OF CHICKPEAS
EXTRA VIRGIN OLIVE OIL
2 GARLIC CLOVES, FINELY CHOPPED
2 SPRIGS OF ROSEMARY, LEAVES STRIPPED OFF THE
  TWIGS
1 x 400 G/14 OZ CAN OF CHOPPED TOMATOES
SALT AND PEPPER

BRUSCHETTA (OPTIONAL)

2 SLICES OF GOOD-QUALITY COARSE WHITE BREAD
  (PREFERABLY A DAY OR TWO OLD) PER PERSON
1 GARLIC CLOVE PER PERSON, HALVED
EXTRA VIRGIN OLIVE OIL

SERVES 6–8

During soaking, the barley will swell considerably. Transfer the swollen barley to a large saucepan and add 2 litres/3½ pints water. Simmer gently for 1 hour.

Meanwhile, open the cans of beans and chickpeas, drain and mix them together. Rinse the mixture very thoroughly in cold water to rid them of the viscous liquid from the tins. Add the beans to the saucepan with the barley and simmer for 15 minutes.

Pour 4 tablespoons olive oil into a large saucepan, place over a low heat and add the garlic and rosemary; leave to infuse for 5–10 minutes, then add the tomatoes and finally the beans and barley.

Simmer for a further 30 minutes, adding a little more water if it becomes really solid – although this is how most Tuscan soups are served. Season to taste and serve in soup plates. Offer more olive oil to add at the table.

For the bruschetta, toast the bread, rub each slice with a cut garlic clove and drizzle with oil. Eat while hot.

Arabella Boxer

BLACK BEAN SOUP
with Bourbon

325 G/12 OZ DRIED BLACK BEANS

1 RED ONION, SLICED

3 WHOLE GARLIC CLOVES

1 BAY LEAF

3 CLOVES

3 TABLESPOONS SUNFLOWER OIL

1 LEEK, FINELY CHOPPED

3 FRESH RED CHILLIES, SEEDED AND FINELY CHOPPED

1 TABLESPOON GROUND CUMIN

1 TABLESPOON GROUND CORIANDER

300–600 ML/½–1 PINT CHICKEN STOCK (PAGE 374)

SEA SALT AND BLACK PEPPER

¼ TEASPOON CAYENNE PEPPER

JUICE OF 2 LIMES OR 1 LEMON

GARNISH

3–4 TABLESPOONS BOURBON WHISKEY (OPTIONAL)

300 ML/½ PINT FROMAGE FRAIS

SALSA FRESCA (PAGE 375)

4 TABLESPOONS COARSELY CHOPPED FRESH
   CORIANDER

SERVES 6

Soak the beans in cold water overnight. Drain and place in a saucepan with 1.5 litres/2½ pints cold water, the onion, garlic, bay leaf and cloves. Bring to the boil and boil fast for 10 minutes, then lower the heat and simmer gently for about 1 hour or until the beans are tender.

Lift out 225 g/8 oz of the beans and reserve. Discard the bay leaf. Purée the remaining beans and cooking liquid in a food processor.

Heat the oil in a large saucepan and cook the leek for 3 minutes. Add the chillies, cumin and ground coriander and cook for a further 3 minutes, stirring frequently. Add 300 ml/½ pint of the stock, with salt, pepper and cayenne to taste. Simmer for 20 minutes, then add the whole and puréed beans and simmer for a further 15 minutes.

Thin the soup with more stock, if needed, and add the lime juice.

Serve hot, with ½ tablespoon bourbon in each bowl, for those who like it. Serve the fromage frais, salsa fresca and chopped coriander in separate bowls.

Arabella Boxer

RUBY RED CONSOMMÉ

675 G/1½ LB SHIN OF BEEF, CUBED
SOME BEEF OR VEAL BONES (E.G. KNUCKLE OF VEAL)
1 ONION, HALVED
1 LEEK, HALVED
1 CARROT, HALVED
1 STICK OF CELERY, HALVED
3 PARSLEY STALKS
1 BAY LEAF
10 BLACK PEPPERCORNS
SEA SALT AND BLACK PEPPER
225 G/8 OZ BEETROOT, RAW OR COOKED, SKINNED
   AND COARSELY GRATED
3 TABLESPOONS LEMON JUICE

SERVES 6

Begin making the consommé the day before you want to serve it. Put the beef and bones into a pressure cooker or deep saucepan. Add 1.7 litres/3 pints cold water and bring very slowly to the boil. As it nears boiling point, skim frequently until the surface is clear. Then add 150 ml/¼ pint cold water, the onion, leek, carrot, celery, parsley, bay leaf and peppercorns. Cover and simmer for 1 hour under pressure, or 3 hours in an ordinary pan. Strain and leave to cool, then chill overnight.

The next day, remove all fat from the surface of the stock; you should be left with about 1.5 litres/2½ pints of stock. Bring back to the boil, adding sea salt and black pepper to taste. Measure 300 ml/½ pint of the boiling stock, pour it over the grated beetroot and leave for 30 minutes.

Strain the red stock back into the consommé. Reheat and add the lemon juice. Serve hot, or chilled, in bowls.

CURRIED LEEK SOUP
with saffron

450 G/1 LB LEEKS, WHITE PARTS ONLY, WEIGHED
    AFTER TRIMMING
50 G/2 OZ BUTTER
1 TABLESPOON SUNFLOWER OIL
2 TABLESPOONS FLOUR
1 TABLESPOON MILD CURRY POWDER
1 LITRE/1¾ PINTS CHICKEN STOCK (PAGE 374)

GARNISH
½ TEASPOON SAFFRON STRANDS
1½ TABLESPOONS SUNFLOWER OIL
1 LEEK, WHITE PART ONLY, THINLY SLICED
85 ML/3 FL OZ SINGLE CREAM

SERVES 6

Slice the leeks. Heat the butter and oil in a large saucepan, add the leeks and cook gently for at least 10 minutes, allowing them to soften but without letting them brown. Add the flour and curry powder and cook gently for 3 minutes, stirring frequently. Heat the stock, add to the pan and bring to the boil, stirring, then lower the heat and simmer for 15 minutes.

Leave to cool slightly, then purée the soup in a liquidizer or food processor and return to the cleaned pan.

Shortly before serving, make the garnish. Warm the saffron in a large metal spoon over a low heat for about 30 seconds. Pound it in a mortar, pour on 1 tablespoon boiling water and leave to infuse. Heat the oil in a small frying pan and fry the sliced leek for 2 minutes, then add the saffron and cook for a further 1 minute, stirring constantly.

Reheat the soup and pour into bowls. Drizzle 1 tablespoon cream over each bowl and scatter some saffron leek rings over the top.

Paul & Jeanne Rankin

CURRY AND COCONUT SOUP

1 TABLESPOON BUTTER

1 ONION, CHOPPED

1 GARLIC CLOVE, CHOPPED

2.5 CM/1 INCH PIECE OF FRESH GINGER, CHOPPED

2 TABLESPOONS HOT (MADRAS) CURRY POWDER

2 x 300 G/11 OZ CANS OF SWEETCORN, DRAINED

600 ML/1 PINT CHICKEN STOCK (PAGE 374)

1 x 400 ML/14 FL OZ CAN OF COCONUT MILK

SALT

TO SERVE

2 TABLESPOONS GREEK YOGURT

1 TEASPOON GARAM MASALA

OPTIONAL CONDIMENTS

SERVES 4–6

Melt the butter in a saucepan over low heat and sweat the onion, garlic and ginger until soft. Add the curry powder and cook for 2 minutes. Add the sweetcorn, chicken stock, coconut milk and salt. Simmer for 10 minutes.

Purée the soup in a liquidizer until smooth. If you prefer a more rustic texture, purée just half of the soup and stir back into the pan.

To serve, ladle the soup into warmed bowls, top with a swirl of the yogurt and a dusting of garam masala. Pass round a selection of condiments, such as chopped green chillies, sliced spring onions and toasted coconut flakes.

Richard Olney

VEGETABLE SOUP

1 LITRE/1¾ PINTS WATER

COARSE SEA SALT

1 SPRIG OF THYME

1 BAY LEAF

2 GARLIC CLOVES, SLICED

2 SMALL CARROTS, ABOUT 125 G/4 OZ, SLICED

1 LEEK, ABOUT 150 G/5 OZ, WHITE AND PALE GREEN
PARTS, SLIT, SOAKED IN COLD WATER, THEN FINELY
SLICED

1–2 POTATOES, ABOUT 225 G/8 OZ, QUARTERED AND
SLICED

1 ONION, FINELY SLICED

1 COURGETTE, SLICED INTO WEDGES

50 G/2 OZ SPAGHETTI OR SPAGHETTINI, BROKEN UP

ABOUT 100 G/3½ OZ GREEN BEANS, TOPPED AND
TAILED, THEN SLICED INTO PEA-SIZE LENGTHS

TO SERVE

FRESHLY GROUND BLACK PEPPER

A WEDGE OF PARMESAN CHEESE

EXTRA VIRGIN OLIVE OIL

SERVES 2

Put the water, salt, herbs and garlic in a large
saucepan over medium-high heat. As you
prepare them, add the carrots, leek, potatoes and
onion. When the water boils, partially cover the
pan and adjust the heat to maintain a light boil.

After 20 minutes, add the courgette and the
pasta, stirring with a wooden spoon. After a
further 5 minutes, stir in the green beans. Cook
for 7–8 minutes longer or until the pasta is
tender (not al dente). Serve in warmed soup
plates.

At table, grind some black pepper over the
soup, grate some cheese on top and drizzle with
olive oil.

Rowley Leigh
WILD GARLIC SOUP

3 POTATOES, SLICED

1 LITRE/1¾ PINTS CHICKEN STOCK, OR WATER

1 LEMON

SALT AND PEPPER

25 G/1 OZ BUTTER

2 ONIONS, SLICED

A COLANDER FULL OF WASHED WILD GARLIC

GRATED NUTMEG

SOUR CREAM OR CRÈME FRAÎCHE

CROÛTONS

25 G/1 OZ BUTTER

3 SLICES OF DAY-OLD COUNTRY-STYLE BREAD, TORN
INTO ROUGH CUBES

SERVES 4

Place the potatoes in a saucepan with the stock or water, a strip of lemon zest and plenty of salt and pepper. Simmer for 10–15 minutes.

Meanwhile, melt the butter in another saucepan and cook the onions over a low heat until soft. Turn up the heat, add the wild garlic, a little lemon juice, salt, pepper and nutmeg and cook until the garlic has wilted considerably. Add to the potatoes and stock and simmer together for 5 minutes, then purée in a liquidizer.

To make the croûtons, melt the butter in a frying pan and fry the cubes of bread until they are crisp and golden.

Serve the soup with a swirl of sour cream or crème fraîche and the buttery croûtons.

THAI FISH SOUP
with tiger prawns

1.2 LITRES/2 PINTS CHICKEN STOCK (PAGE 374)

325 G/12 OZ TIGER PRAWNS, OR OTHER GIANT
PRAWNS IN THEIR SHELLS, UNCOOKED

1 GREEN CHILLI

2 LEMONGRASS STALKS, PEELED AND CRUSHED

2.5 CM/1 INCH PIECE OF FRESH GINGER, SLICED AND
CRUSHED

85 G/3 OZ MANGETOUT

1 FRESH RED CHILLI, SEEDED AND THINLY SLICED IN
RINGS

3 TABLESPOONS FRESH LIME OR LEMON JUICE

2 TABLESPOONS ROUGHLY TORN CORIANDER LEAVES

SERVES 6

Put the stock into a saucepan. Shell the prawns and drop the heads and shells into the stock. Heat slowly, adding the whole green chilli, lemongrass and ginger. When it reaches boiling point, half-cover the saucepan and simmer gently for 20 minutes.

Split open the mangetout, reserve any peas inside, and cut the pods lengthways into thin shreds.

Pour the soup through a muslin-lined sieve into a clean pan and bring back to the boil. Add the shelled prawns and the sliced red chilli and poach gently for 3 minutes, then add the shredded mangetous and cook for a further 3 minutes. Remove from the heat, add the tiny shelled peas and leave to cool.

After 10 minutes, stir in the lime or lemon juice. Divide the prawns between six bowls and spoon the soup over them. Scatter a few torn coriander leaves over each bowl and serve at once.

Arabella Boxer

MEDITERRANEAN FISH SOUP
with rouille

900 G/2 LB MIXED FISH (GREY MULLET, MONKFISH,
   COD, CONGER EEL), FILLETED
25 G/1 OZ BUTTER
1½ TABLESPOONS OLIVE OIL
3 SHALLOTS, CHOPPED
1 LEEK, WHITE PART ONLY, CHOPPED
1 STICK OF CELERY, CHOPPED
1 CARROT, CHOPPED
2 GARLIC CLOVES, CHOPPED
2 TOMATOES, CHOPPED
SEA SALT AND BLACK PEPPER
1 TEASPOON MILD CURRY POWDER
85 ML/3 FL OZ DRY VERMOUTH
1 SMALL BAY LEAF
1 SPRIG OF THYME

GARNISH

6 SLICES OF DAY-OLD FRENCH BREAD, ABOUT 1 CM/½
   INCH THICK
ROUILLE (PAGE 375)
FRESHLY GRATED PARMESAN CHEESE

SERVES 6

Cut the fish into chunks. Heat the butter and oil in a large saucepan and cook the shallots for 3 minutes, then add the leek, celery, carrot, garlic and tomatoes. Cook for a further 3 minutes, then add the pieces of fish, salt, pepper and curry powder. Stir for 2–3 minutes, then pour on the vermouth and 1.2 litres/2 pints hot water. Add the herbs and bring to the boil, then simmer for 1 hour, with the pan half covered.

Meanwhile, heat the oven to 150°C/300°F/Gas Mark 2 and put the bread in to dry out for 20 minutes or until lightly coloured.

Leave the soup to cool slightly, then purée in a liquidizer or food processor and rub through a coarse sieve – leave unsieved if you prefer.

Serve hot, accompanied by the bread, Rouille and grated Parmesan in separate bowls, for guests to help themselves.

Valentina Harris

RICE AND PEA SOUP

2 TABLESPOONS UNSALTED BUTTER

2 TABLESPOONS EXTRA VIRGIN OLIVE OIL

2 ONIONS, CHOPPED

2 STICKS OF CELERY, CHOPPED

450 G/1 LB FRESH PEAS, SHELLED WEIGHT, OR FROZEN
  PETITS POIS

300 G/11 OZ RISOTTO OR PUDDING RICE

1 LITRE/1¾ PINTS CHICKEN OR VEGETABLE STOCK
  (PAGE 374), KEPT HOT

SALT AND FRESHLY GROUND BLACK PEPPER

4 TABLESPOONS DOUBLE CREAM

8 TABLESPOONS FRESHLY GRATED PARMESAN CHEESE

SERVES 4–6

Heat the butter and oil in a wide saucepan, add the onions, celery and peas and fry gently until the onions are completely soft.

Add the rice and stir over medium heat, adding the stock little by little as the rice cooks and absorbs the liquid. Continue to stir and add liquid gradually, keeping the texture very wet and soupy. After about 10 minutes, season with salt and pepper.

As soon as the rice is tender, about 20 minutes, remove the pan from the heat and stir in the cream and the Parmesan. Serve at once.

Follow this soup-cum-risotto with a platter of different kinds of cheese and a tomato salad.

Richard Olney

PUMPKIN AND MUSSEL SOUP

15 G/½ OZ UNSALTED BUTTER

1 SMALL ONION, FINELY CHOPPED

ABOUT 450 G/1 LB PUMPKIN OR OTHER ORANGE-
FLESHED WINTER SQUASH, THICKLY PEELED, SEEDED
AND DICED

COARSE SEA SALT

450 G/1 LB MUSSELS, OPENED IN WHITE WINE
FOR 3–4 MINUTES

4 TABLESPOONS DOUBLE CREAM

TO SERVE

CROÛTONS

FRESHLY GROUND BLACK PEPPER

SERVES 2

Melt the butter in a heavy saucepan over low
heat, add the onion, cover the pan and cook
until softened but not coloured. Add the
pumpkin, a little salt (the mussels' cooking
liquid may be more or less salty) and continue
to cook over low heat, covered, for about 30
minutes, stirring occasionally with a wooden
spoon.

Add the mussels' cooking liquid, bring to the
boil and simmer, partially covered, until the
pumpkin is so tender it is almost
a purée.

If necessary, add a little water to lighten the
body of the soup. Taste and add more salt if
required. Strain the soup through a sieve and
bring it back to the boil. Add the mussels, stir in
the cream and serve at once, in warmed soup
plates. Scatter the surface with croûtons and
grind some black pepper over the soup at table.

Valentina Harris

HEARTY MUSSEL SOUP

1.5 KG/3 LB FRESH, LIVE MUSSELS, CLEANED

2–3 GARLIC CLOVES, LIGHTLY CRUSHED

4 TABLESPOONS EXTRA VIRGIN OLIVE OIL

HANDFUL OF CHOPPED FRESH FLAT-LEAF PARSLEY

2 TABLESPOONS PASSATA

SALT AND FRESHLY GROUND BLACK PEPPER

2 GLASSES OF DRY WHITE WINE

8 SLICES OF CIABATTA BREAD, LIGHTLY TOASTED AND
    RUBBED WITH A HALVED GARLIC CLOVE

OLIVE OIL TO DRIZZLE

SERVES 4

Put all the mussels into a large, wide saucepan with no extra liquid and place over a medium heat. Cover with a lid and shake the pan to help the heat get to all the mussels so they open. Once they are all open, take them out of the pan and strain their liquid. Reserve the liquid, discard all the mussels which remain closed and set the rest aside until required.

In the same pan, fry the garlic in the oil for about 5 minutes. Add the parsley and passata, season and stir well. Add the mussels and the wine and mix thoroughly. Cook over a high heat for about 4 minutes, then remove from the heat.

Arrange the toasted, garlicky bread in a wide bowl. Drizzle a thin stream of olive oil over the bread slices, then pour the mussel soup over the bread. Serve immediately, remembering to place an empty bowl in the middle of the table to collect empty shells. Serve with plenty of ice-cold dry white wine.

Arabella Boxer

GAME CONSOMMÉ
with chervil dumplings

1 PHEASANT, OR 2 PHEASANT CARCASSES

6 GARLIC CLOVES, ROUGHLY CRUSHED

6 LEMONGRASS STALKS, PEELED AND ROUGHLY
   CRUSHED

25 G/1 OZ FRESH GINGER, SLICED AND ROUGHLY
   CRUSHED

8 BLACK PEPPERCORNS, ROUGHLY CRUSHED

1.2 LITRES/2 PINTS CHICKEN STOCK (PAGE 374)

½ TABLESPOON SEA SALT

CHERVIL DUMPLINGS (PAGE 375)

SERVES 6

Begin making the consommé the day before
you want to serve it. Put the bird, or carcasses,
into a large saucepan and add the garlic,
lemongrass, ginger and peppercorns. Add the
stock and bring very slowly to the boil,
skimming frequently as it nears boiling point.
Once the surface is clear, half-cover the pan and
simmer for 2½ hours (or cook for 50 minutes in
a pressure cooker.) If using a raw bird, remove
it after 1 hour (or 20 minutes in a pressure
cooker) and remove the breast fillets, then
return the bird to the pan. When the full time is
up, strain the stock into a bowl. Leave to cool,
then chill overnight.

The next day, remove all fat from the surface
of the stock. If using a whole bird, cut the
reserved breast meat into neat dice, discarding
the skin.

Shortly before serving, make the Chervil
Dumplings. Reheat the soup with the diced
breast meat and adjust the seasoning to taste.
Serve hot, with 2–3 dumplings in each bowl.

Bruno Loubet

CHICKEN AND CORN SOUP
with green peppercorns

50 G/2 OZ BUTTER

225 G/8 OZ LEEKS, WHITE PARTS ONLY, ROUGHLY
  CHOPPED

2 GARLIC CLOVES, CHOPPED

1 LITRE/1¾ PINTS CHICKEN STOCK (PAGE 374)

15 GREEN PEPPERCORNS

100 ML/3½ FL OZ DOUBLE CREAM

2 TABLESPOONS CHOPPED FRESH CHIVES

450 G/1 LB CANNED SWEETCORN, DRAINED

175 G/6 OZ COOKED CHICKEN BREAST, SKINNED AND
  DICED (OPTIONAL)

SALT AND PEPPER

*To achieve the cappuccino effect, top the soup with
milk froth, made by bringing a saucepan of milk to
the boil and then blending with a hand-blender until
froth forms.*

SERVES 6

Melt the butter in a large saucepan, add the
chopped leeks and garlic and cook gently,
without colouring, for about 5 minutes or until
the leeks soften slightly. Add the stock, green
peppercorns and cream and simmer for 30
minutes.

Purée the soup in a liquidizer or with a
hand-blender. Strain into a clean pan, bring to
the boil and then add the chives, the drained
sweetcorn and the diced chicken, if using. Taste
and adjust the seasoning and serve hot.

starters

Aglaia Kremezi

BRUSCHETTA WITH HERBS,
anchovies and peppers

12 SPRIGS OF FLAT-LEAF PARSLEY

6–8 LARGE BASIL LEAVES

4 SPRIGS OF DILL

2 GARLIC CLOVES

4 ANCHOVY FILLETS

2 TABLESPOONS CAPERS, RINSED AND DRAINED

1 TEASPOON BALSAMIC VINEGAR

5 TABLESPOONS FRUITY OLIVE OIL

CAYENNE PEPPER

2 LARGE RED PEPPERS, GRILLED AND PEELED

6 SLICES ITALIAN-STYLE BREAD

SERVES 6

Put the parsley, basil, dill, 1 garlic clove, anchovies and 1 tablespoon of the capers into a food processor or blender and process to make a smooth paste. Add the vinegar, 4 tablespoons olive oil and cayenne pepper to taste and process for a few more seconds. Leave to stand.

Cut the grilled red peppers into thin strips.

Toast the bread on both sides, rub with a garlic clove and drizzle with the remaining olive oil. Spread with the herb mixture and top with red pepper strips and whole capers.

Karen Lee

WHITE BEAN BRUSCHETTA

1 TEASPOON CHOPPED FRESH
   ROSEMARY LEAVES

1½ TABLESPOONS OLIVE OIL

3 GARLIC CLOVES, SLIGHTLY CRUSHED

BRAISED WHITE BEANS (PAGE 378),
   NOT DRAINED, OR 1 x 400 G/14 OZ CAN HARICOT
   OR CANNELLINI BEANS, DRAINED

1 TEASPOON BALSAMIC VINEGAR

⅛ TEASPOON CHILLI FLAKES OR CAYENNE PEPPER

SALT AND FRESHLY GROUND BLACK PEPPER

1 ITALIAN-STYLE LOAF

SERVES 6–8

Mix the chopped rosemary with ½ tablespoon of the olive oil and leave to infuse for at least 30 minutes.

In a small saucepan over the lowest possible heat – or over a heat-diffusing mat if you cannot get a really low heat – cook the garlic in the remaining olive oil for 20–30 minutes or until the garlic has softened and browned; turn the garlic cloves every so often.

Using a fork, mash the softened garlic in the olive oil, then add to the white beans, together with the rosemary and its oil, balsamic vinegar and chilli or cayenne. Mash the beans slightly, using a fork or potato masher. The beans can be prepared up to 8 hours in advance.

To serve, reheat the beans. Taste and adjust the seasoning if required. Slice the bread 1 cm/½ inch thick and toast on both sides. Cut each slice in half and spoon the beans on to the bread.

Aglaia Kremezi

GREEN OLIVES WITH CORIANDER,
lemon, orange and garlic

600 G/1¼ LB GREEN OLIVES IN BRINE, DRAINED

3 TABLESPOONS CORIANDER SEEDS, COARSELY
   CRUSHED

1 LEMON, CUT IN THIN SLICES

PARED ZEST OF 1 ORANGE

2 GARLIC CLOVES, SLICED

2–4 SPRIGS OF THYME

1 FRESH RED CHILLI, SLIT LENGTHWAYS AND SEEDED
   (OPTIONAL)

5 TABLESPOONS LEMON JUICE

3 TABLESPOONS ORANGE JUICE

ABOUT 375 ML/12 FL OZ FRUITY OLIVE OIL

MAKES 1 LITRE/1¾ PINTS

Taste one or two of the olives. If they are very salty, rinse in lukewarm water and dry on paper towels. Place the olives in a bowl, add the coriander, lemon slices, orange zest and garlic and toss to mix thoroughly.

Transfer the olives to a large jar and add the thyme, and the chilli, if you are using it. Beat the lemon and orange juice together with the olive oil and pour over the olives to cover them. Cover the jar and keep at room temperature for 1 day, shaking often. Store in the refrigerator for up to 1 month.

An hour or two before you want to eat them, bring the olives to room temperature. Serve with crusty bread and young, fresh, unsalted cheese, such as a French goats' cheese, Greek manouri or Italian ricotta.

Aglaia Kremezi

AUBERGINE DIP WITH WALNUTS

2 LARGE AUBERGINES, ABOUT 450 G/1 LB EACH

2 TABLESPOONS OLIVE OIL

½–1 FRESH RED CHILLI, SEEDED AND FINELY CHOPPED

125 G/4 OZ WALNUTS

1 LARGE GARLIC CLOVE, FINELY CHOPPED

2–3 TABLESPOONS SHERRY VINEGAR

3–4 TABLESPOONS EXTRA VIRGIN OLIVE OIL

½ TEASPOON SEA SALT

SERVES 10–12

Place the aubergines under a very hot grill, letting the skin blacken and blister to give the aubergines a smoky flavour. Turn from time to time to cook on all sides; this will take about 40 minutes.

Peel off the skins, cut the aubergines in half lengthways and scoop out the flesh. Leave the flesh in a colander to drain for at least 30 minutes.

Meanwhile, heat the olive oil in a small frying pan and sauté the chilli until soft, about 2 minutes.

Place the drained aubergines, the fried chilli with its oil, the walnuts, garlic, 2 tablespoons of the vinegar, 3 tablespoons of the extra virgin olive oil and the salt in a food processor and pulse to make a smooth paste. Taste and add more vinegar, oil or salt if required.

Serve as a dip with crudités, or with fresh bread, pitta bread or crackers.

This will keep for about 1 week in the refrigerator, in a covered bowl.

Aglaia Kremezi

SPINACH AND YOGURT CROSTINI
with pine nuts

675 G/1½ LB SPINACH LEAVES, WASHED WELL AND
  COARSELY CHOPPED
1 BUNCH OF FLAT-LEAF PARSLEY, CHOPPED
600 G/1¼ LB GREEK STRAINED YOGURT
2 GARLIC CLOVES, FINELY CHOPPED
½–1 FRESH CHILLI, FINELY CHOPPED
SALT AND FRESHLY GROUND BLACK PEPPER
40 G/1½ OZ PINE NUTS, TOASTED
CROSTINI

*To make the crostini, cut a baguette into 1 cm/½
slices, brush with olive oil and bake in a hot oven for
about 10 minutes*

SERVES 10–12

Place the spinach in a pan with only the water
left on the leaves after washing. Place the pan
over high heat, cover and let the spinach wilt;
this will take about 2–3 minutes, but remember
to toss the pan once or twice and be careful not
to let the spinach burn. Tip the wilted spinach
into a colander and leave to drain. When the
spinach is cool enough to handle, squeeze out as
much liquid as possible, then chop finely.

Put the spinach in a bowl with the parsley,
yogurt, garlic and chilli, and stir well to mix.
Season to taste. Cover and refrigerate for at least
3 hours or overnight.

To serve, spread the spinach mixture thickly
on crostini and sprinkle with pine nuts.

The mixture will keep for about 4 days in
the refrigerator, in a covered bowl.

Clare Connery

TOMATOES AND MOZZARELLA
with pesto dressing

4–8 LARGE, WELL-FLAVOURED TOMATOES
325–450 G/12 OZ–1 LB BUFFALO MOZZARELLA CHEESE
225 G/8 OZ SMALL, MILD-FLAVOURED SALAD LEAVES
   (OAK LEAF, LAMBS' LETTUCE, LAND CRESS) SALT AND
   COARSELY GROUND BLACK PEPPER
BASIL SPRIGS, TO GARNISH

PESTO DRESSING
50 G/2 OZ FRESH BASIL LEAVES, WASHED AND DRIED
1 LARGE GARLIC CLOVE, CRUSHED
50 G/2 OZ PINE NUTS
JUICE OF 1 SMALL LEMON
175 ML/6 FL OZ OLIVE OIL

SERVES 4

Wash and dry the tomatoes and cut into slices. Drain the mozzarella and cut into 5 mm/¼ inch slices. Wash and dry the salad leaves and refrigerate until required.

To make the pesto dressing, combine the basil leaves with the garlic, pine nuts and lemon juice in a liquidizer or food processor and blend to form a smooth paste. Gradually add the oil to make a thick sauce.

Arrange alternate slices of tomato and mozzarella around one side of four large plates, spoon on a little of the pesto dressing and sprinkle some salt and pepper over the cheese and tomatoes. Serve with the salad leaves and garnish with sprigs of basil.

CURRY PUFFS
with peanut sambal

1 TABLESPOON CURRY POWDER

½ TEASPOON PAPRIKA

2 TABLESPOONS PEANUT OIL

125 G/4 OZ PUMPKIN, PEELED AND CUT INTO SMALL
DICE

1 POTATO, PAR-BOILED AND CUT INTO SMALL DICE

1 SMALL CARROT, CHOPPED

1 ONION, CHOPPED

50 G/2 OZ COOKED PEAS

PINCH OF SUGAR

½ TEASPOON SALT

175 G/6 OZ PUFF PASTRY

VEGETABLE OIL FOR DEEP-FRYING

TO SERVE

PEANUT SAMBAL (PAGE 377)

MAKES 10

Mix the curry powder and paprika together
with a little water to form a paste.

Heat a wok, add the oil and, when hot, add
the curry paste and stir-fry for 2 minutes. Add
the vegetables and stir-fry for a further 2
minutes.

Add 125 ml/4 fl oz water, cover and cook
over a gentle heat until the vegetables are
cooked, soft and dry. Stir in the sugar and salt
and leave to cool.

Roll out the pastry to about 2 mm/¹⁄₁₆ inch
thick. Cut out ten circles, about 10 cm/4 inches
in diameter, using a small saucer or Chinese
bowl as a guide. Place a spoonful of filling in
the centre of each pastry circle.

Moisten the edges with water and fold the
pastry over to form a plump half moon shape,
pressing the edges together to seal. Take a small
section at the top of the curve between thumb
and forefinger, pinch it, pull it slightly, then fold
it back on to the curry puff. Repeat until you
have an attractive crimped edge.

In a wok, heat the oil for deep-frying to
180–190°C/350–375°F or until a cube of bread
browns in 30 seconds. Deep-fry the curry puffs
until golden, then drain on paper towels. Serve
warm, with peanut sambal.

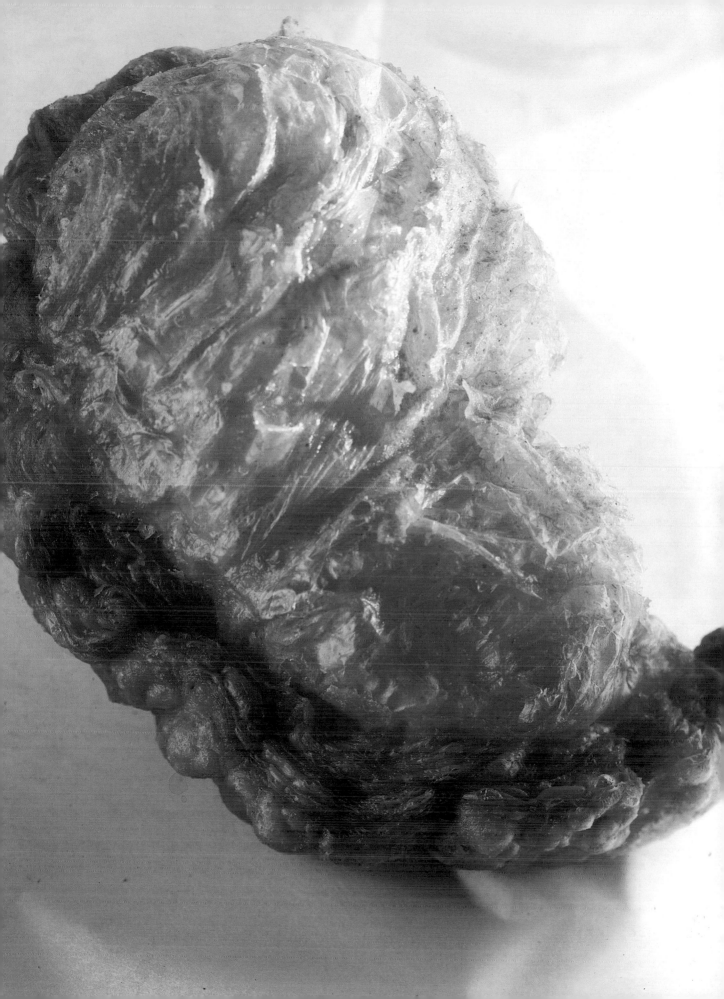

Aglaia Kremezi

GAMBAS AL AJILLO
(Garlic prawns)

ABOUT 5 TABLESPOONS OLIVE OIL

450 G/1 LB UNCOOKED PRAWNS, SHELLED, WITH TAILS LEFT ON

4 GARLIC CLOVES, SLICED

½–1 RED FRESH CHILLI, SEEDED AND FINELY CHOPPED (OPTIONAL)

SALT AND FRESHLY GROUND BLACK PEPPER

3 TABLESPOONS CHOPPED PARSLEY

SERVES 6–8

Heat the olive oil in a heavy frying pan or flameproof dish and add the prawns, garlic and chilli, if you are using it. Cook, stirring with a spatula, for about 3 minutes, until the prawns are firm. Sprinkle with salt, pepper and parsley and serve at once while the prawns are still sizzling, accompanied by crusty bread to dip into the sauce.

VARIATION

You can substitute boned cubed chicken (breast or thigh) for the prawns. It needs to cook for about 10 minutes, so add the garlic and chilli after 6 minutes.

SMOKED HADDOCK PASTIES

with leeks and clotted cream

900 G/2 LB CHILLED PUFF PASTRY
A LITTLE FLOUR
325 G/12 OZ SKINNED UNDYED SMOKED HADDOCK
175 G/6 OZ CLEANED LEEKS
275 G/10 OZ PEELED POTATOES, BOILED
4 TABLESPOONS CLOTTED CREAM
1 TEASPOON SALT
10 TURNS OF THE BLACK PEPPER MILL
1 EGG, BEATEN

MAKES 6

Cut the pastry into six equal pieces. On a lightly floured surface, roll out each piece to about 20 cm/8 inches square, then cut out six 19 cm/7½ inch circles.

Preheat the oven to 200°C/400°F/Gas Mark 6.

Cut the smoked haddock into 2.5 cm/1 inch pieces. Slice the leeks and cut the potatoes into 1 cm/½ inch cubes. Mix together the haddock, leeks, potatoes, clotted cream, salt and pepper.

Divide the fish mixture between the circles of pastry. Moisten one half of each pastry edge with a little beaten egg, bring both edges together over the top of the filling and pinch together well to seal. Crimp the edge of each pasty decoratively between the fingers, transfer to a lightly greased baking sheet and brush all over with more beaten egg. Bake for 35 minutes. Serve hot or cold.

MUSSELS WITH CORIANDER,

chilli, garlic and ginger

2.3 LITRES/4 PINTS MUSSELS, CLEANED
1 TABLESPOON THAI FISH SAUCE
JUICE OF 1 LIME
1 GARLIC CLOVE, FINELY CHOPPED
1 FRESH RED CHILLI, SEEDED AND FINELY CHOPPED
2 TEASPOONS FINELY CHOPPED FRESH GINGER
2 TABLESPOONS SESAME OIL
1 BUNCH OF SPRING ONIONS, THINLY SLICED
2 TABLESPOONS ROUGHLY CHOPPED FRESH CORIANDER

SERVES 4

Place the mussels in a large saucepan with the fish sauce, lime juice, garlic, chilli, ginger and sesame oil. Cover and cook over a high heat for 3 minutes or until the mussels have opened.

Scatter over the sliced spring onions and chopped coriander and turn everything over in the pan. Serve at once.

Jill Dupleix

TUNA WITH WASABI
on chicory

300 g/11 oz very fresh (not previously
   frozen), top-quality raw tuna
1 teaspoon small capers, rinsed and chopped
1 teaspoon chopped gherkins (cornichon
   pickles)
2 anchovy fillets, chopped
2 spring onions, finely chopped
1 tablespoon vegetable oil
1 teaspoon soy sauce
1 egg yolk
1 teaspoon wasabi (Japanese horseradish)
   powder, mixed with water to form a paste
salt and freshly ground black pepper
4 large heads of chicory

MAKES 24 PIECES

Cut the tuna into very small dice.

In a bowl, mix the chopped capers, pickles,
anchovies, spring onions, oil, soy sauce, egg
yolk, wasabi paste and a little salt and pepper.
Add the tuna and toss gently. Taste and adjust
the seasoning if required.

Cut off the chicory roots and carefully pull
the leaves apart. Wash the leaves and pat dry
with paper towels. Arrange on platters, like the
spokes of a wheel. To serve, spoon the
marinated tuna mixture into the hollow base of
each leaf.

Instead of chicory, the tuna mixture can also
be served in small leaves of Cos lettuce.

Jill Dupleix

RAW FISH WITH LIME,
coconut and avocado

400 G/14 OZ VERY FRESH DEEP SEA FISH

5 TABLESPOONS FRESH LIME JUICE

1 SCANT TEASPOON SALT

250 ML/8 FL OZ CANNED COCONUT MILK

1 AVOCADO

4 TOMATOES, SKINNED, SEEDED AND DICED

1 CUCUMBER, PEELED AND DICED

2 TABLESPOONS FRESH CORIANDER LEAVES

SERVES 4

Cut the fish into bite-size pieces or thin slices. Place in a glass bowl, add 4 tablespoons of the lime juice and the salt and leave in the refrigerator to marinate for at least 3 hours, tossing occasionally.

Add the coconut milk and gently mix with the fish.

Peel the avocado, cut into cubes and sprinkle with the remaining lime juice.

Drain the fish and gently toss with the avocado, tomatoes, cucumber and coriander. Divide between four cocktail glasses or serve in a hollowed-out coconut.

Paul & Jeanne Rankin

SPICED BEAN CURD
with a sesame and ginger vinaigrette

450 G/1 LB FRESH BEAN CURD (TOFU)

3 TABLESPOONS PLAIN FLOUR, SIFTED

3 TABLESPOONS SESAME SEEDS

1 TABLESPOON CHILLI POWDER

1 TABLESPOON WHITE PEPPER

2 TABLESPOONS ONION SALT

1 EGG, BEATEN WITH 3 TABLESPOONS MILK

500 ML/16 FL OZ VEGETABLE OIL, FOR FRYING

TO SERVE

3 HEADS OF LITTLE GEM LETTUCE, SHREDDED

SESAME AND GINGER VINAIGRETTE (PAGE 375)

FRESH CORIANDER AND CHIVES

SERVES 4–6 AS A STARTER

Cut the bean curd into wedges, 2 cm/¾ inch thick. Mix the flour, sesame seeds, chilli powder, pepper and onion salt in a wide bowl. Dip each piece of bean curd lightly into the flour, then dip it into the egg and milk mixture and finally into the flour again.

Heat the oil in a wide pan to about 180°C/350°F or until a cube of bread browns in 30 seconds. Fry the bean curd for about 2 minutes on each side, until golden brown. Drain on paper towels.

To serve, pile the shredded lettuce on each plate and top with 3–4 pieces of bean curd. Sprinkle some of the vinaigrette over and around the bean curd. Garnish with the coriander and chives and serve at once.

Jill Dupleix

RICE PAPER ROLLS
with prawns and mint

ABOUT 50 G/2 OZ CELLOPHANE NOODLES (RICE
    VERMICELLI)
12 DRIED RICE PAPER ROUNDS (BANH TRANG), ABOUT
    22 CM/9 INCHES IN DIAMETER
ABOUT 1/2 SMALL ICEBERG LETTUCE, SHREDDED
50 G/2 OZ FRESH BEANSPROUTS, RINSED
3 TABLESPOONS SALTED PEANUTS
HANDFUL OF FRESH MINT
HANDFUL OF FRESH CORIANDER
12 SMALL PRAWNS, LIGHTLY COOKED AND PEELED

TO SERVE
SWEET CHILLI SAUCE (PAGE 377), FOR DIPPING

MAKES 12

Cook the noodles in boiling water for 2
minutes or until tender. Drain and rinse in cold
water, then drain again.

Dunk a rice paper round into simmering
water for a few seconds until soft, then lay on a
serving plate. Top with some shredded lettuce,
noodles, beansprouts, nuts, mint and coriander
leaves, and fold the rice paper towards the
centre to form a firm roll.

Tuck in one small prawn, fold in the ends of
the roll, and continue to roll into a neat sausage
shape. The rice paper will stick to itself and
hold the shape. Continue with the remaining
rice paper rounds. Dip into the sauce and eat
with the fingers.

Jill Dupleix

PACIFIC OYSTERS
with lightly pickled vegetables

1 LARGE KNOB OF FRESH GINGER

1 CUCUMBER

1 CARROT

½ GIANT WHITE RADISH (MOOLI/DAIKON)

250 ML/8 FL OZ WHITE RICE VINEGAR

2 DOZEN FRESHLY OPENED PACIFIC OYSTERS

2 TABLESPOONS FINELY SLICED JAPANESE PICKLED
GINGER

SERVES 4

Peel the ginger, cucumber, carrot and radish.
Cut into 5 cm/2 inch lengths. Cut lengthways
into thin slices, then cut the slices into very fine
matchstick strips. Place the strips in a glass bowl,
add the rice vinegar and leave in the refrigerator
to marinate for at least 1 hour.

Loosen each oyster on its shell and divide the
shells between four platters. Spoon a few of the
marinated vegetables and their dressing on to
each oyster. Top each oyster with a slice of
pickled ginger and serve at once.

For a party, the oysters and their dressing can
be served in small Chinese soup spoons,
arranged on a tray.

Paul & Jeanne Rankin

CHILLI CHICKEN PUFFS
with spicy dipping sauce

200 G/7 OZ CHICKEN FILLET, ROUGHLY CHOPPED

150 G/5 OZ STREAKY BACON, ROUGHLY CHOPPED

1 GARLIC CLOVE, FINELY CHOPPED

2 SPRING ONIONS, FINELY CHOPPED

2 TABLESPOONS CHOPPED FRESH CORIANDER

1 FRESH GREEN CHILLI, CHOPPED

1 EGG

½ TEASPOON SALT

½ TEASPOON PEPPER

A LITTLE FLOUR

1 PACKET (300–350 G/11–13 OZ) FROZEN PUFF
   PASTRY

1 EGG YOLK, BEATEN

2 TABLESPOONS BLACK AND WHITE SESAME SEEDS

TO SERVE

SPICY DIPPING SAUCE (PAGE 377)

MAKES ABOUT 24

Place the chicken and bacon in a food processor with the garlic, spring onions, coriander, chilli, egg, salt and pepper. Pulse until the mixture is well chopped and comes together like sausage meat. Transfer to a piping bag fitted with a 1.5 cm/⅝ inch nozzle.

On a lightly floured surface, roll out the pastry to about 3 mm/⅛ inch thick. Cut the pastry into strips about 6 cm/2½ inches wide.

Pipe the sausage meat along the pastry strips. Lightly brush one edge with egg yolk, then fold the pastry over the meat and press gently to seal; do not seal the ends. Brush the top of the pastry with egg yolk and sprinkle with the sesame seeds. Cut into 6 cm/2½ inch lengths and chill for 15 minutes. Preheat the oven to 200°C/400°F/Gas Mark 6.

Bake the puffs for 10 minutes or until well risen and brown. Reduce the oven temperature to 150°C/300°F/Gas Mark 3 and cook for a further 10 minutes.

Serve warm, accompanied by the dipping sauce.

Antony Worrall Thompson

TWO DIPS
from the Eastern Mediterranean

BABA GHANOUSH

3 LARGE AUBERGINES

OLIVE OIL

4 TABLESPOONS TAHINI (SESAME SEED PASTE)

4 TABLESPOONS GREEK YOGURT

4 GARLIC CLOVES, CRUSHED WITH A LITTLE SALT

JUICE OF 1 LEMON

SALT AND GROUND BLACK PEPPER

POMEGRANATE SEEDS

MINT LEAVES

CUCUMBER, GARLIC AND YOGURT

450 G/1 LB GREEK YOGURT

3 TABLESPOONS CHOPPED FRESH MINT

450 G/1 LB CUCUMBER, PEELED, SEEDED AND SLICED

2 GARLIC CLOVES, CRUSHED WITH A LITTLE SALT

GROUND BLACK PEPPER

Serve both dips with a Mediterranean-style flatbread.

SERVES 6

For the baba ghanoush: prick the aubergines all over with a fork, then rub with a little olive oil. Wrap each aubergine in foil and grill over a fierce flame, barbecue or chargrill for about 15–20 minutes on each side or until the aubergines feel soft and have reduced considerably in size. Remove the foil, drain off any juices and peel away the charred skin. Leave to cool.

Mash the aubergine pulp with a fork or potato masher; it shouldn't be too smooth. Stir in the tahini, yogurt, garlic and lemon juice. Season to taste. Spoon the mixture into a serving bowl and scatter with the pomegranate seeds and a few mint leaves.

For the cucumber, garlic and yogurt dip: combine all the ingredients, then taste and adjust the seasoning as required.

Leave in a cool place for about 1 hour before serving, to allow the flavours to develop.

SALMON TARTARE

Rick Stein

400 G/14 OZ FRESH SALMON FILLET, SKINNED
125 G/4 OZ SMOKED SALMON
1 LARGE GARLIC CLOVE, VERY FINELY CHOPPED
3 SHALLOTS, VERY FINELY CHOPPED
1 TABLESPOON FRESH LEMON JUICE
½ TEASPOON SALT
12 TURNS OF THE BLACK PEPPER MILL
PINCH OF CAYENNE PEPPER
FEW DROPS OF WORCESTERSHIRE SAUCE

TO GARNISH

24–32 SPRIGS OF LAMBS' LETTUCE
EXTRA VIRGIN OLIVE OIL
BALSAMIC VINEGAR
COARSE SEA SALT
COARSELY GROUND BLACK PEPPER

SERVES 4

Cut the salmon fillet and smoked salmon into very small dice. Place in a bowl, add the remaining ingredients and mix well.

Line four 8 cm/3 inch ramekins or similar containers with clingfilm, leaving the edges overhanging. Divide the salmon mixture between the ramekins and press down lightly, so that the tops are smooth. Now invert the ramekins into the centre of four large dinner plates – the bigger the better. Remove the ramekins and the clingfilm.

Arrange 6–8 sprigs of lambs' lettuce around the edge of each plate. Drizzle the rest of the plate, and the leaves, with a little olive oil, add a few drops of balsamic vinegar in between the streaks of oil, and then sprinkle with a little sea salt and black pepper. Serve at once, with a bowl of extra salad if you wish.

Aglaia Kremezi

SMOKED FISH SPREAD

ABOUT 200 G/7 OZ SKINNED AND
  BONED SMOKED FISH (KIPPER,
  SMOKED MACKEREL OR
  SMOKED HADDOCK)
4 SPRING ONIONS, MAINLY WHITE
  PART, ROUGHLY CHOPPED
1 TABLESPOON RED WINE VINEGAR
  OR SHERRY VINEGAR
4–6 TABLESPOONS LEMON JUICE
2–3 POTATOES (300–400 G/11–14 OZ), BOILED AND
  PEELED
125 ML/4 FL OZ OLIVE OIL
FLAT-LEAF PARSLEY, TO GARNISH

SERVES 10–12

Place the smoked fish, spring onions, vinegar and 3 tablespoons of the lemon juice in a food processor and pulse to make a purée. Add 1–2 potatoes and, with the machine running, pour in the olive oil through the funnel. Blend for a few seconds to get a smooth purée. Taste and adjust the flavour with more lemon juice or more potato as required.

Cover and refrigerate for at least 3 hours or overnight.

Garnish with parsley and serve with fresh bread, toast or crackers, or as a dip with crudités.

chapter three

salads

Clare Connery

CAESAR SALAD

2 LARGE HEADS OF COS LETTUCE

GARLIC CROÛTONS

2 GARLIC CLOVES, CRUSHED

5 TABLESPOONS OLIVE OIL

3 SLICES OF WHITE BREAD, ABOUT 5 MM/¼ INCH
    THICK, CRUSTS REMOVED

CAESAR DRESSING

2 EGGS

6 TABLESPOONS OLIVE OIL

JUICE OF 1 SMALL LEMON

1 TABLESPOON WORCESTERSHIRE SAUCE

SALT AND FRESHLY GROUND BLACK
    PEPPER

25–50 G/1–2 OZ PARMESAN CHEESE, GRATED

SERVES 4

Remove the lettuce leaves from the stalks; use
only the tender centre leaves for this salad,
allowing about 10 leaves per person. Wash, dry
and refrigerate until required.

To make the croûtons, stir the garlic into the
oil and leave to infuse for as long as possible. Cut
the bread into 5 mm/¼ inch cubes. Strain the oil
into a frying pan over medium-high heat and
quickly fry the bread cubes until they are an
even golden colour. Drain on paper towels.

To prepare the Caesar dressing, plunge the
eggs into boiling water, bring back to the boil
and boil for 1 minute only. Break the eggs into a
large salad bowl, scraping out the thin layer of
cooked white. Gradually whisk in the oil, then
the lemon juice, Worcestershire sauce, salt and
pepper.

Add the lettuce leaves, croûtons and two-
thirds of the cheese. Toss lightly. Pile on to four
large plates, sprinkle with the remaining cheese
and serve immediately.

Antony Worrall Thompson

GREEK VILLAGE SALAD
(Horiatiki)

4 PLUM TOMATOES, EACH CUT INTO 6 PIECES

½ CUCUMBER, PEELED AND CUT INTO 1 CM/½ INCH
   SLICES

125 G/4 OZ FETA CHEESE, CUBED

50 G/2 OZ KALAMATA OLIVES, STONED

1 SMALL RED ONION, THINLY SLICED

2 TEASPOONS FRESH OREGANO LEAVES

DRESSING

5 TABLESPOONS EXTRA VIRGIN OLIVE OIL

1 TABLESPOON AGED RED WINE VINEGAR

1 TEASPOON DRIED GREEK OREGANO

1 GARLIC CLOVE, FINELY CHOPPED

4 CAPERS, FINELY CHOPPED

1 ANCHOVY, FINELY CHOPPED

GROUND BLACK PEPPER

SERVES 4

Whisk all the dressing ingredients together and leave for 30 minutes for the flavours to meld.

Place all the salad ingredients in a large serving bowl. Shake the dressing and pour over the salad. Toss to combine.

Clare Connery

CRISPY CHICKEN SALAD
with sesame seeds and chilli dressing

325 G/12 OZ MIXED SALAD LEAVES (CHICORY, ROCKET, LAMBS' LETTUCE, YOUNG SPINACH OR SORREL LEAVES)

4 SMALL CHICKEN BREASTS, ABOUT 150 G/5 OZ EACH, CUT INTO STRIPS

50 G/2 OZ PLAIN FLOUR

1 EGG, BEATEN

125 G/4 OZ LIGHT SESAME SEEDS

VEGETABLE OIL FOR DEEP-FRYING

CORIANDER LEAVES, TO GARNISH

CHILLI DRESSING

125 ML/4 FL OZ SUNFLOWER OIL

2 TABLESPOONS SESAME OIL

3 TABLESPOONS RED WINE VINEGAR

2 GARLIC CLOVES, CRUSHED

3 TABLESPOONS SOY SAUCE

1 TEASPOON GROUND SICHUAN PEPPERCORNS

¼ TEASPOON MUSCOVADO SUGAR

½ TEASPOONS TABASCO SAUCE

2 TEASPOONS SWEET CHILLI SAUCE

SERVES 4

Wash and dry the salad leaves and refrigerate until required. Combine all the ingredients for the dressing, whisking well to blend.

Coat the chicken strips in the flour, then dip in the beaten egg and toss in the sesame seeds. Heat the oil to 190°C/375°F or until a cube of bread browns in 30 seconds. Deep-fry the chicken for 3 minutes or until golden brown. Drain on paper towels.

Toss the salad leaves in a little of the dressing and pile in the centre of four large plates. Arrange the chicken on top, sprinkle with a little more dressing and garnish with coriander leaves.

Sean Connery

WILD MUSHROOM SALAD
with chicken

4 LIGHTLY COOKED CHICKEN BREAST FILLETS, SKINNED

225–275 G/8–10 OZ MIXED SALAD LEAVES (CURLY
ENDIVE, LOLLO ROSSO, OAK LEAF, RADICCHIO)

2 TOMATOES, SKINNED, SEEDED AND FINELY DICED

50 G/2 OZ BABY SWEETCORN, LIGHTLY COOKED AND
SLICED IN RINGS

100 ML/3½ FL OZ VINAIGRETTE (PAGE 375)

CHERVIL SPRIGS, TO GARNISH

MUSHROOM SALAD

85 G/3 OZ BUTTON MUSHROOMS

175 G/6 OZ MIXED WILD MUSHROOMS (CHANTERELLES,
CEPS, TROMPET DE MORT, OYSTER MUSHROOMS)

50 G/2 OZ UNSALTED BUTTER

1 TABLESPOON OLIVE OIL

2 SHALLOTS, FINELY CHOPPED

2 GARLIC CLOVES, CRUSHED

2 TABLESPOONS SHERRY VINEGAR

3 TABLESPOONS FINELY CHOPPED CHERVIL

SALT AND FRESHLY GROUND BLACK PEPPER

SERVES 4

Cut the chicken across the fillet into 2 cm/¾ inch slices. Arrange on four large plates like the spokes of a wheel, leaving a space in the centre of the plate.

Combine the salad leaves, tomatoes and half the sweetcorn.

To make the mushroom salad, clean all the mushrooms, trim and cut into even-sized pieces. Fry in batches in the melted butter and oil with the shallots and garlic. Return all the mushrooms to the pan, add the sherry vinegar, fry quickly over medium-high heat, then stir in the chervil and season to taste with salt and pepper.

Toss the salad leaves in a little vinaigrette and pile in the centre of the chicken. Top with a layer of mushroom salad, then more salad leaves, and finish with mushrooms. Scatter any remaining mushrooms and sweetcorn between the chicken pieces, drizzle with vinaigrette, garnish with the chervil and serve immediately.

Sean Connery

WARM CHICKEN LIVER SALAD
with bacon and new potatoes

225–275 G/8–10 OZ MIXED SALAD LEAVES (BATAVIA
    ENDIVE, OAK LEAF, LOLLO ROSSO, ROCKET)
16 TINY NEW POTATOES, SCRUBBED
175 G/6 OZ BACK BACON, CUT INTO THIN STRIPS
25 G/1 OZ UNSALTED BUTTER
1 SHALLOT, FINELY CHOPPED
450 G/1 LB CHICKEN LIVERS, TRIMMED, WASHED AND
    DRIED
100 ML/3½ FL OZ PORT
175 ML/6 FL OZ DOUBLE CREAM
1 TABLESPOON FINELY CHOPPED CHERVIL, TO GARNISH

HERB VINAIGRETTE

3 TABLESPOONS SHERRY VINEGAR
175 ML/6 FL OZ OLIVE OIL
SALT AND FRESHLY GROUND BLACK PEPPER
1 TABLESPOON FINELY CHOPPED CHERVIL
2 TABLESPOONS FINELY CHOPPED CHIVES

SERVES 4

Whisk together all the ingredients for the herb
vinaigrette. Set aside. Wash and dry the salad
leaves and refrigerate until required.

Boil the potatoes until just tender, drain and
keep warm. Fry the bacon in a large frying pan
until crisp, drain and keep warm. Add the butter
to the pan and fry the shallot until soft. Increase
the heat and fry the chicken livers for 1–2
minutes or until seared on all sides. Stir in the
port, cream and salt and pepper to taste. Reduce
the heat and simmer for a further 2 minutes.

Put the bacon and potatoes in a large salad
bowl and moisten with a little of the herb
vinaigrette; add the salad leaves and toss gently.
Arrange the salad in the centre of four large
plates. Remove the chicken livers from the pan
with a slotted spoon, arrange on the salad and
spoon over a little of the warm sauce. Sprinkle
with the chervil and serve immediately.

Jacki Passmore

CHICKEN AND HERB SALAD
(Laab Kai)

450 G/1 LB BONELESS, SKINLESS CHICKEN BREAST

2 SMALL CUCUMBERS

1 ONION

1 RED ONION

6 CHIVES OR GARLIC CHIVES, SNIPPED

SMALL BUNCH OF MINT

SMALL BUNCH OF CORIANDER

SMALL BUNCH OF BASIL

1½ TABLESPOONS THAI FISH SAUCE

2 TABLESPOONS LIME JUICE

1 TABLESPOON SWEET CHILLI SAUCE

1–2 GARLIC CLOVES, FINELY CHOPPED

2½ TEASPOONS SUGAR

SERVES 4

Cut the chicken into 1 cm/½ inch cubes. Heat a nonstick pan and cook the chicken – without adding any oil – for about 3 minutes, shaking the pan and stirring frequently. As soon as the chicken is cooked through, remove from the heat and set aside to cool.

Cut the cucumbers in half lengthways, scoop out and discard the seeds, and slice thinly. Cut the onions in half and slice thinly. Place the cucumber, onions and chives in a salad bowl and toss gently to combine.

Pick off the mint, coriander and basil leaves, reserving a few sprigs for garnish. Add the leaves to the salad.

Put the remaining ingredients in a bowl and whisk together to make the dressing. Add the chicken and mix well, then add to the salad and toss gently to combine. Serve garnished with the reserved herbs.

Clave Connery

BEEF TAPENADE
with watercress and lambs' lettuce

450 G/1 LB RARE ROAST BEEF, CUT INTO 1 CM/½ INCH
   SLICES
1 LARGE RED AND GREEN PEPPER, SEEDED AND CUT
   INTO 5 MM X 5 CM/¼ X 2 INCH STRIPS
275 G/10 OZ WATERCRESS AND LAMBS' LETTUCE
12 BLACK OLIVES, STONED
1 TEASPOON CAPERS, DRAINED

TAPENADE DRESSING
150 G/5 OZ BLACK OLIVES, STONED
50 G/1¾ OZ CANNED ANCHOVY FILLETS, DRAINED AND
   RINSED
3 TABLESPOONS CAPERS, DRAINED
50 G/2 OZ CANNED TUNA, DRAINED
JUICE OF 1 SMALL LEMON
½ TEASPOON DIJON MUSTARD
4 TABLESPOONS OLIVE OIL
4 TABLESPOONS VINAIGRETTE (PAGE 375)

HERB CROSTINI
2 TABLESPOONS OLIVE OIL
2 TABLESPOONS FINELY CHOPPED PARSLEY, CHERVIL
   AND CHIVES
4 SLICES OF FRENCH BREAD, ABOUT 2 CM/¾ INCH
   THICK

SERVES 4

To make the tapenade dressing, blend the olives, anchovies, capers, tuna, lemon juice and mustard to form a smooth paste. Gradually blend in the oil. Put 4–5 tablespoons of the tapenade paste into a large bowl (refrigerate the remainder for use in another dish). Add the vinaigrette and mix well. Stir in the beef and peppers, cover and refrigerate for a few hours before serving.

To make the herb crostini, preheat the oven to 200°C/400°F/Gas Mark 6. Combine the oil and herbs and brush over the bread. Bake for about 10 minutes until crisp and golden.

Mix the watercress and lambs' lettuce and divide between four large plates. Set a crostini in the centre of each plate and arrange a pile of beef tapenade on top. Sprinkle the olives and capers over the salad and serve immediately.

GREEN BEAN SALAD
with balsamic vinaigrette

450 G/1 LB GREEN BEANS

3–4 SPRING ONIONS, THINLY SLICED

2 TABLESPOONS CHOPPED FRESH DILL

SALAD LEAVES, TO SERVE

BALSAMIC VINAIGRETTE

½ TEASPOON SALT

¾ TABLESPOON BALSAMIC VINEGAR

¾ TABLESPOON RED WINE VINEGAR

1 TEASPOON DIJON MUSTARD

⅛ TEASPOON FRESHLY GROUND BLACK PEPPER

3 TABLESPOONS OLIVE OIL

SERVES 4–6

To make the balsamic vinaigrette: dissolve the salt in the vinegars in a screw-topped glass jar. Add the mustard, pepper and olive oil and shake vigorously. The vinaigrette can be kept in the refrigerator for up to 5 days.

Steam the green beans for 3–4 minutes, then plunge them into ice cold water for 2 minutes to stop the cooking and hold the colour. Drain well and trim the stem ends. The beans can be prepared up to 8 hours in advance.

Place the beans in a serving bowl. Add the spring onions, dill and dressing and toss until combined. Serve at once or within 1 hour, on a bed of salad leaves.

Jill Dupleix

HOT AND SOUR BEEF SALAD

300 G/11 OZ FILLET STEAK
1 TEASPOON FISH SAUCE

DRESSING

2 TABLESPOONS UNCOOKED JASMINE RICE
2 DRIED RED CHILLIES (OR ½ TEASPOON CHILLI
   POWDER)
4 RED SHALLOTS, FINELY SLICED
LARGE HANDFUL OF FRESH MINT LEAVES
SMALL HANDFUL OF FRESH CORIANDER LEAVES
2 SPRING ONIONS, FINELY SLICED
2 TABLESPOONS LIME JUICE
2 TABLESPOONS FISH SAUCE
½ TEASPOON SUGAR

**SERVES 2 FOR LUNCH,
4 AS PART OF A THAI MEAL**

Heat a heavy-bottomed frying pan, add the rice
and toast over medium heat until golden. Grind
or pound the rice to a powder and set aside.
Reheat the frying pan and add the dried chillies.
Toast until smoky, then grind or pound to a
powder and set aside.

Grill or pan-sear the steak quickly, leaving it
quite rare. Sprinkle with the fish sauce and leave
to rest for 10 minutes.

Mix ½ teaspoon of the ground roasted chilli
powder (store the rest) and the rice powder with
the shallots, mint, coriander, spring onions, lime
juice, fish sauce and sugar. Taste and adjust the
seasoning if required: it should be hot, sour and
salty.

Slice the beef thinly and toss through the
salad, together with any juices. Pile high on a
plate and serve at once.

As a simple lunch, it can be accompanied by a
platter of crunchy lettuces and cucumber.

Richard Olney

COMPOSED SALAD

2 EGGS

275 G/10 OZ SMALL, FIRM-FLESHED POTATOES

HANDFUL OF SMALL GREEN BEANS, TOPPED, TAILED
   AND CUT INTO 2.5 CM/1 INCH SECTIONS

HANDFUL OF BLACK OLIVES

4 SALTED ANCHOVIES, BRIEFLY SOAKED IN COLD
   WATER, FILLETED, RINSED, PATTED DRY BETWEEN
   PAPER TOWELS

1 TABLESPOON FINELY CHOPPED FLAT-LEAF PARSLEY

VINAIGRETTE

SALT AND FRESHLY GROUND BLACK PEPPER

1 TABLESPOON RED WINE VINEGAR

3 TABLESPOONS OLIVE OIL

1 SHALLOT, VERY FINELY CHOPPED

SERVES 2

Place the eggs in a saucepan of cold water, bring
to the boil and simmer for 9 minutes. Immerse
in a bowl of cold water and set aside.

Boil the potatoes in their skins until just done,
about 25 minutes.

While the potatoes are cooking, prepare the
vinaigrette. Grind salt and pepper into the salad
bowl, add the vinegar, swirl it to dissolve the
salt, add the olive oil and stir in the shallot with
a salad serving spoon and fork.

Cook the beans in boiling water until barely
tender, 2–5 minutes. Drain, but do not refresh in
cold water.

Drain the potatoes and peel them while still
boiling hot, protecting your hands with a tea
towel. Slice them directly into the vinaigrette
and toss them immediately – only when hot will
they absorb its flavours correctly.

Shell the eggs and slice thinly over the potatoes – the yolks will crumble coarsely. Scatter
over the beans, olives, anchovies and parsley, in
that order. Present the salad before tossing it at
the table.

Clare Connery

SMOKED SALMON SALAD
with potato cakes and sour cream

125 G/4 OZ LAMBS' LETTUCE

125 G/4 OZ ROCKET

85 G/3 OZ CHICORY, CUT INTO SLIVERS

325 G/12 OZ SMOKED SALMON,
   CUT INTO STRIPS

2 TOMATOES, SEEDED AND DICED

4 TABLESPOONS SOUR CREAM

8 CHIVES, TO GARNISH

POTATO CAKES

225 G/8 OZ COOKED, MASHED POTATOES

25 G/1 OZ BUTTER, MELTED

50 G/2 OZ PLAIN FLOUR, PLUS
   EXTRA FOR SHAPING AND
   COOKING

LEMON DRESSING

6 TABLESPOONS OLIVE OIL

2–3 TABLESPOONS LEMON JUICE

SALT AND FRESHLY GROUND BLACK PEPPER

2 TABLESPOONS CHOPPED CHIVES

SERVES 4

First make the potato cakes. Mix the potatoes, butter and flour together to form a light dough. Roll out on a lightly floured surface to about 2 cm/½ inch thick. Using a 6 cm/2½ inch round cutter, cut into four circles. Heat a large heavy frying pan, dust with a little flour and cook the potato cakes until lightly browned on each side. Remove from the pan and leave to cool.

Combine the salad leaves in a bowl. Whisk together the dressing ingredients and moisten the salad with 1–2 tablespoons.

Scatter the leaves over four large plates, set a potato cake in the centre of each and pile the salmon around the edge of the cakes. Arrange the tomato dice on the potato cakes, top with sour cream, garnish each with two strips of chives and finish with a dusting of freshly ground black pepper. Serve any extra dressing separately.

Antony Worrall Thompson

SALMON TABBOULEH

450 G/1 LB SALMON FILLET, IN ONE PIECE,
    THOROUGHLY SCALED
SALT
175 ML/6 FL OZ EXTRA VIRGIN OLIVE OIL
50 G/2 OZ FINE BULGAR WHEAT (CRACKED WHEAT)
450 G/1 LB PLUM TOMATOES, SEEDED AND DICED
1 BUNCH OF SPRING ONIONS, FINELY SLICED
225 G/8 OZ FLAT-LEAF PARSLEY, STEMMED AND
    CHOPPED BY HAND
50 G/2 OZ MINT, STEMMED AND CHOPPED BY HAND
½ TEASPOON GROUND CINNAMON
½ TEASPOON GROUND ALLSPICE
½ TEASPOON GROUND BLACK PEPPER
JUICE OF 2 LIMES
18 SMALL COS LETTUCE LEAVES

SERVES 6

Season the salmon, rub with a little olive oil and grill, with the skin side towards the heat, until the skin is slightly charred and very crispy. Turn the salmon over and grill for a further 2 minutes. Leave to cool. Remove and dice the skin; set aside. Flake the salmon flesh – not too small – and set aside.

Rinse the bulgar wheat in several changes of water. For the last change of water, leave the wheat to soak for 15 minutes.

Drain the bulgar wheat and combine with the diced tomatoes, spring onions, herbs, spices and lime juice. Gently mix in the salmon. Season to taste.

Arrange the lettuce leaves around a bowl and fill the centre with the tabbouleh. Scatter the crisp diced salmon skin over the top. Use the lettuce leaves to scoop up the tabbouleh.

Alastair Little

PRAWN SALAD
with taramasalata dressing

40 TIGER PRAWNS (ABOUT 1 KG/2¼ LB), HEADLESS BUT
   WITH SHELLS ON

1 GARLIC CLOVE, FINELY CHOPPED

1 LARGE FRESH RED CHILLI, SEEDED AND FINELY
   CHOPPED

SALT AND PEPPER

EXTRA VIRGIN OLIVE OIL

24 RIPE CHERRY TOMATOES

ABOUT 8 LARGE HANDFULS OF MIXED SALAD LEAVES

1 BUNCH OF CHIVES, SNIPPED INTO 1 CM/½ INCH
   LENGTHS

TARAMASALATA DRESSING

2 TABLESPOONS GOOD-QUALITY TARAMASALATA

JUICE OF 1 LEMON

6 TABLESPOONS EXTRA VIRGIN OLIVE OIL

SERVES 4

Peel the prawns and slit along their backs to
devein them. Continue cutting until the prawns
are nearly in two parts and then press them flat
to butterfly them. Place them in the grill pan
and scatter with the garlic and chilli. Season with
salt and drizzle on a little oil. Rub gently into
the prawns and ensure that the chilli is evenly
distributed. Heat the grill, but don't begin to
cook the prawns until everything else is ready.

Cut the tomatoes in half, season and drizzle
with olive oil. Wash and spin-dry the salad.

To make the dressing, put the taramasalata in
a bowl, whisk in the lemon juice, and then
gradually whisk in the oil.

Put the prawns under the hot grill for 2–3
minutes or until they change colour, becoming
opaque. They may need turning, but they must
not overcook.

Meanwhile, dress the salad leaves and pile on
to four plates. Arrange the prawns and tomatoes
around the edge of the salad and scatter with the
snipped chives.

Sean Connery

MARINATED HERRING SALAD
with sour cream dressing

4 LARGE HERRINGS, GUTTED, BONED AND FILLETED
225 G/8 OZ MIXED SALAD LEAVES
3 TABLESPOONS VINAIGRETTE
8 SMALL POTATOES, COOKED AND SLICED
1 TABLESPOON FINELY CHOPPED CHIVES

MARINADE
150 ML/5 FL OZ CIDER VINEGAR
150 ML/5 FL OZ WATER
3 TABLESPOONS CASTER SUGAR
1 SMALL ONION, SLICED
2 BAY LEAVES
8 PEPPERCORNS
8 ALLSPICE BERRIES
FEW FENNEL STALKS

SOUR CREAM DRESSING
300 ML/10 FL OZ SOUR CREAM
1 SMALL RED ONION, QUARTERED AND THINLY SLICED
4 TABLESPOONS CHOPPED SPRING ONION
FRESHLY GROUND BLACK PEPPER

SERVES 4
Cut the herrings into 2.5 cm/1 inch pieces and place in a large glass bowl. Put all the ingredients for the marinade into a saucepan, bring to the boil, then simmer for about 2 minutes. Leave until completely cold. Pour the cold marinade over the herrings, cover and refrigerate overnight.

Mix all the ingredients for the dressing in a large bowl. Drain the herrings from the marinade, pat dry and mix into the dressing.

Toss the salad leaves with the vinaigrette and divide between four large plates. Arrange the potatoes on the plates in overlapping slices. Pile the herrings on top of the potatoes, sprinkle with chives and serve immediately.

Sean Connery

TOASTED GOATS' CHEESE SALAD
with walnuts and creamy mustard dressing

225 G/8 OZ MIXED SALAD LEAVES (CURLY ENDIVE,
    ROCKET, LOLLO ROSSO, YOUNG SPINACH LEAVES)
2 TOMATOES, SKINNED, SEEDED AND DICED
SMALL BUNCH OF CHERVIL AND TARRAGON
4 SMALL FIRM-TEXTURED GOATS' CHEESES OR 325
    G/12 OZ GOATS' CHEESE LOG, CUT INTO 4 SLICES
50 G/2 OZ BUTTER, SOFTENED
85 G/3 OZ WALNUT PIECES, CHOPPED
4 SLICES OF FRENCH BREAD

MUSTARD DRESSING
5 TABLESPOONS WALNUT OIL
1 TABLESPOON WHOLE GRAIN MUSTARD
½ TABLESPOON DIJON MUSTARD
1 GARLIC CLOVE, FINELY CHOPPED
2 TABLESPOONS RED WINE VINEGAR
1 TABLESPOON DOUBLE CREAM

GARNISH
2 TABLESPOONS BLACK POPPY SEEDS
2 TABLESPOONS FINELY CHOPPED CHIVES

SERVES 4

Combine the salad leaves, diced tomatoes and herbs in a large bowl. Place all the ingredients for the dressing in a screw-topped jar and shake well to blend.

Place the cheeses on a baking sheet, spread with the softened butter and cover with the walnuts. Cook under a very hot grill for 2–3 minutes or until evenly browned and warmed through. Toast the bread at the same time.

Pour a little dressing over the salad leaves to moisten them. Toss gently and arrange on one side of four large plates. Set a piece of toasted bread on the other side and carefully lift the toasted cheese on top. Drizzle a little of the remaining dressing over the cheese. Sprinkle with the poppy seeds and chives and serve immediately.

Sean Connery

SPICY CABBAGE AND NOODLES
with warm scallops

12 SMALL SCALLOPS

125 G/4 OZ VERMICELLI NOODLES

3 TABLESPOONS SUNFLOWER OIL

1 LARGE ONION, THINLY SLICED

2 GARLIC CLOVES, CRUSHED

1 SMALL RED CHILLI, SEEDED AND FINELY CHOPPED

8 THIN SLICES OF FRESH GINGER

2 LARGE RED PEPPERS, SEEDED AND CUT INTO STRIPS

1 SMALL SAVOY CABBAGE, QUARTERED, CORE
   REMOVED
   AND FINELY SHREDDED

50 G/2 OZ BEANSPROUTS

3 TABLESPOONS CHOPPED CORIANDER, PLUS EXTRA
   TO GARNISH

SPICY DRESSING

6 TABLESPOONS SUNFLOWER OIL

2 TABLESPOONS SESAME OIL

2 GARLIC CLOVES, CRUSHED

4 TABLESPOONS RED WINE VINEGAR

4 TABLESPOONS TERIYAKI SAUCE

2 TABLESPOONS THAI FISH SAUCE

PINCH OF MUSCOVADO SUGAR

1–2 TEASPOONS SWEET CHILLI SAUCE

SERVES 4

Place all the ingredients for the dressing in a screw-topped jar and shake well to blend.

Wash and trim the scallops and pat dry.

Cook the noodles according to the packet instructions, then drain. Heat 2 tablespoons of the oil in a wok and fry the onion, garlic, chilli and ginger until soft. Add the peppers, then the cabbage, tossing quickly until slightly wilted. Add the drained noodles and the beansprouts. Pour over the dressing, bring to the boil, then stir-fry for a few minutes. Stir in the coriander.

Brush each scallop with a little sunflower oil and sear on a very hot cast-iron pan for 30 seconds each side.

Pile the cabbage mixture on to four large plates and arrange the scallops on top. Garnish with coriander and serve immediately.

eggs
and
cheese

Richard Olney

SCRAMBLED EGGS
with asparagus

1 GARLIC CLOVE, PEELED

45 G/1½ OZ COLD UNSALTED BUTTER, DICED

6 EGGS

SALT AND FRESHLY GROUND BLACK PEPPER

225 G/½ LB ASPARAGUS, STEMS PEELED, SLICED THINLY
ON THE DIAGONAL, PARBOILED IN HEAVILY SALTED
WATER FOR A FEW SECONDS ONLY, THEN DRAINED

CROÛTONS, TO SERVE

*The eggs are cooked in a bain-marie; I use a heavy
saucepan placed on a trivet in a larger saucepan that is
filled with water to about the level of the eggs in the
smaller pan. To gauge the amount of water, assemble
the pans and trivet in advance.*

SERVES 2

Rub a wooden spoon with the garlic. Butter the
smaller saucepan. Place 15 g/½ oz of the butter
in a bowl, break over the eggs, season and beat
lightly with a fork.

Pour the eggs into the smaller saucepan, place
it on the trivet in the larger pan and heat until
the water is nearly boiling. Keeping the water
just below the boil, stir the eggs slowly and
regularly with the garlicky spoon, scraping the
sides, corners and bottom of the pan.

Melt 15 g/½ oz butter in an omelette pan and
sauté the parboiled asparagus over high heat, just
long enough to heat through. Stir into the eggs.

As the eggs begin to thicken, watch them
closely, stirring more rapidly. As they approach a
creamy but pourable consistency, remove the
pan from the water. Add the remaining butter
and stir for half a minute. Serve in warmed plates
and scatter with croûtons.

Aglaia Kremezi

TORTILLA
(Potato and onion omelette)

4 TABLESPOONS OLIVE OIL

1 KG/2¼ LB LARGE POTATOES, PEELED, CUT IN HALF
LENGTHWAYS AND SLICED

3 ONIONS, DICED

1 GREEN PEPPER, DICED

5 EGGS, BEATEN

SALT AND FRESHLY GROUND BLACK PEPPER

SERVES 8

Heat the oil in a nonstick frying pan and sauté the potatoes, onions and pepper for a few minutes, stirring frequently. Cover and cook over medium heat for 10–15 minutes, stirring occasionally, until tender. Drain in a colander, then return to the frying pan.

Season the eggs generously with salt and pepper, then pour the eggs over the vegetables and cook over low heat, shaking the pan often, until the omelette no longer sticks to the sides of the pan.

Place a large plate over the omelette and invert the frying pan. Slide the omelette back into the pan and cook for another minute or so. Transfer to a plate, cut into squares and serve warm or at room temperature.

Richard Olney

FLAT COURGETTE OMELETTE

2 FIRM COURGETTES, ABOUT 325 G/12 OZ

SALT

2 TABLESPOONS OLIVE OIL

15 G/½ OZ COLD UNSALTED BUTTER, DICED

1 TABLESPOON LEAVES AND UNOPENED FLOWER BUDS
OF TENDER FRESH MARJORAM, FINELY CHOPPED

3 EGGS

FRESHLY GROUND BLACK PEPPER

HANDFUL OF FRESHLY GRATED PARMESAN CHEESE

SERVES 2

Shred the courgettes with the medium shredding blade of a food processor, or grate them coarsely. Layer the shreds in a bowl, sprinkling each layer with salt, and leave for at least 30 minutes. Squeeze tightly and transfer to a plate, discarding the liquid.

Heat the grill. Heat half the olive oil in an omelette pan, add the courgettes and sauté for 2–3 minutes, until lightly coloured.

Put the butter and marjoram in a bowl with the eggs, salt and pepper. Stir with a fork and add the courgettes, stirring briskly.

Replace the pan over high heat, add the remaining oil, swirl to coat the pan and add the egg mixture. Stir with the fork, tines facing up, without scraping the pan, for about 30 seconds. Sprinkle the cheese over the omelette, taking care not to touch the pan.

Place the pan under the hot grill for 1–2 minutes or until the eggs are nearly set at the centre. Shake the pan gently, to be certain the omelette slips freely, and slide it on to a warmed platter. Serve cut into wedges.

Rowley Leigh

OMELETTE WITH MOUSSERONS

3 EGGS

50 G/2 OZ BUTTER

A HANDFUL OF MOUSSERON MUSHROOMS, CLEANED
   (PAGE 374)

SALT AND PEPPER

LEMON JUICE

SERVES 1

Break the eggs into a bowl and beat them lightly until they are thoroughly mixed.

Heat half the butter in a saucepan until it is foaming; fry the mushrooms very quickly and season with a little salt, pepper and lemon juice.

Place an omelette pan over a fairly high heat and add the remaining butter; when it is foaming, pour in the eggs, add the mushrooms and season well. Do nothing for 10 seconds, but wait for the eggs to bubble up in the middle of the pan. Stir quickly and lightly with the back of a fork or a wooden spoon, then move the omelette off the centre of the pan towards the edge of the pan furthest away from you. Speed is of the essence; the omelette should remain creamy in the centre and should take no more than 45 seconds to cook. Give the pan a little knock to nudge the omelette against the edge. Tip the omelette on to a warmed plate and serve at once, either on its own or with some fried potatoes.

Aglaia Kremezi

SPICY FETA AND PEPPER SPREAD

3 TABLESPOONS OLIVE OIL

1 LARGE RED PEPPER, SEEDED AND
   COARSELY CHOPPED

1 SMALL FRESH RED CHILLI, SEEDED AND CHOPPED, OR
   ½–1 TEASPOON CAYENNE PEPPER

450 G/1 LB FETA CHEESE, OR 300 G/11 OZ FETA
   CHEESE AND 150 G/5 OZ COTTAGE CHEESE

SERVES 10–12

Heat the olive oil in a frying pan and sauté the pepper together with the chilli, if you are using it, until soft, about 5 minutes. If you are using cayenne pepper, add it to the pan a few seconds before removing it from the heat.

Taste the feta and if it is very salty, rinse in cold water. Crumble it with a fork and place it in a food processor. Add the sautéed peppers and their oil, and pulse to make a smooth paste.

Serve with fresh bread, toast or crackers.

This will keep for about 1 week in the refrigerator, in a covered bowl. Bring to room temperature before serving.

Valentina Harris

POLENTA PASTICCIATA

300 G/11 OZ YELLOW POLENTA FLOUR
SALT
4 TABLESPOONS OLIVE OIL
2 ONIONS, FINELY CHOPPED
1 GARLIC CLOVE, FINELY CHOPPED
1 STICK OF CELERY, CHOPPED
1 CARROT, CHOPPED
50 G/2 OZ PANCETTA, CHOPPED
500 ML/16 FL OZ PASSATA
1 BAY LEAF
SALT AND FRESHLY GROUND BLACK PEPPER
300 G/11 OZ MOZZARELLA CHEESE, CUBED
200 G/7 OZ PARMESAN CHEESE, GRATED
3 TABLESPOONS EXTRA VIRGIN OLIVE OIL

SERVES 6

Bring 2 litres/3½ pints water to the boil, add two pinches of salt and then rain the polenta into the boiling water, whisking vigorously. As soon as the polenta begins to thicken, take a large wooden spoon and stir constantly until the polenta comes away from the sides of the pan: this will take 50 minutes. Turn the cooked polenta on to a wooden board and leave until cold. This can be made the day before. Cut the cold polenta into strips about 8 cm/3 inches wide.

Heat the oil in a saucepan and fry the onions, garlic, celery, carrot and pancetta until the vegetables are soft. Add the passata and the bay leaf. Season, cover and simmer gently for about 45 minutes.

Preheat the oven to 190°C/375°F/Gas Mark 5.

Oil an ovenproof dish and arrange a layer of polenta on the bottom. Cover with a thin layer of the tomato sauce, then sprinkle with mozzarella and Parmesan. Drizzle with a little oil, then repeat the layers until all the sauce and cheese have been used up.

Bake the polenta for about 30 minutes. Serve piping hot.

If you have some polenta left over, grill it and drizzle it with a little oil. You can eat this while you wait for the main dish.

This is a very filling dish, so to follow I would recommend nothing more substantial than a little salad and fruit, preferably some refreshing citrus fruit.

Aglaia Kremezi

YOGURT CHEESE WITH HERBS
and garlic

600 G/1¼ LB GREEK STRAINED YOGURT

1–2 GARLIC CLOVES, FINELY CHOPPED

1½ TEASPOONS SEA SALT

½–1½ TEASPOONS GROUND WHITE PEPPER

3 BUNCHES OF DILL, CHOPPED

6 SPRIGS OF CORIANDER, CHOPPED

7 SPRIGS OF FLAT-LEAF PARSLEY, CHOPPED

SERVES 8–10

Put all the ingredients into a bowl and stir well to mix. (You can vary the herbs according to taste or availability. For example you can use only dill, or you can substitute parsley for the dill and complement it with mint or basil.)

Line another bowl with a double layer of muslin or a linen tea towel and pour in the yogurt mixture. Gather the ends of the cloth and tie them together with a piece of kitchen string, making a loop so you can hang it from a large wooden spoon, keeping it well clear of the bottom of the bowl. Leave to drain for 8–12 hours or overnight.

Untie the cloth and remove the soft cheese. Serve with fresh bread, toast or crackers.

This will keep for about 1 week in the refrigerator, in a covered bowl.

Karen Lee

CREAMY POLENTA
with three cheeses

500 ML/16 FL OZ SKIMMED MILK

500 ML/16 FL OZ WATER

1½ TEASPOONS SALT

¼ TEASPOON GROUND WHITE PEPPER

225 G/8 OZ COARSE CORNMEAL
  (POLENTA)

175 G/6 OZ MIXED PARMESAN, CHEDDAR AND GOATS'
  CHEESE, GRATED OR CHOPPED

SERVES 6–8

Bring the milk and water to the boil in a heavy-based saucepan. Add the salt and pepper, then add the cornmeal in a slow and steady stream, stirring continuously until all the cornmeal is absorbed, about 3 minutes.

Reduce the heat to very low and, using a large wooden spoon or spatula, stir the cornmeal in a figure-of-eight motion almost constantly for 18–20 minutes (or less if using quick-cooking polenta). The polenta is done when it adheres to itself and pulls away from the sides of the pan.

Remove from the heat, add the cheese and stir until melted, about 1–2 minutes.

Serve piping hot. Alternatively, place in a buttered or oiled heatproof dish, leave to cool, then cover and store in the refrigerator. To serve, brush with butter or olive oil and place under a hot grill for 2–3 minutes or until lightly browned. Then bake in a preheated oven at 190°C/375°F/Gas Mark 5 for 5–10 minutes.

Alastair Little

TOMATO AND MUSTARD TARTS

with Cheddar cheese and thyme

250 G/9 OZ PUFF PASTRY
SALT AND PEPPER
8 RIPE PLUM TOMATOES, SKINNED AND THINLY SLICED
4 TABLESPOONS DIJON MUSTARD
250 G/9 OZ MILD CHEDDAR CHEESE, THINLY SLICED
A LITTLE FRESH THYME
EXTRA VIRGIN OLIVE OIL

SERVES 4

Preheat the oven to 180°C/ 350°F/Gas Mark 4 and lightly butter a baking sheet. On a lightly floured surface, roll out the puff pastry fairly thinly and cut out four circles, about 10 cm/4 inches in diameter. Transfer these upside down to the baking sheet.

Season the tomato slices generously. Spread 1 teaspoon of the mustard on each pastry circle, leaving a 5 mm/¼ inch border. Arrange a circle of overlapping tomato and cheese slices on top, again leaving the border uncovered. Arrange more cheese and tomato slices to fill the centres. Sprinkle the tarts with thyme and drizzle lightly with olive oil.

Using the back of a knife blade, feather the edges of the pastry, pushing up the borders to form a low wall.

Bake for 10 minutes or until the pastry has risen. Reduce the oven temperature to 160°C/ 325°F/Gas Mark 3 and bake for a further 10 minutes. Serve immediately, with a green salad.

Valentina Harris

COURGETTE AND CHEESE GRATIN

5 LARGE COURGETTES, TOPPED, TAILED AND WASHED
4 TABLESPOONS EXTRA VIRGIN OLIVE OIL
1 LARGE RED ONION, THINLY SLICED
5 FRESH EGGS, BEATEN THOROUGHLY
6 TABLESPOONS FRESHLY GRATED PARMESAN CHEESE
150 G/5 OZ MOZZARELLA CHEESE, CUT INTO SMALL
  CUBES
2 TABLESPOONS CHOPPED FRESH FLAT-LEAF PARSLEY
SALT AND FRESHLY GROUND BLACK PEPPER
3 TABLESPOONS DRIED WHITE BREADCRUMBS

SERVES 4–6

Preheat the oven to 180°C/350°F/Gas Mark 4.

Cut the courgettes into cubes. Heat the oil in a frying pan, add the onion and fry until soft. Add the courgette cubes and fry gently until softened, turning frequently.

Oil an ovenproof dish large enough to hold all the ingredients with space at the top. Scatter a layer of the courgette and onion mixture in the dish. Cover with a thin layer of eggs and sprinkle with Parmesan, mozzarella and a little parsley; season with salt and pepper. Repeat until all the ingredients have been layered in the dish. Make sure the top is covered with beaten egg. Sprinkle the breadcrumbs on the top and bake for about 30 minutes or until well browned and crisp.

Serve with crusty bread and a crisp green salad. Some torn basil leaves are a good addition to the salad, since the flavour of basil goes very well with courgettes.

Aglaia Kremezi

CHEESE AND SPINACH TRIANGLES
with leek and fennel

ABOUT 125 ML/4 FL OZ OLIVE OIL

1 LEEK, THINLY SLICED

1 FENNEL BULB, FINELY CHOPPED

225 G/8 OZ FROZEN SPINACH, CHOPPED

1 BUNCH OF PARSLEY, CHOPPED

85 G/3 OZ PECORINO OR FETA CHEESE, GRATED

85 G/3 OZ PARMESAN OR MATURE CHEDDAR CHEESE,
 GRATED

1 EGG

SALT AND FRESHLY GROUND BLACK PEPPER

14 FILO PASTRY SHEETS

MAKES 28

Preheat the oven to 200°C/400°F/Gas Mark 6.

Heat 3 tablespoons of the olive oil in a frying pan and sauté the leek and fennel until tender, about 8 minutes. Add the spinach and parsley and sauté, stirring, until dry. Remove from the heat, stir in the cheeses and egg; season to taste.

Work with one sheet of filo pastry at a time, keeping the rest covered with a damp tea towel to prevent it from drying out. Lightly brush a sheet of filo with olive oil and fold it in half lengthways. Brush the top with oil and cut it into two strips. Place 1 heaped tablespoon of the spinach mixture at the end of a strip of filo. Fold the corner of the pastry over the filling to reach the other edge, making a triangle. Fold the triangle up over the pastry strip. Then continue folding the triangle across and up until all the pastry is folded around the filling. Brush with a little more oil and place on an oiled baking sheet. Repeat to make 28 parcels.

Bake for about 35 minutes, until golden brown. Serve warm or at room temperature.

If fresh (not frozen) filo pastry is used, the uncooked parcels can be frozen; cook from frozen.

Paul & Jeanne Rankin

GOATS' CHEESE FRITTERS
with Jalapeño chillies

325 G/12 OZ FRESH GOATS' CHEESE

1 SMALL JAR (ABOUT 175 G/6 OZ OR SMALLER) SLICED
   JALAPEÑO CHILLIES

A LITTLE FLOUR

125 G/4 OZ GROUND ALMONDS

125 G/4 OZ DRIED BREADCRUMBS

1 TABLESPOON CHOPPED FRESH PARSLEY

1 EGG, BEATEN WITH 2 TABLESPOONS MILK

1 SMALL JAR (ABOUT 200 G/7 OZ) ROASTED RED
   PEPPERS (PIMENTOS)

100 ML/3½ FL OZ VINAIGRETTE

1 TEASPOON CHILLI SAUCE

VEGETABLE OIL FOR DEEP-FRYING

TO SERVE

BUNCH OF ROCKET

ROUGHLY CHOPPED CHIVES AND TOASTED PINE NUTS
   (OPTIONAL)

SERVES 4

Using a small knife, remove the skin from the goats' cheese. Drain 1–2 tablespoons of the chillies – depending on how hot you like your food – and pat them very dry on paper towels. Place the cheese and chillies in a food processor and pulse for about 15 seconds or until the cheese softens slightly. Tip the mixture on to a clean surface and divide it into 12 pieces. Sprinkle lightly with flour and roll between your hands to form perfect balls.

Mix together the almonds, breadcrumbs and parsley. Dip each cheese ball into the egg and milk mixture and then into the almond and breadcrumb mixture. Refrigerate for at least 2 hours, until they are quite firm.

Drain any excess liquid from the pimentos and chop finely to form a rough purée. Stir in the vinaigrette and chilli sauce. Taste and adjust the seasoning.

Heat the oil to 180°C/350°F or until a cube of bread browns in 30 seconds. Fry the cheese balls until just golden (don't fry them for too long or they will burst).

Arrange a bed of rocket on four plates and spoon a generous portion of the pimento vinaigrette around the plate. Place the cheese fritters on the rocket and serve at once, garnished with chives and toasted pine nuts.

rice

Michele Scicolone

TOMATO AND BASIL RISOTTO

1.5 LITRES/2½ PINTS CHICKEN STOCK (PAGE 374)

3 TABLESPOONS UNSALTED BUTTER

1 TABLESPOON OLIVE OIL

2–3 SHALLOTS OR 1 ONION, FINELY CHOPPED

400 G/14 OZ MEDIUM-GRAIN RICE

125 ML/4 FL OZ DRY WHITE WINE

450 G/1 LB FRESH TOMATOES, SEEDED AND CHOPPED,
   OR
   400 G/14 OZ CANNED TOMATOES, PASSED THROUGH
   A FOOD MILL

SALT AND FRESHLY GROUND BLACK PEPPER

LARGE BUNCH OF BASIL, CHOPPED

50 G/2 OZ PARMESAN CHEESE, GRATED

SERVES 4–6

Heat the stock to just below simmering point.

In a large saucepan, melt 2 tablespoons of the butter with the oil over medium heat. Add the shallots or onion and cook until tender, about 3 minutes.

Add the rice and stir for 2 minutes, until it is coated with the butter. Add the wine and continue to cook and stir until the liquid is absorbed. Add the tomatoes and cook for 1 minute further.

Add the hot stock, 125 ml/4 fl oz at a time, stirring constantly and making sure the liquid has been absorbed before adding more. After about 10 minutes, stir in salt and pepper to taste. If more liquid is required, use hot water. The risotto is done when the rice grains are tender, yet still firm to the bite.

Remove the pan from the heat and stir in the remaining butter, the basil and the Parmesan cheese. Serve at once.

TIPS FOR MAKING PERFECT RISOTTO

Use a medium-grain Italian rice such as arborio, carnaroli or vialone nano.

Use homemade chicken, beef, veal, fish or vegetable stock as appropriate. As an alternative, use a good-quality chilled or canned chicken or meat stock. Taste several brands to see which is best. Some commercially made stock is salty, so taste carefully before adding salt. Dilute canned stock with an equal amount of water.

Cook risotto in a heavy-based, wide saucepan that is not too deep, about 25 cm/10 inches in diameter and 10 cm/4 inches deep.

Cooking time is approximately 20 minutes from the first addition of stock, but exact cooking times will vary according to the variety of rice, the flavouring ingredients and the type of pan used. Depending on the variety of rice, you may need to use less or more liquid. Keep a kettle of hot water ready while cooking the risotto; if the stock runs out before the rice is cooked, add hot water instead.

Risotto needs constant stirring – enlist a friend to keep you company and to help stir the pot.

Risotto is ready to eat when it is al dente, tender yet still firm to the bite. The centre of each grain of rice should be neither chalky and hard, nor soft and mushy. It does not reheat well, so serve it as soon as it is ready. Risotto should be served in shallow bowls and eaten with a fork. It is served as a separate course - not a side dish. The only exception is Risotto Milanese, which is often served as an accompaniment to Osso Buco.

Leftover risotto can be used to make a Risotto al Salto, crispy rice pancakes. Mix about 500 ml/16 fl oz of risotto (any flavour) with a beaten egg. Melt some butter in a small frying pan. Scoop up about 4 tablespoons of the rice mixture, place it in the pan and flatten slightly. Cook until golden brown and crisp on both sides. Repeat with the remaining rice, to make 8 pancakes. Serve hot.

Michele Scicolone

ITALIAN SAUSAGE RISOTTO
with mushrooms

1.5 LITRES/2½ PINTS CHICKEN STOCK (PAGE 374)
2 TABLESPOONS UNSALTED BUTTER
1 TABLESPOON OLIVE OIL
1 ONION, FINELY CHOPPED
225 G/8 OZ ITALIAN SAUSAGES, CASINGS REMOVED
225 G/8 OZ MUSHROOMS, SLICED
400 G/14 OZ MEDIUM-GRAIN RICE
125 ML/4 FL OZ DRY WHITE WINE
SALT AND FRESHLY GROUND BLACK PEPPER
50 G/2 OZ PARMESAN CHEESE, GRATED

SERVES 4–6

Heat the stock to just below simmering point.

In a large saucepan, melt the butter with the oil over medium heat. Add the onion and cook until tender, about 5 minutes.

Add the sausages and cook, stirring frequently to break up the lumps. When the sausages are lightly browned, add the mushrooms and cook for 2 minutes or until just wilted.

Add the rice and stir for 2 minutes, until it is coated with the butter. Add the wine and stir until the liquid is absorbed.

Add the hot stock, 125 ml/4 fl oz at a time, stirring constantly and making sure the liquid has been absorbed before adding more. After about 10 minutes, stir in salt and pepper to taste. If more liquid is required, use hot water. The risotto is done when the rice grains are tender, yet still firm to the bite.

Remove the pan from the heat and stir in the Parmesan cheese. Serve at once.

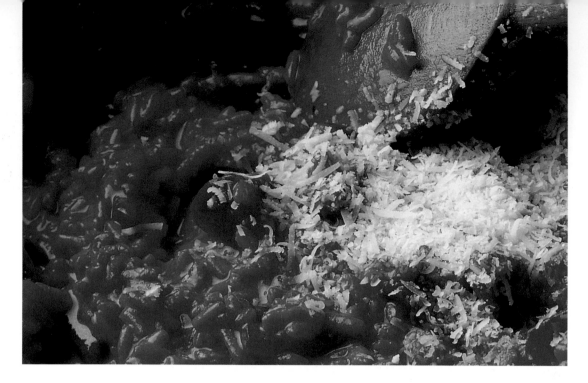

Michele Scicolone

ROASTED BEETROOT RISOTTO

4 BEETROOT, TRIMMED

1.5 LITRES/2½ PINTS CHICKEN STOCK (PAGE 374)

3 TABLESPOONS UNSALTED BUTTER

1 TABLESPOON OLIVE OIL

1 ONION, FINELY CHOPPED

400 G/14 OZ MEDIUM-GRAIN RICE

175 ML/6 FL OZ DRY WHITE WINE

SALT AND FRESHLY GROUND BLACK PEPPER

50 G/2 OZ PARMESAN CHEESE, GRATED

SERVES 4–6

Preheat the oven to 230°C/450°F/Gas Mark 8. Place the beetroot on a sheet of foil and bake in the preheated oven for 45–60 minutes or until tender when pierced with a knife. Leave to cool. Peel off the skins and chop the beetroot.

For the risotto, heat the stock to just below simmering point.

In a large saucepan, melt 2 tablespoons of the butter with the oil over medium heat. Add the onion and cook until tender.

Add the rice and stir for 2 minutes. Add the wine and continue to cook and stir until the liquid is absorbed. Add the beetroot and cook for 1 minute.

Add the hot stock, 125 ml/4 fl oz at a time, stirring constantly and making sure the liquid has been absorbed before adding more. After about 10 minutes, stir in salt and pepper to taste. If more liquid is required, use hot water. The risotto is done when the rice grains are tender, yet still firm to the bite.

Remove the pan from the heat and stir in the remaining butter and the cheese. Serve at once.

Michele Scicolone

RED WINE RISOTTO

1.5 LITRES/2½ PINTS CHICKEN STOCK (PAGE 374)

3 TABLESPOONS UNSALTED BUTTER

1 TABLESPOON OLIVE OIL

1 ONION, FINELY CHOPPED

1 LARGE GARLIC CLOVE, FINELY CHOPPED

400 G/14 OZ MEDIUM-GRAIN RICE

2 TEASPOONS TOMATO PURÉE

250 ML/8 FL OZ DRY RED WINE, SUCH AS BARBERA

SALT AND FRESHLY GROUND BLACK PEPPER

50 G/2 OZ PARMESAN CHEESE, GRATED

SERVES 4–6

Heat the stock to just below simmering point.

In a large saucepan, melt 2 tablespoons of the butter with the oil over medium heat. Add the onion and cook until tender, about 5 minutes. Add the garlic and cook for a further 1 minute.

Add the rice and stir for 2 minutes, until it is heated and coated with the butter.

Mix the tomato purée with 125 ml/4 fl oz of the stock. Add to the rice and stir until the liquid is completely absorbed. Add the wine and continue to cook, stirring, until the liquid is absorbed.

Add the remaining hot stock, 125 ml/4 fl oz at a time, stirring constantly and making sure the liquid has been absorbed before adding more. After about 10 minutes, stir in salt and pepper to taste. If more liquid is required, use hot water. The risotto is done when the rice grains are tender, yet still firm to the bite.

Remove the pan from the heat and stir in the remaining butter and the cheese. Serve at once.

Michele Sciadone

RISOTTO WITH FENNEL

450 G/1 LB FENNEL (1 LARGE BULB)
1.5 LITRES/2½ PINTS CHICKEN STOCK (PAGE 374)
2 TABLESPOONS UNSALTED BUTTER
2 TABLESPOONS OLIVE OIL
3–4 SPRING ONIONS, FINELY CHOPPED
400 G/14 OZ MEDIUM-GRAIN RICE
SALT AND FRESHLY GROUND PEPPER
125 G/4 OZ PARMESAN CHEESE, GRATED

SERVES 4–6

Trim off the dark green feathery leaves of the fennel and trim the stalks down to the rounded bulb. Cut a slice off the stem end and pare off any bruises on the outer leaves. Cut the fennel into quarters lengthways, then into thin slices.

Heat the stock to just below simmering point.

In a large saucepan, melt 1 tablespoon of the butter with the oil over medium-low heat. Add the spring onions and cook until tender, about 3 minutes. Add the fennel and cook for 10 minutes, stirring occasionally.

Add the rice and stir for 2 minutes. Add the hot stock, 125 ml/4 fl oz at a time, stirring constantly and making sure the liquid has been absorbed before adding more. After about 10 minutes, stir in salt and pepper to taste. If more liquid is required, use hot water. The risotto is done when the rice grains are tender, yet still firm to the bite.

Remove the pan from the heat and stir in the remaining butter and the cheese. Serve at once.

Michele Scicolone

PRAWN AND SCALLOP RISOTTO

3 TABLESPOONS OLIVE OIL

2 LARGE GARLIC CLOVES, FINELY CHOPPED

3 TABLESPOONS CHOPPED FRESH PARSLEY

450 G/1 LB UNCOOKED PRAWNS, SHELLED AND
DEVEINED AND CUT INTO 3 OR 4 PIECES

125 G/4 OZ SCALLOPS, HALVED OR QUARTERED IF
LARGE

SALT AND FRESHLY GROUND PEPPER

125 ML/4 FL OZ DRY WHITE WINE

1.5 LITRES/2½ PINTS CHICKEN OR FISH STOCK (PAGE
374)

3 TABLESPOONS UNSALTED BUTTER

1 ONION, FINELY CHOPPED

400 G/14 OZ MEDIUM-GRAIN RICE

SERVES 6

In a saucepan, heat 2 tablespoons of the oil with the garlic and 2 tablespoons of the parsley over medium heat. Cook until the garlic begins to colour slightly.

Add the prawns, scallops, salt and pepper. Cook until the prawns turn pink, about 2 minutes. Add the wine and bring to a simmer.

With a slotted spoon, remove the seafood and set aside. Pour the stock into the pan and heat it to just below simmering point.

In a large saucepan, melt 2 tablespoons of the butter with the remaining oil, add the onion and cook until golden.

Add the rice and stir for 2 minutes. Add the hot stock, 125 ml/4 fl oz at a time, stirring constantly and making sure the liquid has been absorbed before adding more. After about 10 minutes, stir in salt and pepper to taste. If more liquid is required, use hot water. When the rice is just tender, stir in the seafood and heat through. Remove from the heat and stir in the remaining butter and parsley. Serve at once.

Michele Scicolone

GOLDEN CARROT RISOTTO
with vegetable confetti

1.5 LITRES/2½ PINTS CHICKEN STOCK (PAGE 374)

3 TABLESPOONS UNSALTED BUTTER

1 TABLESPOON OLIVE OIL

1 ONION, FINELY CHOPPED

400 G/14 OZ MEDIUM-GRAIN RICE

6–8 CARROTS, SLICED

SALT AND FRESHLY GROUND BLACK PEPPER

85 G/3 OZ SHELLED FRESH OR FROZEN PEAS

1 SMALL RED PEPPER, FINELY DICED

1 COURGETTE, FINELY DICED

2 TABLESPOONS CHOPPED FRESH BASIL

50 G/2 OZ PARMESAN CHEESE, GRATED

SERVES 4–6

Heat the stock to just below simmering point.

In a large saucepan, melt 2 tablespoons of the butter with the oil over medium heat. Add the onion and cook until tender, about 5 minutes.

Add the rice and stir for 2 minutes, until it is coated with the butter. Add the carrots and cook for 1 minute.

Add the hot stock, 125 ml/4 fl oz at a time, stirring constantly and making sure the liquid has been absorbed before adding more. After about 10 minutes, stir in salt and pepper to taste. If more liquid is required, use hot water.

After a further 5 minutes, stir in the peas, red pepper and diced courgette. The risotto is done when the rice grains are tender, yet still firm to the bite.

Remove the pan from the heat and stir in the remaining butter and the cheese. Serve at once.

Michele Scicolone

LEEK AND PANCETTA RISOTTO

2 LEEKS
1.5 LITRES/2½ PINTS CHICKEN STOCK (PAGE 374)
2 TABLESPOONS UNSALTED BUTTER
1 TABLESPOON OLIVE OIL
50 G/2 OZ CHOPPED PANCETTA OR BLANCHED BACON
400 G/14 OZ MEDIUM-GRAIN RICE
125 ML/4 FL OZ DRY WHITE WINE
SALT AND FRESHLY GROUND BLACK PEPPER
50 G/2 OZ PARMESAN CHEESE, GRATED

SERVES 4–6

Trim the leeks and cut them in half lengthways. Rinse well, then cut into thin slices.

Heat the stock to just below simmering point.

In a large saucepan, melt the butter with the oil over medium heat. Add the pancetta or bacon and cook until lightly browned, about 5 minutes. Add the leeks and cook until tender, about 5 minutes.

Add the rice and stir for 2 minutes, until it is coated with the butter. Add the wine and stir until the liquid is absorbed.

Add the hot stock, 125 ml/4 fl oz at a time, stirring constantly and making sure the liquid has been absorbed before adding more. After about 10 minutes, stir in salt and pepper to taste. If more liquid is required, use hot water. The risotto is done when the rice grains are tender, yet still firm to the bite.

Remove the pan from the heat and stir in the Parmesan cheese. Serve at once.

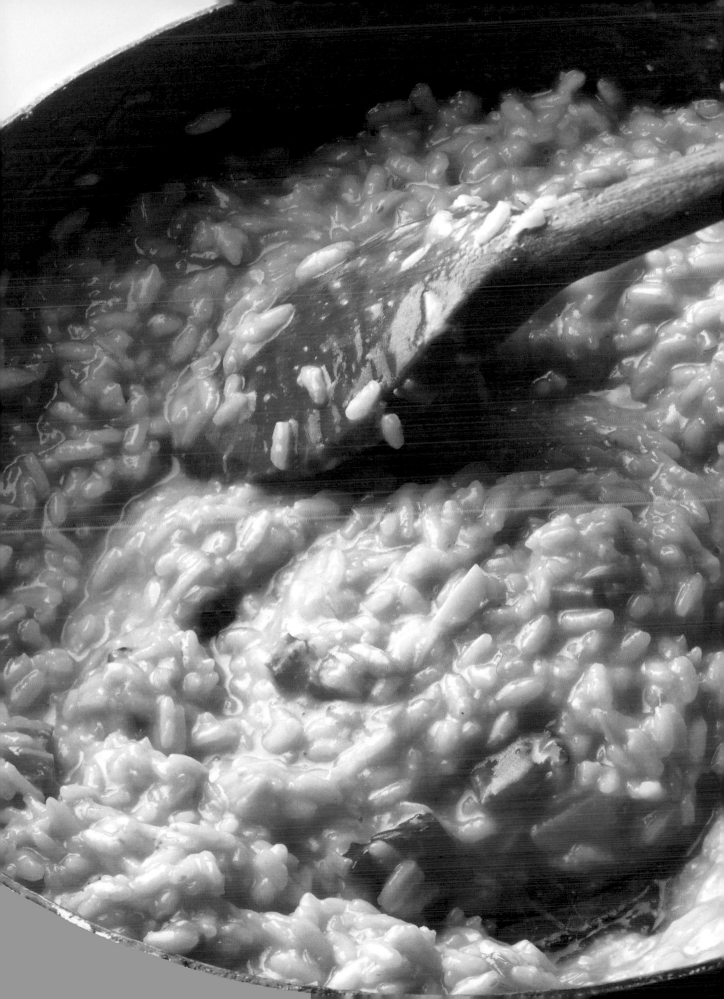

Michele Scicolone
ORANGE RISOTTO

1 ORANGE

1.5 LITRES/2½ PINTS CHICKEN STOCK (PAGE 374)

3 TABLESPOONS UNSALTED BUTTER

1 TABLESPOON SUNFLOWER OIL

1 ONION, FINELY CHOPPED

400 G/14 OZ MEDIUM-GRAIN RICE

125 ML/4 FL OZ DRY WHITE WINE

SALT AND FRESHLY GROUND PEPPER

½ TEASPOON GRATED LEMON ZEST

85 G/3 OZ PARMESAN CHEESE, GRATED

SERVES 4–6

Scrub the orange and dry it well. Grate the zest, being careful not to remove any of the white pith; you should have about 1 teaspoon of zest. Cut the orange in half and squeeze the juice; there should be about 125 ml/4 fl oz.

Heat the stock to just below simmering point.

In a large saucepan, melt 1 tablespoon of the butter with the oil over medium-low heat. Add the onion and cook until tender and golden, about 5 minutes.

Add the rice and stir for 2 minutes. Add the wine and cook, stirring, until it is absorbed.

Stir in the orange juice. Add the hot stock, 125 ml/4 fl oz at a time, stirring constantly and making sure the liquid has been absorbed before adding more. After about 10 minutes, stir in salt and pepper to taste. If more liquid is required, use hot water.

When the rice is tender, yet still firm to the bite, remove from the heat. Stir in the grated orange and lemon zest, the remaining butter and the cheese. Serve at once.

Michele Scicolone

PEAR AND PARMESAN RISOTTO

1.5 LITRES/2½ PINTS CHICKEN STOCK (PAGE 374)
3 TABLESPOONS UNSALTED BUTTER
1 TABLESPOON OLIVE OIL
1 ONION, FINELY CHOPPED
400 G/14 OZ MEDIUM-GRAIN RICE
175 ML/6 FL OZ DRY WHITE WINE
2 PEARS, PEELED, CORED AND CHOPPED
SALT AND FRESHLY GROUND BLACK PEPPER
50 G/2 OZ PARMESAN CHEESE, GRATED

SERVES 4–6

Heat the stock to just below simmering point.

In a large saucepan, melt 2 tablespoons of the butter with the oil over medium heat. Add the onion and cook until tender, about 5 minutes.

Add the rice and stir for 2 minutes, until it is heated and coated with the butter. Add the wine and cook, stirring, until it is absorbed. Add the pears and cook for 1 minute.

Add the hot stock, 125 ml/4 fl oz at a time, stirring constantly and making sure the liquid has been absorbed before adding more. After about 10 minutes, stir in salt and pepper to taste. If more liquid is required, use hot water. The risotto is done when the rice grains are tender, yet still firm to the bite.

Remove the pan from the heat and stir in the remaining butter and the cheese. Serve at once.

Antony Worrall Thompson

PAELLA
with shellfish and chicken

6 TABLESPOONS EXTRA VIRGIN OLIVE OIL

12 LARGE UNCOOKED PRAWNS

1 LARGE ONION, FINELY DICED

12 CHICKEN THIGHS OR RABBIT PIECES

4 GARLIC CLOVES, CRUSHED WITH A LITTLE SALT

2 SPRIGS OF THYME

6 SMALL SQUID, CLEANED AND CUT INTO ROUNDS

175 ML/6 FL OZ DRY WHITE WINE

450 G/1 LB CLAMS, CLEANED

450 G/1 LB MUSSELS, CLEANED

600 G/1¼ LB SHORT-GRAIN RICE

PINCH OF SAFFRON, SOAKED IN A LITTLE WARM WATER

1 TEASPOON PAPRIKA

4 LARGE TOMATOES, SKINNED AND CHOPPED

3 TABLESPOONS CHOPPED FLAT-LEAF PARSLEY

SALT AND GROUND BLACK PEPPER

SERVES 6

Heat half the oil in a paella pan or large frying pan and cook the prawns over a high heat for 2 minutes. Remove and set aside.

Add the remaining oil to the pan, with the onion, chicken, garlic, thyme and squid. Fry until all is golden, about 10 minutes.

Meanwhile, bring the wine to the boil in a large saucepan, add the clams and mussels, cover and cook over a high heat until the shellfish have opened. Strain the cooking liquid through a fine sieve and set aside. When cool enough to handle, shell half the mussels and clams; discard the empty shells.

Add the rice, saffron and paprika to the pan with the chicken, stir to combine. Pour in 2½ litres/4½ pints water and cook for 10 minutes over a high heat.

Reduce the heat to medium and cook for a further 10 minutes.

In the last 3 minutes of cooking, stir in the tomatoes, prawns, clams, mussels and parsley. Season to taste and serve immediately, from the paella dish.

Karen Lee

THREE-GRAIN FRIED RICE

85 G/3 OZ SHORT-GRAIN BROWN RICE

85 G/3 OZ BROWN SWEET RICE (AVAILABLE FROM
HEALTH FOOD SHOPS), OR BASMATI RICE (BROWN
OR WHITE)

85 G/3 OZ WHOLE WHEAT BERRIES

1½ TABLESPOONS PEANUT OIL

ABOUT 325 G/12 OZ MIXED VEGETABLES, SUCH AS RED
AND YELLOW PEPPERS, MANGETOUT, SPRING
ONIONS, CARROTS, CUT INTO MATCHSTICKS

1 TABLESPOON SOY SAUCE

½ TABLESPOON OYSTER SAUCE (OPTIONAL)

1 TABLESPOON SESAME SEEDS, ROASTED

SERVES 4

Wash all the rice and wheat berries and leave to
drain. While they are draining, bring 375 ml/12
fl oz water to a rolling boil over high heat. Add
the grains and return to the boil. Stir, cover,
reduce the heat to low and simmer for 30
minutes.

Remove the pan from the heat and leave to
stand for 30 minutes. Spread the grains on a
plate; when cool, cover and refrigerate for at
least 3 hours or up to 3 days.

Place a wok over high heat until it begins to
smoke. Add 1 tablespoon of the oil, swirl it
around the wok, then add the cold grains.
Reduce the heat and stir-fry for about 2–3
minutes, pushing down with the back of a
spatula so that the grains scorch. Remove the
grains from the wok.

Return the wok to a high heat, add the
remaining oil and the vegetables and stir-fry for
2–3 minutes. Return the grains to the wok with
the soy and oyster sauces, and stir-fry for 1–2
minutes. Serve at once, topped with the roasted
sesame seeds.

Yon-Rit So

FLAVOURED GLUTINOUS RICE

500 G/1 LB 2 OZ THAI GLUTINOUS RICE, RINSED THEN
    SOAKED IN 5 CM/2 INCHES OF COLD WATER FOR AT
    LEAST 4 HOURS

5 TABLESPOONS PEANUT OR CORN OIL

4 LARGE SPRING ONIONS, CUT INTO SMALL ROUNDS

40 G/1½ OZ DRIED SHRIMPS, RINSED, SOAKED IN JUST
    ENOUGH WATER TO COVER FOR 1 HOUR, THEN
    DRAINED

25 G/1 OZ CHINESE DRIED BLACK MUSHROOMS,
    RINSED, SOAKED IN 300 ML/½ PINT HOT WATER FOR
    2–3 HOURS, DRAINED THEN DICED

325 G/12 OZ LEAN BACON, FRIED THEN DICED

LARGE BUNCH OF CORIANDER LEAVES (WITHOUT MAIN
    STALKS)

SALT

SOY SAUCE

SERVES 3-4

Drain the rice, then stir in 1 tablespoon of the
oil. Smear 1 tablespoon oil over a perforated
steamer container with fine holes and spread the
rice over it. (If the holes are too large, cover
them with muslin.) Cover and steam over
boiling water for 30–40 minutes or until the rice
is cooked.

Heat a wok over high heat until smoke rises.
Add the remaining oil and swirl it around. Add
the spring onions, stir, then add the dried
shrimps and the diced mushrooms and stir until
piping hot. Remove from the heat and add the
hot sticky rice; mix well, breaking up any lumps.
Mix in the bacon and the coriander leaves. Taste
and add salt and soy sauce if required. Serve hot.

*This can be prepared in advance. To reheat, add 1
tablespoon oil to a warm wok and spread the rice
mixture over the base. Place over medium-low heat
until the bottom has formed a crisp crust. Turn the
mixture and toast the other side, adding a little more
oil if necessary.*

Valentina Harris

BAKED STUFFED TOMATOES
with Italian sausage

6 LARGE, FIRM, ROUND BEEFSTEAK TOMATOES

200 G/7 OZ LONG-GRAIN OR RISOTTO RICE

2 GARLIC CLOVES, LIGHTLY CRUSHED IN THEIR SKINS

6–7 TABLESPOONS EXTRA VIRGIN OLIVE OIL

2 ONIONS, CHOPPED

200 G/7 OZ FRESH ITALIAN SAUSAGE, PEELED AND
    CRUMBLED, OR MINCED PORK

A FEW LEAVES OF FRESH BASIL

LARGE PINCH OF DRIED THYME

SALT AND FRESHLY GROUND BLACK PEPPER

¼ TEASPOON BEEF EXTRACT, DILUTED IN 125 ML/4 FL
    OZ HOT WATER

HANDFUL OF FRESHLY GRATED PARMESAN CHEESE

SERVES 4

Preheat the oven to 200°C/400°F/Gas Mark 6.
Cut the tops off the tomatoes and scoop out the
seeds and cores. Turn them upside down to
drain for 30 minutes. Boil the rice in plenty of
salted water until just tender. Drain and set aside.

Fry the garlic in 4 tablespoons of the oil until
browned, then discard. Add the onions and fry
until soft, then add the sausage or minced pork
and stir thoroughly. Add the basil and thyme and
season lightly. Simmer until the meat is cooked
through, adding a little water or stock
occasionally to prevent it from drying out.

When the meat is thoroughly cooked, mix it
with the rice and use to fill the tomatoes. Pour
the diluted beef extract into a baking dish and
arrange the tomatoes in the dish. Sprinkle with
olive oil and plenty of grated Parmesan. Bake for
30 minutes. Serve warm.

A salad of boiled green beans or lightly boiled
chard dressed with lemon juice and olive oil is
ideal with this dish.

pasta

SOBA NOODLES
with chicken and ginger

500 G/1¼ LB DRIED SOBA (BUCKWHEAT) NOODLES

1 TABLESPOON SESAME OIL

1 WHOLE CHICKEN, POACHED OR STEAMED

1 CUCUMBER

1 TABLESPOON FRESH CORIANDER LEAVES

DRESSING

BUNCH OF SPRING ONIONS

8 TABLESPOONS FRESH (UNUSED) PEANUT OIL

2 TABLESPOONS SHREDDED FRESH GINGER

1 TEASPOON SALT

SERVES 4

Cook the noodles in boiling water for a few minutes, separating them carefully, until tender but still firm. Drain, refresh in cold water, drain again and toss in sesame oil. Chill until ready to serve.

Shred the chicken, discarding the bones and most of the skin; do not chill or it will numb the flavour.

Peel the cucumber, cut in half lengthways, scoop out the seeds with a teaspoon and cut the flesh into matchstick strips.

For the dressing, finely chop the green stems of the spring onions. Gently warm the peanut oil in a small saucepan with the ginger and salt, stirring until the salt dissolves. Add the spring onions and stir for a few seconds until they wilt and soften, then remove from the heat.

In a bowl, combine the shredded chicken, cucumber, noodles, coriander and half the warm dressing; toss gently. To serve, twirl the noodles on a large fork and arrange in a pyramid in the centre of each plate. Top each pyramid with a spoonful of the remaining spring onion dressing.

Antony Worrall Thompson

PENNE WITH SPINACH,
Gorgonzola and pine nuts

1 TABLESPOON EXTRA VIRGIN OLIVE OIL

2 GARLIC CLOVES, CRUSHED WITH A LITTLE SALT

½ ONION, FINELY DICED

150 ML/¼ PINT DRY WHITE WINE

450 ML/¾ PINT DOUBLE CREAM

450 G/1 LB PENNE PASTA

85 G/3 OZ BABY SPINACH

125 G/4 OZ GORGONZOLA, CRUMBLED

GROUND BLACK PEPPER

3 TABLESPOONS FRESHLY GRATED PARMESAN CHEESE

50 G/2 OZ PINE NUTS, TOASTED

SERVES 4

Heat the olive oil in a large saucepan and add the garlic and onion. Cook over a medium heat until soft but not brown.

Add the wine and cook over a high heat until the wine has reduced and become syrupy.

Stir in the cream and continue to cook over a high heat until the cream has reduced by half. Strain the sauce through a fine sieve and return to the saucepan.

Meanwhile, bring a large saucepan of salted water to the boil and cook the pasta until al dente.

Fold the spinach and Gorgonzola into the cream sauce and cook until the spinach has wilted and the Gorgonzola has started to melt. Season to taste with black pepper.

When the pasta is cooked, drain and fold into the Gorgonzola cream. Add the Parmesan and stir to combine. Tip the pasta into a large warmed bowl and scatter with the toasted pine nuts.

Alastair Little

TAGLIATELLE WITH SOY SAUCE
and mustard

2 TABLESPOONS JAPANESE SOY SAUCE

1 TABLESPOON ENGLISH MUSTARD POWDER, MIXED
  WITH 1 TABLESPOON WATER

2 TABLESPOONS SUNFLOWER OIL

1 BUNCH OF SPRING ONIONS, CUT INTO 1 CM/½ INCH
  DIAGONAL SLICES

COOKED CHICKEN BREAST, SKINNED AND DICED
  (OPTIONAL)

400 G/14 OZ GOOD-QUALITY EGG TAGLIATELLE

TO GARNISH (OPTIONAL)

FRESH CORIANDER LEAVES

FRESH RED CHILLI, FINELY SHREDDED

FRESH GINGER, FINELY SHREDDED

SERVES 4

Put 4 litres/7 pints water into a large saucepan, salt it very lightly and bring to the boil. Mix the soy sauce and mustard together in a small bowl. Heat the oil in a large frying pan over a low heat and gently cook the spring onions until soft, together with the diced chicken, if using.

When you are ready to eat, drop the pasta into the boiling water and cook for 1½–2 minutes or until al dente (just tender, but remaining firm to the bite). Drain the pasta, reserving 4 tablespoons of the cooking water, and tip the pasta into the frying pan with the spring onions. Add the soy and mustard mixture, turn up the heat and toss thoroughly. If the pasta is not coated with the dressing, add a little of the reserved water. Serve at once, with coriander, chilli and/or ginger scattered over if you like.

Karen Lee

FARFALLE WITH PORCINI
and tomato sauce

40 G/1½ OZ DRIED PORCINI MUSHROOMS (CEPS)

1 TABLESPOON OLIVE OIL

1 TABLESPOON CHOPPED GARLIC

2–3 SHALLOTS, CHOPPED

½ RECIPE TOMATO SAUCE (PAGE 378)

1 TABLESPOON CREAM

1 TABLESPOON MILK

2 TABLESPOONS CHOPPED FRESH FLAT–LEAF PARSLEY

1 TEASPOON SALT

225 G/8 OZ DRIED FARFALLE (BOW–TIE PASTA)

50 G/2 OZ PARMESAN CHEESE, GRATED

SERVES 2

Place the ceps in a bowl and cover with 250 ml/8 fl oz cold water. Leave to soak for 30 minutes or until soft. Squeeze the mushrooms over the bowl, then cut into dice. Strain the liquid into a small saucepan and boil until reduced to 4 tablespoons. Set aside.

Place a frying pan over medium heat, add the olive oil and reduce the heat to low. Add the garlic and sauté for about 2 minutes. Add the shallots and porcini and sauté for a further 2 minutes or until the shallots are soft. Add the tomato sauce, simmer for 1 minute, then add the cream, milk and parsley and simmer for a further 1 minute.

The sauce can be prepared in advance and stored in the refrigerator for up to 3 days.

To serve, cook the pasta in a large saucepan of boiling water with the salt for 9–10 minutes or until just tender. Drain well.

Bring the sauce to a simmer and add the porcini liquid. Add the pasta and toss over low heat for about 1 minute. Add the cheese, mix briefly and serve at once.

LINGUINE WITH TOMATO SAUCE
and sautéed aubergine

450 G/1 LB AUBERGINE, CUT INTO THIN STRIPS

2 TEASPOONS SALT

5 TABLESPOONS OLIVE OIL

4 GARLIC CLOVES, CHOPPED

TOMATO SAUCE (PAGE 378)

4 TABLESPOONS DRY WHITE WINE

¼ TEASPOON FRESHLY GROUND BLACK PEPPER

¼ TEASPOON CAYENNE PEPPER

1 TABLESPOON CHOPPED FRESH OREGANO, OR 1
   TEASPOON DRIED OREGANO

325 G/12 OZ DRIED LINGUINE OR SPAGHETTI

85–125 G/3–4 OZ PARMESAN CHEESE, GRATED

SERVES 3–4

Place the aubergine strips in a bowl with 1 teaspoon of the salt. Toss to mix and leave for 1 hour.

Rinse the aubergine in cold water, then drain and pat dry.

Place a large, heavy-based saucepan over high heat, add 1 tablespoon of the olive oil and reduce the heat to low. Add the garlic and sauté for 2 minutes or until it has just begun to turn golden. Add the tomato sauce, wine, black and cayenne pepper and the oregano; simmer for about 3 minutes.

Cook the pasta in a large saucepan of boiling water with 1 teaspoon of salt for about 7–9 minutes, or until just tender. Drain, reserving the cooking water.

Heat a large frying pan over high heat, add the remaining olive oil and sauté the aubergine for about 5 minutes or until crisp.

Bring the sauce to a simmer and add the pasta, aubergine and 4 tablespoons of the pasta cooking water. Toss over low heat for about 1 minute. Add the grated cheese, mix briefly and serve at once.

THAI NOODLES
(Pad Thai)

300–325 G/11–12 OZ RICE STICKS
   (FLAT RICE NOODLES)
2–2½ TABLESPOONS VEGETABLE OR PEANUT OIL
1 ONION, FINELY SLICED
2 GARLIC CLOVES, SLICED
175 G/6 OZ BONELESS, SKINLESS CHICKEN BREAST
150 G/5 OZ SMALL PEELED PRAWNS
2–3 SPRING ONIONS, CHOPPED
175 G/6 OZ FRESH BEANSPROUTS
3–4 TABLESPOONS THAI FISH SAUCE
SALT AND PEPPER
2–3 TABLESPOONS ROASTED PEANUTS, CHOPPED
1 FRESH RED CHILLI, SEEDED AND FINELY SHREDDED
   (OPTIONAL)
LIME WEDGES, TO GARNISH

SERVES 4

Bring a large saucepan of water to the boil and add the noodles. Cook for about 3 minutes, until just tender, but still firm to the bite, then drain and set aside.

Heat the oil in a wok or large frying pan. Sauté the onion and garlic until lightly browned, about 4 minutes.

Cut the chicken into 1 cm/½ inch cubes. Push the onion to the side of the pan, add the chicken and stir-fry until evenly browned, then add the prawns, spring onions and beansprouts and cook over high heat for about 2½ minutes, stirring constantly.

Add the drained noodles and stir-fry until heated through, keeping them moving to prevent sticking. Season to taste with fish sauce, salt and pepper.

Serve on a large platter or individual plates and scatter over the peanuts and shredded chilli, if using. Garnish with lime wedges for squeezing.

Valentina Harris

SPINACH AND TOMATO LASAGNE

400 G/14 OZ LASAGNE SHEETS

1 KG/2¼ LB FRESH SPINACH OR 500 G/1 LB 2 OZ
  FROZEN LEAF SPINACH

4 TABLESPOONS EXTRA VIRGIN OLIVE OIL

2 GARLIC CLOVES, CHOPPED

500 ML/16 FL OZ PASSATA

1 TABLESPOON CHOPPED FRESH FLAT-LEAF PARSLEY

SALT AND FRESHLY GROUND BLACK PEPPER

2 TABLESPOONS MELTED BUTTER

BÉCHAMEL SAUCE (PAGE 376)

250 G/9 OZ MOZZARELLA CHEESE, CUBED

150 G/5 OZ PARMESAN CHEESE, GRATED

SERVES 4–6

Bring a large saucepan of salted water to the boil. Cook the lasagne sheets four or five at a time, making sure they don't stick together. As soon as they are tender, remove them from the water and lay them on damp, clean tea towels, without touching, while you cook the remaining lasagne.

Cook the spinach in a little boiling water until just wilted, cool under running water, drain and squeeze dry.

Heat the olive oil in a saucepan, add the garlic and fry gently for about 5 minutes, then add the passata. Stir, then simmer for about 15 minutes. Add the parsley and seasoning and set aside.

Preheat the oven to 180°C/350°F/Gas Mark 4.

Brush an ovenproof dish with the melted butter. Pour a little béchamel sauce in the bottom of the dish and arrange a layer of lasagne sheets on top, slightly overlapping. Scatter over some spinach, mozzarella and Parmesan. Cover with the tomato sauce, then another layer of lasagne sheets.

Repeat the layers until all the ingredients have been used up, ending with a layer of béchamel sauce over the tomato sauce. Bake for about 45 minutes or until bubbling and lightly browned.

Serve with a salad of baby spinach and lambs' lettuce, dressed with a little balsamic vinegar and extra virgin olive oil, and plenty of bread or warmed focaccia for mopping up extra sauce.

Paul & Jeanne Rankin

SPAGHETTINI WITH PRAWNS,
rocket and chilli

450 G/1 LB SPAGHETTINI
175 ML/6 FL OZ EXTRA VIRGIN OLIVE OIL
450 G/1 LB FRESH PRAWNS, PEELED
SALT AND PEPPER
½ TEASPOON DRIED CHILLI FLAKES
2 TEASPOONS CHOPPED GARLIC
125 ML/4 FL OZ DRY WHITE WINE
1 TABLESPOON FRESH LEMON JUICE
SMALL BUNCH OF ROCKET

SERVES 4–6

Bring a large saucepan of salted water to a vigorous boil. Add the pasta and cook until al dente (just firm to the bite), about 6 minutes.

While the pasta is cooking, heat a large sauté pan over high heat until very hot. Add 3 tablespoons of the olive oil and then add the prawns. Season with salt and pepper and the chilli flakes. After about 1 minute, the prawns will turn pink; at this stage, add the garlic. Cook for another 30 seconds and then add the wine, lemon juice and 4 tablespoons water. When the wine boils vigorously, remove the pan from the heat.

When the pasta is done, drain well and toss with the remaining olive oil, the prawns and the rocket. Serve on individual warmed plates.

LINGUINE WITH PRAWNS,
dill and courgettes

2 COURGETTES

SALT AND FRESHLY GROUND BLACK PEPPER

225 G/8 OZ DRIED LINGUINE PASTA

2 TABLESPOONS EXTRA VIRGIN OLIVE OIL

175 G/6 OZ COOKED PEELED PRAWNS, THAWED IF
    FROZEN

1 TABLESPOON CHOPPED FRESH DILL

SERVES 4

Trim the ends of the courgettes, then cut across the courgettes to make 4 cm/1½ inch pieces; cut each piece lengthways into 3 mm/⅛ inch thick slices, then cut each slice lengthways into 3 mm/⅛ inch batons.

Place 1.7 litres/3 pints water in a large saucepan, add 3 teaspoons salt and bring to the boil. Add the pasta, bring back to the boil and boil for 10 minutes or until al dente – just tender but still slightly firm to the bite.

When the pasta is almost ready, warm the olive oil in a small saucepan over a low heat. Add the courgettes and cook gently for 1 minute, but don't let them fry. Add the prawns and heat through for about 30 seconds, then add the dill and season to taste. Drain the pasta, tip into a large bowl and add the prawn mixture. Toss together and serve at once.

Gordon Ramsay

SAUCE ANTIBOISE

3 LARGE PLUM TOMATOES
200 ML/7 FL OZ OLIVE OIL
3 LARGE SHALLOTS, FINELY CHOPPED
2 GARLIC CLOVES, CRUSHED
6 LARGE FRESH BASIL LEAVES
2 SPRIGS OF CORIANDER
3 SPRIGS OF TARRAGON
1 TABLESPOON FRESH LEMON JUICE
SEA SALT AND FRESHLY GROUND BLACK PEPPER

SERVES 4

Score the base of each tomato with a sharp knife, place in a bowl and cover with boiling water. Leave for about 1 minute. Drain and rinse in cold water, then slip off the skins. Quarter the tomatoes, remove the seeds and cores and chop the flesh into fine dice. Set aside.

Heat the oil in a saucepan over low heat and cook the shallots and garlic for about 5 minutes or until softened. Remove from the heat.

Meanwhile, remove the stalks from the herbs if necessary; cut the leaves into thin julienne strips. Stir into the shallots and oil and leave to infuse for 5 minutes, then mix in the tomato dice.

Return to the heat and heat gently until piping hot. Add the lemon juice, season to taste, then toss with freshly cooked spaghetti.

SAFFRON VELOUTÉ
with scallops

4 SHALLOTS, THINLY SLICED
15 G/½ OZ UNSALTED BUTTER
½ TEASPOON SAFFRON STRANDS
250 ML/8 FL OZ DRY WHITE WINE
250 ML/8 FL OZ DRY VERMOUTH
500 ML/16 FL OZ FISH, VEGETABLE OR CHICKEN STOCK
    (PAGE 374)
SEA SALT AND FRESHLY GROUND BLACK PEPPER
250 ML/8 FL OZ DOUBLE CREAM
250 ML/8 FL OZ SINGLE CREAM

TO SERVE
4–12 SCALLOPS (DEPENDING ON SIZE)
1 TABLESPOON CHOPPED CHERVIL

SERVES 4

In a wide saucepan, gently cook the shallots with the butter for about 5 minutes, then crush in the saffron strands and continue cooking very, very gently for another 5 minutes.

Stir in the wine and vermouth and simmer, uncovered, until the liquid has reduced down to a thin syrupy glaze, about 10 minutes. Add the stock and simmer until reduced by half. Season to taste.

Stir in the two creams and simmer, still uncovered, for about 10 minutes or until the consistency is smooth and velvety.

Meanwhile, steam the scallops or sear in a hot nonstick pan.

Strain the sauce through a fine sieve, then toss with freshly cooked tagliatelle. Serve at once, with the scallops, sprinkled with the chervil.

Salmon or another fish can be used instead of the scallops.

PARSLEY CREAM SAUCE

100 G/3½ OZ CURLY LEAF PARSLEY
100 G/3½ OZ WATERCRESS
4 TABLESPOONS DOUBLE CREAM
SEA SALT AND FRESHLY GROUND BLACK PEPPER
ABOUT 200 ML/7 FL OZ CHICKEN OR VEGETABLE
    STOCK (PAGE 374)

SERVES 4

Wash the parsley and watercress thoroughly. Pick off and discard the thick stalks. Drain well.

Blanch the parsley in a large saucepan of boiling water for 4 minutes, then add the watercress and continue cooking for a further 1–2 minutes.

Drain well in a sieve, then tip the blanched leaves into an old, clean tea towel. Roll up and squeeze the towel tightly to extract all the water.

Place the leaves in a food processor with the cream and seasoning and blend to a smooth purée, scraping down the sides frequently. The secret of this sauce is to run the machine until the parsley and watercress become very smooth and glossy. When the consistency is quite silky, blend in the stock and return the sauce to the saucepan.

Return to a gentle boil for 1–2 minutes, taste and adjust the seasoning if required, then toss with freshly cooked pasta.

Gordon Ramsay

LEMONGRASS PRIMAVERA SAUCE

2 STALKS OF FRESH LEMONGRASS

125 ML/4 FL OZ OLIVE OIL

100 G/3½ OZ FINE GREEN BEANS

3 TABLESPOONS FRESH YOUNG PEAS

4 PLUM TOMATOES

1 SHALLOT, FINELY CHOPPED

GRATED RIND OF 1 SMALL LEMON

SQUEEZE OF FRESH LEMON JUICE

SEA SALT AND FRESHLY GROUND BLACK PEPPER

FINELY CHOPPED STONED BLACK OLIVES, TO GARNISH

SERVES 4

Trim the lemongrass, then cut in half lengthways. Slice finely and place in a saucepan with the oil; heat slowly until hot but not boiling. Remove from the heat and leave to infuse for about 5 minutes.

Meanwhile, trim the beans and cut into 2.5 cm/1 inch lengths. Blanch in boiling water for 2 minutes, then add the peas and cook for another minute. Drain and rinse in cold running water. Drain and dry on paper towels.

Score the base of each tomato with a sharp knife, place in a bowl and cover with boiling water. Leave for about 1 minute. Drain and rinse in cold water, then slip off the skins. Quarter the tomatoes, remove the seeds and cores and cut the flesh into fine dice.

Strain the infused oil through a sieve and discard the lemongrass.

Mix the oil with the shallot, lemon rind and juice and the beans, peas and diced tomatoes; season to taste. Toss with freshly cooked pasta and serve at once, as a warm salad, garnished with chopped black olives.

Gordon Ramsay

ROSEMARY CREAM SAUCE
with beans, bacon and asparagus

1 LITRE/1¾ PINTS CHICKEN STOCK (PAGE 374)

150 ML/¼ PINT DOUBLE CREAM

1 TEASPOON CHOPPED FRESH ROSEMARY

150 G/5 OZ ASPARAGUS TIPS

175 G/6 OZ LEAN BACON, IN ONE PIECE

1 TABLESPOON OLIVE OIL

200 G/7 OZ COOKED WHITE HARICOT OR CANNELLINI
  BEANS

SEA SALT AND FRESHLY GROUND BLACK PEPPER

SERVES 4

Put the stock in a saucepan and boil to reduce by half. Add the cream and rosemary and continue boiling until reduced to about 500 ml/16 fl oz. Remove from the heat and set aside.

Meanwhile, blanch the asparagus tips in boiling water for 2 minutes. Drain and rinse in cold running water. Drain well.

Cut the bacon into dice or narrow strips. Heat the oil in a frying pan and, when hot, fry the bacon, stirring occasionally, until golden brown and crisp. Drain on paper towels.

Return the sauce to a medium heat and stir in the white beans and half the crisp bacon. Simmer for 1–2 minutes, then taste and adjust the seasoning if required. Toss with freshly cooked pasta and serve at once, sprinkled with the asparagus tips and the remaining crisp bacon.

Gordon Ramsay

SWEET PEPPER SAUCE
with clams

500 G/1 LB 2 OZ FRESH CLAMS (OR MUSSELS) IN THEIR
  SHELLS, THOROUGHLY SCRUBBED

1 LARGE BOUQUET GARNI OF FRESH HERBS

300 ML/½ PINT DRY WHITE WINE

50 G/2 OZ BUTTER

2 RED PEPPERS, SEEDED AND FINELY CHOPPED

2 YELLOW PEPPERS, SEEDED AND FINELY CHOPPED

6 SHALLOTS, FINELY CHOPPED

1 SPRIG EACH OF TARRAGON, CHERVIL AND THYME

1 FRESH BAY LEAF

3 TABLESPOONS DRY VERMOUTH

2 TEASPOONS WHITE WINE VINEGAR

SEA SALT AND FRESHLY GROUND BLACK PEPPER

1 TABLESPOON CHOPPED FRESH BASIL

SERVES 4

Rinse the clams two or three times in cold water, then place in a saucepan with the bouquet garni and white wine. Cover and cook over a medium heat for about 5 minutes, shaking the pan occasionally. Drain the clams through a muslin-lined sieve, reserving the cooking liquid. Discard any clams that have not opened. Remove most of the clams from their shells and reserve, discarding the empty shells.

Melt half the butter in a saucepan and gently fry the chopped peppers and shallots with the herbs for about 10 minutes or until softened.

Add the vermouth and cook, uncovered, for about 3 minutes or until reduced, then add the vinegar and cook for a further 1 minute or until evaporated.

Add the reserved clam cooking liquid and simmer, uncovered, for about 10 minutes. Remove the herb sprigs.

The sauce can be left chunky with pieces of pepper or, if you prefer a smooth sauce, tip the contents of the pan into a liquidizer or food processor and purée, then rub through a sieve.

Season to taste, then add the clams, reheat and briskly stir in the remaining butter. Toss with freshly cooked pasta and serve at once, sprinkled with the basil.

Gordon Ramsay

WHITE BEAN CAPPUCCINO

500 ML/16 FL OZ CHICKEN OR VEGETABLE STOCK
  (PAGE 374)
250 G/9 OZ COOKED WHITE HARICOT OR CANNELLINI
  BEANS
150 ML/¼ PINT DOUBLE CREAM
2 TEASPOONS TRUFFLE OIL
SEA SALT AND FRESHLY GROUND BLACK PEPPER
15 G/½ OZ ICE-COLD BUTTER, CUT INTO SMALL PIECES
1 TABLESPOON CHOPPED FRESH CHIVES
SPRIGS OF CHERVIL

*This sauce is designed to go with ravioli or cannelloni.
Buy or make your own favourite ravioli, or make fresh
lasagne pasta (page 161), blanch, drain well and roll
around one of the following fillings:*
* *ratatouille*
* *blanched baby spinach leaves with fried, sliced
    mushrooms*
* *flaked white crab meat mixed with flaked cooked
    salmon, moistened with a little cream*
* *shredded cooked pheasant mixed with finely
    shredded, sautéed Savoy cabbage*

SERVES 4

Boil the stock until reduced to about 300 ml/½
pint.

Meanwhile, purée the beans in a liquidizer or
food processor, then scrape into a bowl. Using a
hand-held multi-blender, slowly whisk in the
stock, cream and truffle oil. Season to taste, then
pour the sauce into a saucepan.

When ready to serve, place your ravioli or
cannelloni on four warmed plates. Return the
sauce to a gentle boil and whisk back to a froth
with the hand-held blender. While you whisk,
add the pieces of ice-cold butter – this helps to
stabilize the foam.

Spoon the top of the foam over the pasta,
continuing to reheat and whisk the sauce as you
serve. Garnish with chives and chervil.

Gordon Ramsay

TOMATO AND CARDAMOM COULIS
with vegetable brunoise

2 SHALLOTS, SLICED

1 GARLIC CLOVE, PEELED AND LEFT WHOLE

8 TABLESPOONS OLIVE OIL

4 CARDAMOM PODS, SPLIT

1 SPRIG EACH OF THYME, BASIL AND TARRAGON

3 TABLESPOONS DRY WHITE WINE

500 G/1 LB 2 OZ RIPE PLUM TOMATOES, SKINNED AND
    CHOPPED

1 TABLESPOON TOMATO PURÉE

SEA SALT AND FRESHLY GROUND BLACK PEPPER

VEGETABLE BRUNOISE

1 SMALL AUBERGINE

1 YELLOW PEPPER

2 SMALL COURGETTES

SERVES 4

Put the shallots and garlic into a saucepan with 2 tablespoons of the oil. Cover and cook over a low heat for 5 minutes, then add the cardamom pods and herbs and cook for a further 2 minutes.

Stir in the wine and cook for 1–2 minutes, until it evaporates, then mix in the chopped tomatoes and tomato purée. Season well with salt and pepper, then cover and simmer very gently for about 15 minutes.

Meanwhile, cut the aubergine, pepper and courgettes into large dice. Heat 2 tablespoons of the oil in a large frying pan and fry the aubergine for 5–7 minutes or until almost tender. Add the pepper and courgette dice and continue to fry, stirring frequently, for a further 5–7 minutes; they should be hot through but should remain firm.

Remove the garlic clove from the tomato mixture, then purée the mixture with the remaining oil in a liquidizer or food processor. Rub the purée through a fine sieve, season to taste and serve with freshly cooked tagliatelle, sprinkled with the vegetable brunoise.

GLAZED BABY ONIONS
and light curry sauce

ABOUT 24 BABY ONIONS OR SMALL SHALLOTS,
   UNPEELED

200 G/7 OZ CARROTS, CUT INTO THIN BATONS OR
   JULIENNE STRIPS

25 G/1 OZ BUTTER

1 TABLESPOON OLIVE OIL

200 ML/7 FL OZ SWEET WHITE WINE

200 ML/7 FL OZ CHICKEN OR VEGETABLE STOCK
   (PAGE 374)

1 TEASPOON MILD CURRY PASTE

3 TABLESPOONS DOUBLE CREAM

100 G/3½ OZ YOUNG SPINACH LEAVES

SEA SALT AND FRESHLY GROUND BLACK PEPPER

SERVES 3–4

Blanch the onions or shallots briefly in boiling water, then drain and skin (blanching makes them easier to peel). Blanch the carrots in boiling water for 2 minutes, then drain and set aside.

Heat the butter and oil in a sauté pan and gently fry the onions or shallots for about 10 minutes, shaking the pan occasionally, until softened and golden brown.

In a saucepan, boil the wine until reduced by half, then add the stock and curry paste and boil again until reduced to about
300 ml/½ pint. Stir in the cream and cook for 2 minutes.

Remove any thick stalks from the spinach leaves and add to the sauce, stirring until just wilted. Add the onions and carrots, then season to taste. Toss with freshly cooked pasta and serve at once.

Gordon Ramsay

WILD MUSHROOM SAUCE

100 G/3½ OZ SELECTION OF WILD MUSHROOMS

100 G/3½ OZ BUTTON MUSHROOMS

3 TABLESPOONS OLIVE OIL

1 TABLESPOON FRESH LEMON JUICE

SEA SALT AND FRESHLY GROUND BLACK PEPPER

VELOUTÉ SAUCE, OMITTING SAFFRON (PAGE 149)

FLAT-LEAF PARSLEY, TO GARNISH

SERVES 4

Pick over the wild mushrooms and wipe clean with a damp cloth if necessary. Chop both wild and button mushrooms very finely.

Place the chopped mushrooms in a wide shallow saucepan with the oil and cook gently until liquid starts to seep out. Add the lemon juice and seasoning and cook gently, stirring occasionally, until the liquid has evaporated away. This may take 20–30 minutes.

Bring the velouté sauce to simmering point and stir in the mushroom mixture. Taste and adjust the seasoning if required. Toss with freshly cooked pasta and serve at once, garnished with flat-leaf parsley.

MAKING FRESH PASTA

You will need a pasta rolling machine and a food processor

225 G/8 OZ PLAIN FLOUR
GOOD PINCH OF SEA SALT
2 EGGS (SIZE 2)
3 EGG YOLKS
1 TABLESPOON OLIVE OIL

Sift the flour and salt together, then place in a food processor with the remaining ingredients and process until the mixture forms coarse crumbs. Test the texture by pressing a small amount between your finger and thumb. If it cracks, then process for a few more seconds.

Tip the mixture on to a work surface and knead until you have a ball of smooth dough that feels soft but not sticky. Wrap in clingfilm and leave to rest for an hour or so.

Divide the dough into large walnut-size balls and feed through a pasta rolling machine several times, according to the manufacturer's instructions, until you have long, thin sheets of pasta.

For lasagne or cannelloni, cut the sheets to the required lengths. For tagliatelle or spaghetti, cut each sheet into ribbons using the special machine cutters.

Blanch in boiling salted water for 30 seconds to 1 minute. Drain and plunge into ice-cold water. Drain again and set aside.

To serve, reheat in a little boiling water with a knob of butter for 1–2 minutes.

PASTA GARNISHES

• wafer-thin shavings of fresh Parmesan or pecorino cheese
• chopped fresh herbs (parsley, chervil, dill, basil, coriander)
• a concassé of finely chopped olives mixed with finely diced skinned tomatoes
• julienne strips of Parma ham
• crisp-fried vegetables (celeriac, beetroot, carrot, whole baby spinach leaves). Cut root vegetables first into thin slices, then into fine julienne strips. Leave to dry on paper towels for 20 minutes.

Shallow fry the vegetable strips or whole spinach leaves in hot olive oil to cover for 3–5 minutes or until cooked but not coloured. Drain on paper towels placed on a baking sheet.

Heat the oven to its lowest setting and dry the shredded vegetables in the oven, with the door slightly open, until crisp but not browned. Change the paper towels once or twice during this drying-out period.

vegetables

Paul Gayler

CHARGRILLED POTATOES
with asparagus and porcini

275 G/10 OZ NEW POTATOES

150 G/5 OZ ASPARAGUS

150 G/5 OZ PORCINI MUSHROOMS (OR CHESTNUT OR
    STRAW MUSHROOMS), SLICED ABOUT
    1 CM/½ INCH THICK

6 TABLESPOONS EXTRA VIRGIN OLIVE OIL

3 TEASPOONS BALSAMIC VINEGAR

SEA SALT AND COARSELY GROUND BLACK PEPPER

SERVES 4

Cook the new potatoes in their skins in boiling
salted water until just tender. Leave to cool
slightly before peeling them. Cut into
1 cm/½ inch thick slices.

Preheat the grill to very hot. Brush the
asparagus, mushrooms and potatoes with 4
tablespoons of the olive oil and place under the
hot grill, turning them until they are golden and
beginning to brown in places.

Serve immediately, drizzled with the balsamic
vinegar and the remaining olive oil and
sprinkled with sea salt and freshly ground black
pepper.

Paul Gayler

PAN-FRIED POTATO TERRINE
with dried fruits

25 G/1 OZ SMOKED BACON, FINELY DICED

½ ONION, FINELY CHOPPED

675 G/1½ LB WAXY POTATOES

SALT AND FRESHLY GROUND BLACK PEPPER

125 G/4 OZ MIXED DRIED FRUITS (PRUNE, APPLE, APRICOT), CUT INTO 1 CM/½ INCH DICE

2 EGGS

85 ML/3 FL OZ DOUBLE CREAM

25 G/1 OZ GRUYÈRE CHEESE, GRATED

GRATED NUTMEG

25 G/1 OZ BUTTER

SERVES 8–10

Begin making the terrine a day or two before you want to serve it. Preheat the oven to 180°C/350°F/Gas Mark 4.

Heat a frying pan until hot, add the bacon and sauté over a high heat to release its fat, add the onion and sauté together until lightly golden. Leave to cool.

Grate the potatoes coarsely and place in a bowl. Add the bacon and onion and season lightly. Add the dried fruits, eggs, cream and cheese and mix well. Season again with salt, pepper and nutmeg.

Line a 900 g/2 lb loaf tin with clingfilm. Pack the tin with the potato mixture and place in the oven to cook for up to 3 hours, until tender when tested with a skewer. Leave to cool completely.

To serve, cut the terrine into 1–2 cm/½–¾ inch thick slices and fry in the butter until golden and slightly crisp. Serve hot.

Paul Gayler

POTATO AND WALNUT GNOCCHI
with gorgonzola and basil sauce

85 G/3 OZ WALNUTS, GROUND

85 G/3 OZ GORGONZOLA CHEESE, CRUMBLED

325 G/12 OZ PEELED POTATOES (KING EDWARDS OR
   MARIS PIPER), BOILED UNTIL TENDER, THEN WELL
   MASHED, HOT

15 G/½ OZ BUTTER, SOFTENED

2 EGG YOLKS

125 G/4 OZ PLAIN FLOUR

SALT AND FRESHLY GROUND BLACK PEPPER

SAUCE

125 G/4 OZ BUTTER

50 G/2 OZ GORGONZOLA CHEESE, CRUMBLED

SMALL HANDFUL OF FRESH BASIL LEAVES, ROUGHLY
   TORN

50 G/2 OZ PARMESAN CHEESE, GRATED

SERVES 4

Add the ground walnuts and Gorgonzola to the hot mashed potato and beat to allow the cheese to melt. Add the butter, egg yolks, half of the flour and a little salt and pepper; mix well.

Turn the mixture on to a lightly floured surface and gently knead in the remaining flour, a little at a time, to form a smooth dough. Leave to cool.

Roll the dough into long, 2.5 cm/1 inch diameter cylinders, then cut into 2 cm/¾ inch pieces. Roll each piece over the prongs of a fork to form a decorative shape. Place the gnocchi on a floured tray and leave to dry for about 1 hour.

Poach the gnocchi, a few at a time, in plenty of boiling salted water for 2–3 minutes or until they float to the surface. Remove with a slotted spoon and keep warm.

For the sauce, place the butter in a saucepan with 3 tablespoons water, bring to the boil, then whisk in the Gorgonzola. Add the basil and season to taste. Roll the gnocchi in the sauce and serve sprinkled with the Parmesan.

Paul Gayler

TWICE-COOKED CHICORY
with orange and cardamom

8 HEADS OF CHICORY (BELGIAN ENDIVE)
85 G/3 OZ BUTTER
JUICE OF ½ LEMON
2 TEASPOONS SUGAR
SALT
JUICE AND GRATED ZEST OF 1 ORANGE
1 TEASPOON CARDAMOM SEEDS

SERVES 4

Preheat the oven to 180°C/350°F/Gas Mark 4.

Cut a thin slice off the bottom of each head of chicory and remove a little of the core, using a small knife. Wash them carefully, without separating the leaves.

Using 25 g/1 oz of the butter, butter an ovenproof lidded dish just large enough to hold all the chicory in a single layer. Add the chicory, 6 tablespoons water and the lemon juice; sprinkle with half the sugar and a little salt. Cover with buttered greaseproof paper and top with a plate to keep the chicory submerged during cooking. Cover with a lid and bake for 30–40 minutes or until tender when tested with the point of a knife. Drain and set aside. This may be prepared a day in advance.

To serve, squeeze the chicory gently to remove excess liquid, then dry well in a clean tea towel. Cut them in half lengthways.

Heat the remaining butter in a large frying pan until foaming, add the orange zest, cardamom seeds and the remaining sugar and cook over a fairly high heat for 30 seconds or until lightly caramelized. Reduce the heat, add the halved chicory and cook gently, turning once, until caramelized and golden on both sides. Pour the orange juice over the chicory, then transfer to a serving dish and pour over the caramelized pan juices.

Paul Gayler

BRAISED ARTICHOKES
with lemon mint pesto broth

4 GLOBE ARTICHOKES
SALT AND FRESHLY GROUND BLACK PEPPER
175 ML/6 FL OZ DRY WHITE WINE
6 TABLESPOONS OLIVE OIL
1 GARLIC CLOVE, CRUSHED

LEMON MINT PESTO
4 TABLESPOONS FRESH MINT LEAVES
GRATED ZEST OF ½ LEMON
1 GARLIC CLOVE, CRUSHED
4 TABLESPOONS OLIVE OIL
PINCH OF SUGAR

SERVES 4

Preheat the oven to 150°C/300°F/Gas Mark 2. Prepare the artichokes (page 374) and season all over with salt and pepper.

Place the artichokes upside down in an ovenproof dish. Whisk the wine and oil together, stir in the crushed garlic and pour over the artichokes. Cover the dish with foil or a lid, place in the oven and braise for about 45 minutes or until tender. Drain, reserving the cooking liquid, and leave to cool.

For the pesto, place all the ingredients in a liquidizer and blend to a purée.

To serve, cut the artichokes in half. Add the pesto to the cooking liquid, taste and adjust the seasoning. Pour over the artichokes and serve at room temperature.

Paul Gayler

VEGETABLE FRITTERS
in Indian spiced batter

1 AUBERGINE, SLICED INTO 1 CM/½ INCH CUBES

8 CAULIFLOWER FLORETS

2 COURGETTES, THICKLY SLICED

125 G/4 OZ FRENCH BEANS, BLANCHED AND DRAINED

VEGETABLE OIL FOR DEEP-FRYING

SALT

SPICY BATTER

175 G/6 OZ CHICKPEA FLOUR

½ TEASPOON BAKING POWDER

1 TEASPOON CORNFLOUR

½ TABLESPOON EACH OF GROUND CUMIN, CORIANDER, MILD CURRY POWDER AND TURMERIC

CHUTNEY MAYONNAISE

1 TABLESPOON MANGO CHUTNEY, CHOPPED

125 ML/4 FL OZ MAYONNAISE

1 TABLESPOON GRATED FRESH GINGER

SERVES 4

Place all the batter ingredients in a large bowl, mix well, then stir in enough water to form a light batter. Place all the vegetables in the batter, stir well to coat and leave for 30 minutes.

Make the chutney mayonnaise by mixing all the ingredients together in a small bowl. Chill.

Heat the oil to 180°C/350°F or until a cube of bread browns in 30 seconds. Drop tablespoons of the vegetables in batter, one by one, into the hot oil and fry until golden and crisp. Drain on paper towels and season lightly with a little salt.

When all the vegetable fritters are cooked, serve hot, accompanied by chutney mayonnaise or your favourite dip or sauce.

GADO GADO

125 G/4 OZ NEW POTATOES

2 CARROTS, CUT INTO MATCHSTICKS

125 G/4 OZ FRENCH BEANS

85 G/3 OZ CUCUMBER, CUT INTO MATCHSTICKS

50 G/2 OZ BEANSPROUTS

2 TABLESPOONS VEGETABLE OIL

275 G/10 OZ FIRM TOFU, CUT INTO 1 CM/½ INCH
    SLICES

SALT AND FRESHLY GROUND BLACK PEPPER

½ A CHINESE CABBAGE OR ICEBERG LETTUCE, LEAVES
    SEPARATED

8 QUAILS' EGGS, HARD-BOILED AND HALVED

PEANUT SAUCE

6 TABLESPOONS SESAME OIL

1 FRESH RED CHILLI, SEEDED AND CHOPPED

125 G/4 OZ CRUNCHY PEANUT BUTTER

6 TABLESPOONS VEGETABLE STOCK

1 GARLIC CLOVE, CRUSHED

1 TABLESPOON SOY SAUCE

2 TABLESPOONS SUGAR

JUICE OF 1 LEMON

SERVES 4

Boil the new potatoes until tender. Drain, then peel them while they are still hot, slice and keep them warm.

Cook the carrots and beans separately in boiling salted water, retaining their crispness. Drain them and add to the potatoes; keep warm. Add the cucumber and beansprouts to the vegetables.

Heat the oil in a frying pan and fry the tofu slices until golden. Season well and drain on paper towels.

For the sauce, heat 3 tablespoons of the sesame oil in a small saucepan and fry the chilli until soft. In another pan, heat the peanut butter, add the stock and boil for 2 minutes. Add the chilli and its oil and remove from the heat, then add the garlic, soy sauce, the remaining sesame oil and the sugar. Season to taste and add the lemon juice; the dressing may separate slightly.

To serve, season the warm vegetables. Arrange the Chinese cabbage or lettuce leaves on the serving plates. Top with the tofu, the warm vegetables and the quails' eggs. Coat lightly with the sauce.

Paul Gayler

MY FAVOURITE GRATIN

15 G/½ OZ BUTTER

200 G/7 OZ PARSNIPS, THINLY SLICED

SALT AND FRESHLY GROUND BLACK PEPPER

GRATED NUTMEG

200 G/7 OZ SWEDE, THINLY SLICED

200 G/7 OZ POTATOES, THINLY SLICED

450 ML/¾ PINT DOUBLE CREAM

150 ML/¼ PINT MILK

1 GARLIC CLOVE, CRUSHED

50 G/2 OZ CHEDDAR CHEESE, GRATED (OPTIONAL)

SERVES 4

Preheat the oven to 180°C/350°F/Gas Mark 4. Butter a 25 cm/10 inch diameter (about 1.5 litre/2 pint) gratin dish.

Arrange the parsnips in overlapping slices in the dish and season with salt, pepper and nutmeg. Top with neat layers of swede and season again, then top with the potato slices and season once more.

Bring the cream, milk and garlic to the boil, then pour through a strainer on to the vegetables, ensuring that the liquid covers them. (It may be necessary to top up with more milk.) Sprinkle over the cheese, if using, then bake for 45–50 minutes or until the vegetables are tender and the top is golden and crusty.

Valentina Harris

CAULIFLOWER AND RICE BAKE

1 CAULIFLOWER, BROKEN INTO FLORETS

8 HEAPED TABLESPOONS RISOTTO RICE

1 ONION, THINLY SLICED

85 G/3 OZ UNSALTED BUTTER

4 TABLESPOONS DRIED WHITE BREADCRUMBS

SALT AND FRESHLY GROUND PEPPER

6 HEAPED TABLESPOONS FRESHLY GRATED PARMESAN
 CHEESE

1 LITRE/1¾ PINTS BÉCHAMEL SAUCE (PAGE 376)

TOMATO AND OLIVE SAUCE

2 GARLIC CLOVES, CHOPPED

4 TABLESPOONS OLIVE OIL

2 TABLESPOONS FINELY CHOPPED CAPERS

2 TABLESPOONS FINELY CHOPPED BLACK OLIVES

500 ML/16 FL OZ PASSATA

LARGE PINCH OF DRIED OREGANO

SERVES 4

Preheat the oven to 230°C/450°F/Gas Mark 8. Steam the cauliflower florets until only just tender, about 10 minutes.

Boil the rice in salted water for 10 minutes, then drain. Fry the onion gently in half the butter in a large, wide frying pan. Add the partly cooked rice and mix together for about 3 minutes, using two forks in order to keep the rice grains separate.

Thoroughly butter an ovenproof dish and sprinkle with breadcrumbs. Arrange half the cauliflower in the dish, season lightly, then cover with half the rice, half the Parmesan and half the béchamel sauce. Repeat the layers and sprinkle the remaining breadcrumbs on top. Dot with the remaining butter and bake for 15–20 minutes.

Meanwhile, make the sauce; fry the garlic in the oil for 5 minutes. Add the capers and olives and fry for a further 5 minutes. Add the passata, simmer for about 10 minutes, then add the oregano and season to taste. Keep warm until ready to serve with the bake.

Serve with a leafy green salad containing plenty of spicy-tasting rocket (arugula).

Pat Chapman

PAKISTANI VEGETABLE BALTI

400 G/14 OZ CANNED CHICKPEAS

4 TABLESPOONS VEGETABLE OIL

4 GARLIC CLOVES, FINELY CHOPPED

2 SMALL ONIONS, SLICED

1 RED PEPPER, CHOPPED

½ YELLOW PEPPER, CHOPPED

2–3 GREEN CHILLIES, SLICED (OPTIONAL)

400 G/14 OZ SPINACH

150 G/5 OZ MUSHROOMS, QUARTERED

1 TABLESPOON TOMATO KETCHUP

6 CHERRY TOMATOES, HALVED

2 TEASPOONS CHOPPED MANGO CHUTNEY

1 TABLESPOON EACH OF CHOPPED FRESH MINT
   AND CORIANDER LEAVES

SALT

WHOLE SPICES

1 TEASPOON CORIANDER SEEDS

½ TEASPOON EACH OF CUMIN SEEDS AND FENNEL SEEDS

6 WHOLE GREEN CARDAMOM PODS

GROUND SPICES

2 TEASPOONS DRIED FENUGREEK LEAVES

½ TEASPOON EACH OF BLACK PEPPER, TURMERIC
   AND CLOVES

⅓ TEASPOON CINNAMON

SERVES 4

Heat a wok or karahi over fairly high heat, adding no oil. Add the whole spices and dry-fry, stirring constantly, for about 30 seconds. Leave to cool, then grind in a coffee grinder. Add the ground spices and mix well. Drain the can of chickpeas, reserving the liquid.

Heat the oil in a wok or karahi and stir-fry over high heat for 10–15 minutes with the garlic, spices and onions, gradually lowering the heat.

Increase the heat and add the peppers and chillies, if using. Stir-fry for about 3 minutes.

Add the spinach and some of the chickpea liquid and stir-fry for a further 2–3 minutes. Add the chickpeas, the remaining liquid and all the remaining ingredients, except the salt.

Add just enough water to create the desired gravy consistency and stir-fry for 2–3 minutes or until well mixed and hot through. Season to taste, garnish and serve.

Pat Chapman

COCHIN VEGETABLE CURRY

125 G/4 OZ NEW POTATOES, HALVED

125 G/4 OZ CANNED RED KIDNEY BEANS

4 TABLESPOONS SUNFLOWER OIL

2 GARLIC CLOVES, SLICED

1 SMALL RED ONION, SLICED

2–4 FRESH RED CHILLIES, CHOPPED (OPTIONAL)

125 G/4 OZ GREEN BEANS, TOPPED AND TAILED

½ AUBERGINE, DICED

2 SMALL CARROTS, DICED

10–12 DRIED OR FRESH CURRY LEAVES

300 ML/10 FL OZ NATURAL YOGURT

1 TABLESPOON CHOPPED FRESH CORIANDER LEAVES

SALT

SPICES

1 TEASPOON EACH OF BLACK MUSTARD SEEDS AND
   SESAME SEEDS

½ TEASPOON EACH OF CRUSHED BLACK PEPPERCORNS
   AND TURMERIC

⅓ TEASPOON CHOPPED DRIED RED CHILLIES

SERVES 4

Boil the potatoes until tender. Drain and rinse the kidney beans.

Heat the oil in a wok or karahi and stir-fry over high heat for 10–15 minutes with the garlic, spices and onions, gradually lowering the heat.

Add the chillies, if using, beans, aubergine and carrots, and stir-fry for about 3 minutes.

Gradually add the curry leaves and yogurt, little by little over 5 minutes, stirring frequently and ensuring that the mixture simmers but does not boil.

Add the potatoes and coriander leaves and simmer for a further 4–5 minutes or until hot through. Season to taste, garnish and serve.

Yon-Rit So

STIR-FRIED BEANSPROUTS
with courgettes

3–4 TABLESPOONS PEANUT OR CORN OIL

1½–2 TABLESPOONS SHREDDED FRESH GINGER

400 G/14 OZ BEANSPROUTS

400 G/14 OZ COURGETTES, TOPPED AND TAILED,
   THEN CUT INTO THIN STICKS ABOUT 5 CM/
   2 INCHES LONG

½ TEASPOON SALT

2–3 TEASPOONS THIN OR LIGHT SOY SAUCE

1 TABLESPOON SESAME OIL

SERVES 3–4 VEGETARIANS, 6 WITH OTHER DISHES

Heat a wok over high heat until smoke rises. Add the oil and swirl it around. Add the ginger and let it sizzle for a few seconds. Add the beansprouts and courgettes, season with the salt and turn and toss vigorously until the beansprouts begin to release their water.

Add the soy sauce and continue to stir and turn for about 5 minutes, varying the heat between high and medium, until most of the moisture has evaporated. Add the sesame oil and transfer the mixture to a serving dish. Serve at once.

Paul Gayler

FRAGRANT THAI VEGETABLES
with spiced coconut

4 TABLESPOONS PEANUT OIL

50 G/2 OZ BUTTER

1 GARLIC CLOVE, CRUSHED

25 G/1 OZ FRESH GINGER, CUT INTO MATCHSTICKS

1 SMALL AUBERGINE, CUT INTO 1 CM/½ INCH CUBES

1 CARROT, SLICED

150 G/5 OZ SHIITAKE MUSHROOMS

2 COURGETTES, CUT INTO 5 MM/¼ INCH SLICES

4 SMALL BOK CHOY, HALVED LENGTHWAYS

225 G/8 OZ MANGETOUT

125 G/4 OZ CUCUMBER, HALVED, SEEDS REMOVED,
CUT INTO BATONS

FRESHLY GRATED COCONUT

1 FRESH RED CHILLI, SEEDED AND FINELY CHOPPED

SERVES 4

Heat the peanut oil and butter in a wok or deep-sided frying pan over a fairly high heat. Add the garlic and ginger and cook for 30 seconds to release the fragrance.

Add the vegetables to the pan in the order listed and toss together until they are cooked but retaining their crispness.

Mix the coconut with the chilli and sprinkle over the vegetables; serve at once.

Jameen Garlin

ROSEMARY ROASTED VEGETABLES

6–7 TABLESPOONS EXTRA VIRGIN OLIVE OIL
3 LARGE BAKING POTATOES, SCRUBBED
3 TABLESPOONS FRESH ROSEMARY, BRUISED
COARSE SALT
FRESHLY GROUND BLACK PEPPER
3 LARGE ONIONS
450 G/1 LB BABY CARROTS, PEELED
450 G/1 LB ASPARAGUS, PEELED AND TOUGH ENDS
  REMOVED

Almost any combination of vegetables can be used: try parsnips, aubergines, peppers. Roasting times may vary, depending on the variety, size and age of the vegetables, so check them every so often. Roast one vegetable at a time and be sure to stir or turn them over occasionally so that they brown on all sides.

SERVES 6

Preheat the oven to 200°C/400°F/Gas Mark 6. Lightly grease four baking sheets with olive oil.

Cut the potatoes into quarters lengthways. Place them on one of the baking sheets, cut side down. Drizzle with olive oil and sprinkle on a little rosemary, salt and pepper. Roast for 50 minutes–1 hour or until tender when tested with the point of a fork.

Keeping the skin on the onions, trim off the roots but leave the root end intact. Cut into quarters and place cut side down on a baking sheet. Drizzle with olive oil, rosemary, salt and pepper. Roast for about 45 minutes or until the onions are browned, caramelized and soft. Peel off the skin before serving.

Arrange the carrots in a single layer on a baking sheet. Drizzle with olive oil, rosemary, salt and pepper. Roast for about 45 minutes or until tender when tested with the point of a fork.

Arrange the asparagus in a single layer on a baking sheet. Drizzle with olive oil, rosemary, salt and pepper. Roast for 15–20 minutes or until tender when tested with the point of a fork.

To serve as a side dish, arrange the roasted vegetables on a platter and reheat if necessary. To serve as a first course, toss with hot pasta.

Rowley Leigh

CEPS WITH PARSLEY AND GARLIC

450 G/1 LB CEPS, CLEANED (PAGE 374)
3–4 TABLESPOONS OLIVE OIL
6 GARLIC CLOVES, FINELY CHOPPED
6 SPRIGS OF PARSLEY, FINELY CHOPPED
SALT AND PEPPER

SERVES 4

Slice the ceps quite thinly and sauté in olive oil in a very hot frying pan for 3–4 minutes. Using a slotted spoon, remove the ceps from the pan and keep warm.

Add a little more oil to the pan if necessary, then reduce the heat and add the garlic; cook for about 5 minutes, then return the ceps to the pan, add the parsley and season well. Serve immediately, either on their own or with a good steak.

Karen Lee

CRISPY BROCCOLI

½ HEAD OF BROCCOLI
2 TABLESPOONS OLIVE OIL
⅓ TEASPOON SALT
2 TABLESPOONS SLICED GARLIC
⅛ TEASPOON CAYENNE PEPPER

SERVES 2–4

Wash and drain the broccoli. Cut off and discard about 5 cm/2 inches of the stem. Peel the remaining stem, then slice into 1 cm/½ inch thick pieces; when you come to the florets, break them up.

Place a frying pan over medium heat, add the olive oil and salt and heat for 1 minute, then reduce the heat to low, add the garlic and sauté for 2 minutes.

Add the broccoli and cayenne pepper and toss to mix well. Sauté over medium heat for 5 minutes, tossing occasionally until the broccoli is cooked through but still a little crunchy. Serve hot or at room temperature.

Yan-Kit So

STIR-FRIED CHINESE LEAF
with oyster mushrooms

1 HEAD OF CHINESE LEAVES,
  ABOUT 600–675 G/1¼–1½ LB
150–175 G/5–6 OZ OYSTER MUSHROOMS
4 TABLESPOONS PEANUT OR CORN OIL
6 SLICES OF FRESH GINGER, PEELED
4 LARGE SPRING ONIONS, CUT INTO 4 CM/1½ INCH
  SECTIONS, WHITE AND GREEN PARTS SEPARATED
¾–1 TEASPOON SALT
1½–1¾ TABLESPOONS WINE VINEGAR OR CHINESE RICE
  VINEGAR

SERVES 2–3 VEGETARIANS, 4–6 WITH OTHER DISHES

Separate the Chinese leaves and rinse the outer ones to remove any dirt. Cut the leaves in half lengthways, then cut crossways into 5 cm/2 inch sections, separating the stalks and leafy parts. Set aside.

Cut the oyster mushrooms lengthways into strips.

Heat a wok over high heat until smoke rises. Add the oil and swirl it around. Add the ginger, stir, add the white spring onions and stir for a few seconds. Add the reserved stalks, turn and toss vigorously for a few seconds.

Reduce the heat to medium. Add the salt, which will draw out moisture from the Chinese leaves. Add the vinegar, stir, add the oyster mushrooms, stir, then add the leafy parts. Continue to stir and cook for about 5 minutes, depending on how crisp you like the Chinese leaves. Add the green spring onions, stir to mix, then transfer to a serving dish. Serve hot.

Karen Lee

SAUTÉED PEPPERS
with garlic and capers

2 RED OR YELLOW PEPPERS, SEEDED AND CUT INTO
   LARGE SQUARES
1½ TABLESPOONS OLIVE OIL
1 LARGE GARLIC CLOVE, SLICED
1 TABLESPOON CAPERS, RINSED AND DRAINED
4 TABLESPOONS DRY WHITE WINE
SALT AND FRESHLY GROUND BLACK PEPPER

SERVES 2–4

Sauté the peppers in the olive oil over medium heat for about 5–10 minutes or until they soften and are cooked through – it does not matter if they brown slightly. After about 4 minutes, add the garlic and stir occasionally – the garlic should brown slightly.

Add the capers, stir briefly, then, using a slotted spoon, transfer the contents of the pan to a warmed serving dish.

Add the white wine to the pan and stir over low heat to deglaze the pan and reduce the liquid by half. Taste the liquid and adjust the seasoning if required, then pour over the peppers. Serve hot or at room temperature, with warm bread or over rice or pasta.

Karen Lee

BRAISED GREENS

325 G/12 OZ MIXED GREENS, SUCH AS KALE, SWISS
  CHARD
1½ TABLESPOONS OLIVE OIL
⅓ TEASPOON SALT
2 GARLIC CLOVES, CHOPPED
1½ LEEKS, CUT INTO 1 CM/½ INCH PIECES
ABOUT 125 ML/4 FL OZ VEGETABLE STOCK (PAGE 374)
¼ TEASPOON FRESHLY GROUND BLACK PEPPER

SERVES 2–4

Wash and drain the greens. Remove and discard
any tough kale stems. Cut the greens into
2.5 cm/1 inch pieces, keeping the Swiss chard
stems separate.

Place a wok or large saucepan over high heat
for 1 minute, then reduce the heat to very low
and add the olive oil, salt, garlic and leeks; sauté
for about 10 minutes. The garlic and leeks
should not burn, so use a heat-diffusing mat if
you cannot get a really low heat.

Add the stock and bring to the boil. If using
Swiss chard, add the stems, cover and cook for
3 4 minutes, then add the leaves, cover and
cook for a further 6–10 minutes, stirring until
slightly wilted. Season to taste with the black
pepper. Serve hot or at room temperature. Do
not reheat.

fish

Antony Worrall Thompson

GRILLED TUNA
with celeriac skordalia, rocket salad

4 TUNA LOIN STEAKS, ABOUT 175 G/6 OZ EACH
EXTRA VIRGIN OLIVE OIL
SALT AND GROUND BLACK PEPPER
4 LEMON WEDGES

CELERIAC SKORDALIA
325 G/12 OZ CELERIAC, CUBED
125 G/4 OZ POTATO, CUBED
5 GARLIC CLOVES, CRUSHED WITH A LITTLE SALT
250 ML/8 FL OZ EXTRA VIRGIN OLIVE OIL
85 ML/3 FL OZ WARM MILK

ROCKET SALAD
85 G/3 OZ ROCKET LEAVES, WASHED AND DRIED
4 TABLESPOONS EXTRA VIRGIN OLIVE OIL

SERVES 4

To make the skordalia, boil the celeriac and potato in salted water until tender, about 20–30 minutes.

Drain and return the vegetables to a pan over a low heat to dry out. Place the warm vegetables in a food processor and blend until smooth. With the machine running, add the garlic and slowly pour in the oil and milk as if you were making a mayonnaise. Season to taste.

To cook the tuna, preheat a grill. Rub the tuna lightly with the olive oil, salt and pepper. Cook for 1–2 minutes on each side, depending on how rare you like the tuna. (Well-done tuna is a waste of good fish, and if this is your preference then you may as well open a can.)

Season the rocket leaves and toss with the olive oil. Arrange the celeriac skordalia on four plates, top with the tuna and serve the rocket on the side, with a wedge of lemon.

Alastair Little

BAKED COD
with potato crust

2 BAKING POTATOES, PEELED

SALT AND PEPPER

4 COD FILLET STEAKS WITH SKIN, ABOUT 250 G/9 OZ
EACH (FROZEN ONES FROM THE SUPERMARKET ARE
GENERALLY EXCELLENT)

A PLATE OF SEASONED FLOUR

100 G/3½ OZ UNSALTED BUTTER

2 LEMONS, HALVED

SERVES 4

Preheat the oven to its highest setting. Butter a
baking sheet. Slice the potatoes as thinly as
possible, rinse thoroughly, then dry with paper
towels.

Season the fish on the flesh side and arrange
the potato slices on this side, overlapping like
scales. Season the potatoes and, using a fish slice,
carefully transfer the fish to the seasoned flour,
skin side down. Flour on the skin side only,
then equally carefully transfer to the buttered
baking sheet. Dot the potato scales with small
pieces of butter, then place in the oven and
bake for 15 minutes.

Meanwhile, heat the grill (if you have a dual-
function oven simply switch from oven to grill
function). Finish browning and crisping the
potato under the grill.

Very carefully transfer the fish to four serving
plates, pour over any buttery juices and serve a
half lemon on each plate. A simple green
vegetable such as sugar snap peas would be an
ideal companion.

Roger Vergé

JOHN DORY
with spring vegetables

1 JOHN DORY, ABOUT 900 G/2 LB, FILLETED AND
  SKINNED, OR FILLETS OF SOLE, MONKFISH, TURBOT
  OR BASS
1 POTATO, DICED
20 TINY GREEN BEANS
1 CARROT, CUT IN JULIENNE STRIPS
1 LEEK, WHITE PART ONLY, CUT IN JULIENNE STRIPS
1 CELERY STALK, FROM THE INSIDE OF THE HEAD OF
  CELERY, CUT IN JULIENNE STRIPS
25 G/1 OZ BUTTER
6 TABLESPOONS DOUBLE CREAM
SALT AND PEPPER
1 BUNCH OF CHIVES, FINELY CHOPPED

SERVES 2

Cut the fish fillets into strips about 1 cm/½ inch wide.

Cook the potato in lightly salted boiling water until tender. Cook the beans in lightly salted boiling water until just tender; drain and refresh in cold water. Put the julienne vegetable strips in a small saucepan with a pinch of salt, 3 tablespoons water and 1 teaspoon of the butter. Cook over high heat until the carrots are just tender and the liquid has almost evaporated. Keep all the vegetables hot.

Put the cream in a saucepan, add a little salt and the strips of fish. Bring to the boil and simmer for 2 minutes – not a second more. Place a strainer over a liquidizer and pour in the cream. Return the fish to the saucepan and add the drained beans and the vegetables cut in julienne strips.

Add half the cooked potato to the liquidizer and purée until smooth. Add the remaining butter and blend briefly. Season to taste. Pour over the fish and vegetables and bring to the boil over high heat. Stir in the chives and serve

Roger Vergé

MONKFISH CÔTE D'AZUR

675–800 G/1½–1¾ LB MONKFISH FILLETS

SALT AND PEPPER

1 SPRIG OF SAGE

8 BABY CARROTS

8 BABY TURNIPS

1 HEAD OF BROCCOLI, CUT INTO FLORETS

4 SMALL COURGETTES

12 SMALL NEW POTATOES

225 G/8 OZ MANGETOUT, SHELLED PEAS OR GREEN
    BEANS

1 BUNCH EACH OF SAGE AND ROSEMARY

THE SAUCE

1 TABLESPOON EACH OF CHOPPED FRESH PARSLEY AND
    CHERVIL

½ TABLESPOON EACH OF CHOPPED FRESH BASIL,
    TARRAGON, CHIVES AND CELERY LEAVES

1 GARLIC CLOVE

3 TABLESPOONS EXTRA VIRGIN OLIVE OIL

1 TABLESPOON WINE VINEGAR

1 TABLESPOON SMALL CAPERS

2 SMALL RIPE TOMATOES, SKINNED, SEEDED AND DICED

½ RED PEPPER, GRILLED, PEELED AND DICED

3 TABLESPOONS PITTED BLACK OLIVES

SERVES 4

Remove the membrane from the monkfish. Place the fish on a piece of clingfilm, sprinkle with salt and pepper and add a leaf of sage every 1 cm/½ inch. Roll up very tightly to make a neat cylindrical shape. Place on a steamer rack and leave in a cool place.

Prepare all the vegetables, wash and arrange on a steamer rack; sprinkle with coarse salt.

Fill the bottom of a steamer with water, add the sage and rosemary and bring to the boil. Place the rack of vegetables over the water and steam for 10 minutes. Place the fish on its rack over the vegetables and steam for a further 10 minutes, or until both the fish and vegetables are tender.

Meanwhile, chop all the herbs for the sauce together with the garlic and mix with the oil, vinegar and salt and pepper to taste. Stir in the remaining ingredients.

Slice the monkfish and serve with the vegetables, with the sauce served separately.

Roger Vergé

STUFFED SEABASS

1 SEA BASS, ABOUT 900 G/2 LB, CLEANED, SCALED AND
   BONED, BONE RESERVED
SALT AND PEPPER
2 SMALL SHALLOTS, CHOPPED
50 ML/2 FL OZ DRY VERMOUTH
200 ML/7 FL OZ DRY WHITE WINE
100 G/3½ OZ BUTTER
100 ML/3½ FL OZ WATER
1 SMALL SPRIG OF THYME
1 SMALL BAY LEAF
150 ML/5 FL OZ DOUBLE CREAM

STUFFING

ABOUT 200 G/7 OZ WHITE FISH FILLET, WITH ITS BONE
1 OR 2 EGG WHITES
200 ML/7 FL OZ DOUBLE CREAM
125 G/4 OZ PEELED COOKED PRAWNS
2 TABLESPOONS PITTED SMALL BLACK OLIVES, CHOPPED
2 TABLESPOONS CHOPPED FRESH PARSLEY OR MIXED
   HERBS

SERVES 6

Preheat the oven to 160°C/325°F/Gas Mark 3.

All the ingredients for the stuffing must be cold. Place the white fish fillet in a food processor with a little salt and pepper and purée briefly. Add the egg whites and mix for a few seconds, then add the cream and mix for a few seconds more. Transfer to a bowl and stir in the prawns, olives and half the herbs.

Season inside the sea bass and fill with the stuffing. Butter a flameproof dish or baking tin and sprinkle with salt, pepper and 1 chopped shallot. Place the sea bass on top and pour in the vermouth and half the wine. Bring to the boil over medium-high heat, then cover and bake for 40 minutes.

Sweat the remaining shallot in a little butter with the fish bone for 2–3 minutes. Add the remaining wine, bring to the boil, then add the water, thyme, bay leaf and a little pepper. Simmer very gently for 10 minutes, then strain.

When the fish is cooked, pour the cooking liquid into a saucepan. Boil to reduce, add the strained fish stock and boil to reduce by half. Add the cream and boil for 1–2 minutes. Remove from the heat and whisk in the remaining butter, cut into dice. Stir in the remaining herbs and serve with the sea bass.

Valentina Harris

BAKED HERRINGS

with potatoes and button onions

1 KG/2¼ LB FRESH HERRINGS, HEADS AND SPINES
   REMOVED
300 G/11 OZ POTATOES
250 G/9 OZ BUTTON ONIONS, PEELED
85 G/3 OZ UNSALTED BUTTER
FRESHLY GROUND BLACK PEPPER
HANDFUL OF CAPERS PRESERVED IN SALT
FRESH FLAT-LEAF PARSLEY, CHOPPED

SERVES 4

Preheat the oven to 180°C/350°C/Gas Mark 4.
Clean the herrings very thoroughly. Slice the
potatoes thickly. If the onions are larger than a
walnut, cut them in half. Put 1 tablespoon
butter in a frying pan and add the onions. Sauté
the onions for about 5 minutes to soften them
slightly.

Generously butter a large ovenproof dish and
lay the herrings in the dish with the potatoes
and onions. Season with pepper. Bake for about
10 minutes, then add the capers and parsley and
continue cooking, basting frequently with the
butter from the dish, for about 1 hour or until
the potatoes are tender. Serve piping hot.

I like to serve this with a simple, really
crunchy coleslaw salad, with a little wholegrain
mustard added to the dressing.

Rowley Leigh

STEAMED TURBOT
with horns of plenty

A HANDFUL OF HORN OF PLENTY MUSHROOMS,
  CLEANED
2 TABLESPOONS EXTRA VIRGIN OLIVE OIL
1 SMALL TURBOT, ABOUT 900 G/2 LB, CLEANED,
  SKINNED AND FILLETED
1–2 GARLIC CLOVES, FINELY CHOPPED
1 TABLESPOON SNIPPED FRESH CHIVES

BEURRE BLANC
2 TABLESPOONS DRY WHITE WINE
1 TABLESPOON WHITE WINE VINEGAR
1 SHALLOT, FINELY CHOPPED
125 G/4 OZ COLD UNSALTED BUTTER, CUBED

SERVES 2

To make the butter sauce, put the wine, vinegar and chopped shallot in a small, heavy saucepan and boil until the liquid is reduced almost to nothing. Add the butter a little at a time, whisking vigorously, until it forms a creamy sauce – this should take no more than 2–3 minutes. Still whisking vigorously, increase the heat and bring the sauce to just below boiling point, then season to taste and remove from the heat. Keep warm by sitting the pan in a larger pan filled with very hot water.

Sauté the mushrooms in olive oil for about 2 minutes or until tender. Keep warm.

Steam the turbot fillets for 7–8 minutes or until cooked.

Serve at once, on warmed plates; top with the sauce, the mushrooms and a sprinkling of garlic and chives.

Roger Vergé

RED MULLET EN BARIGOULE

3 GLOBE ARTICHOKES

1 LEMON, HALVED

500 ML/16 FL OZ EXTRA VIRGIN OLIVE OIL

2 SMALL CARROTS, SLICED THINLY

2 SMALL ONIONS, SLICED THINLY

1 GARLIC CLOVE, CRUSHED

1 SPRIG OF THYME

2 BAY LEAVES

SALT AND PEPPER

150 ML/5 FL OZ DRY WHITE WINE

250 ML/8 FL OZ WHITE STOCK

2 LARGE RIPE TOMATOES, SKINNED, SEEDED AND
   DICED

1 RED PEPPER, GRILLED, PEELED AND DICED

ABOUT 15 G/½ OZ EACH OF FRESH CHERVIL, DILL,
   TARRAGON, BASIL

4 SMALL RED MULLET, ABOUT 200–225 G/7–8 OZ
   EACH, FILLETED

SERVES 4

Prepare the artichoke hearts (page 374) and leave them in the water.

Heat 200 ml/7 fl oz of the oil in a saucepan over low heat and sweat the carrots and onions until softened, about 5 minutes.

Add the garlic, thyme and bay leaves. Cut the artichoke hearts into quarters and add them to the pan with a little salt and pepper, the wine and stock. Simmer, uncovered, until the artichokes are tender and the sauce has almost evaporated, about 20 minutes.

Mix the diced tomatoes and pepper with most of the remaining olive oil; season to taste. Pick off the smallest, most tender herb leaves and chop them, but do not add them until the last moment.

Lightly brush the red mullet fillets with olive oil and place on a lightly oiled grill pan, skin side up. Place under a hot grill for 3–4 minutes, until just cooked.

Divide the artichokes between four plates and arrange the mullet on top. Mix the herbs with the tomato and pepper mixture and spoon over the fish.

SUPREME OF BRILL
with mussels and spinach

1 KG/2¼ LB MUSSELS, CLEANED

250 ML/8 FL OZ DRY WHITE WINE

1 KG/2¼ LB SPINACH

A LITTLE UNSALTED BUTTER

4 FILLETS OF BRILL (OR HALIBUT OR TURBOT), ABOUT
    800 G/1¾ LB – YOU WILL PROBABLY HAVE TO BUY A
    1.5 KG/3 LB BRILL AND ASK YOUR FISHMONGER TO
    FILLET IT

200 ML/7 FL OZ DOUBLE CREAM

PINCH OF SAFFRON

SALT AND PEPPER

SERVES 4

Put the mussels in a large saucepan with the wine over a high heat. As soon as the shells open, tip the mussels into a colander over a bowl to catch the cooking liquid. Strain the liquid through a fine sieve into a clean pan and place over a high heat to boil until reduced by half. Leave to cool. Shell the mussels and place in a bowl with a little of the cooking liquid; keep chilled.

Wash the spinach, boil for 1 minute, then refresh in cold water, drain and squeeze dry. Preheat the oven to 180°C/350°F/Gas Mark 4.

Butter a gratin dish and arrange the spinach in the dish to form a bed for the brill. Dot the fish with more butter, cover loosely with foil and bake for 12–15 minutes or until the fish is opaque.

While the brill is cooking, add the cream to the reduced mussel liquid. Bring back to the boil and simmer until slightly thickened. Add the saffron and season to taste. When the brill is nearly cooked, add the mussels to the sauce and heat through gently. Pour over the fish and serve from the gratin dish.

Roger Vergé

BRAISED TURBOT WITH SORREL

1 SMALL TURBOT, ABOUT 900 G/2 LB, GUTTED, GILLS
    AND FINS REMOVED
2 BUNCHES OF SORREL, ABOUT 85 G/3 OZ IN TOTAL
SALT AND PEPPER
2 SHALLOTS, FINELY CHOPPED
85 ML/3 FL OZ DRY WHITE WINE
85 ML/3 FL OZ DOUBLE CREAM
25 G/1 OZ BUTTER, CUT INTO SMALL CUBES

SERVES 2

Begin by soaking the fish in ice-cold water for
5–6 hours.

Preheat the oven to 200°C/ 400°F/Gas Mark
6. Dry the fish thoroughly.

Pull the tender parts of the sorrel leaves away
from the tough central ribs. Wash the leaves and
pat dry, then roll up each leaf tightly like a cigar
and cut into very fine ribbons (a chiffonade).

Season the turbot on both sides. Butter a
baking dish and sprinkle with the chopped
shallots. Place the fish on top, dark skin
upwards, and pour in the wine. Cook in the
preheated oven for 20–25 minutes.

When the fish is cooked, transfer to a dish to
keep hot. Pour the cooking liquid and shallots
into a saucepan over high heat. Boil until the
liquid is syrupy and reduced to 2–3 tablespoons.
Add the cream and bring briefly to the boil,
then stir in the chiffonade of sorrel. Bring back
to the boil and season to taste. Remove from
the heat and beat in the butter, little by little.
Keep the sauce warm.

Peel off the dark skin from the fish and
remove the fringe of bones by running a sharp
knife around the edge of the fish and pushing
the bones outwards. Place it on a hot, lightly
buttered serving dish and pour over some of the
sorrel sauce. Serve the remaining sauce
separately.

Jameen Garlin

CORIANDER-CRUSTED SALMON
and leeks

2–3 TABLESPOONS EXTRA VIRGIN OLIVE OIL

1 STICK OF CELERY, CHOPPED

25 G/1 OZ BUTTER

3 LEEKS (MOSTLY WHITE PART), CUT INTO FINE STRIPS

85 ML/3 FL OZ WHITE WINE

COARSE SALT

FRESHLY GROUND BLACK PEPPER

1.6 KG/3½ LB WHOLE SALMON, SCALED AND GUTTED
   (OR A TAIL OR CENTRE-CUT SECTION)

2 TABLESPOONS CRUSHED CORIANDER SEEDS

FRESH PARSLEY, TO GARNISH

SERVES 6

Preheat the oven to 200°C/400°F/Gas Mark 6. Lightly grease a large baking sheet with olive oil. Spread the celery over the baking sheet.

Melt the butter in a saucepan and add the leeks and wine. Cover and cook over very low heat until the leeks are limp, about 5 minutes. Season to taste and leave to cool.

Generously season the fish inside and out. Place half of the leeks inside the fish and scatter the remainder over the celery. Place the fish on the bed of vegetables.

Drizzle olive oil over the fish, then press coriander seeds into the skin on the top side of the fish to form a crust.

Roast the fish for 20–30 minutes (about 10 minutes per 2.5 cm/1 inch thickness.) The fish is done when it is aromatic, the skin on the tail bubbles, and there is no raw red colour near the bone when pierced with a skewer.

Transfer the fish to a warm platter and serve with the roasted leeks. Garnish with parsley.

Rowley Leigh

WILD SALMON WITH SORREL

EXTRA VIRGIN OLIVE OIL

4 THICK SALMON STEAKS, SKIN ON

1 LARGE BUNCH OF SORREL LEAVES, WASHED

1 LEMON

SEA SALT

COARSELY GROUND BLACK PEPPER

SERVES 4

Heat a heavy frying pan with a little oil, add the salmon steaks, skin side down, and cook very slowly for 10 minutes, or until the salmon is cooked half way through.

Pour out any excess oil and add the washed sorrel leaves. Turn the salmon steaks and squeeze in the juice of the lemon. Enrobe each steak with the wilted sorrel leaves, then remove from the pan while they are still very pink on the side away from the skin.

Serve at once, on warmed plates; pour the pan juices over the steaks, drizzle on a little extra virgin olive oil and scatter with sea salt and coarsely ground pepper.

SEA TROUT FILLET
with a horseradish crust

2 KG/4½ LB SEA TROUT, CLEANED, SKINNED AND
   FILLETED, BONES RESERVED
50 G/2 OZ BUTTER
2 SHALLOTS, SLICED
1 GLASS OF DRY WHITE WINE
6 BLACK PEPPERCORNS
A SPRIG OF THYME
100 ML/3½ FL OZ DOUBLE CREAM
SALT AND PEPPER
LEMON
100 G/3½ OZ HORSERADISH, PEELED
100 G/3½ OZ DRIED BREADCRUMBS
4 TABLESPOONS FLOUR
1 EGG, BEATEN

SERVES 6

Rub your fingers over the fish to make sure no small bones remain; if you feel any, pull them out with a pair of tweezers.

Heat half the butter in a saucepan over a low heat and cook the shallots until soft but not browned. Add the chopped backbone of the trout, turn to seal in the butter, then add the wine, peppercorns and thyme and cook very gently for 10 minutes.

Add the cream and cook for another 10 minutes. Season well with salt, pepper and a squeeze of lemon juice. Strain through a fine sieve and boil to reduce slightly if the sauce is too thin. Keep warm.

Grate the horseradish very finely (this might make you cry) and mix with the breadcrumbs and a little salt and pepper. Dredge the trout fillets in a little flour and shake off any excess. Dip one side of each fillet in a little beaten egg and then into the breadcrumb and horseradish mixture.

Heat the remaining butter in a frying pan and fry the fillets, crumb side first, for about 4 minutes on each side. They should be very moist and remain slightly pink in the middle.

Serve the trout fillets on a bed of spinach, surrounded by the creamy sauce.

Jill Dupleix

SEARED SALMON
with a spice crust

1 TEASPOON GROUND CUMIN

1 TEASPOON GROUND CORIANDER

1 TEASPOON FENNEL SEEDS

½ TEASPOON SEA SALT

4 THICK, WIDE FILLETS OF FRESH SALMON, WITH SKIN

1 TABLESPOON OLIVE OIL

SERVES 4

Mix the cumin, coriander, fennel seeds and salt together in a bowl.

Run your fingers gently over the salmon fillets to feel where the bones lie and use a pair of tweezers to remove all the bones.

Brush a little olive oil on the salmon skin and rub the spice mixture into the skin. Heat a heavy-bottomed frying pan and add a very light film of olive oil.

When it is hot, add the salmon, skin side down, and cook gently for 4–5 minutes without turning. You will see the flesh turn pale as it cooks. If you like, flip it over and cook the other side for the last minute. The skin should be quite crisp and the flesh inside still a deep pink.

Serve on a bed of spiced red lentils or puréed potato spiked with cumin, accompanied by a good mango chutney.

Paul & Jeanne Rankin

CARPACCIO OF SALMON
with avocado, lime and fresh coriander

275 G/10 OZ FRESH SALMON FILLET

125 ML/4 FL OZ FRESH LIME JUICE

1 TEASPOON GRATED LIME ZEST

SALT AND PEPPER

2 FRESH CHILLIES, THINLY SLICED

1 SMALL RED ONION, FINELY CHOPPED

2 PLUM TOMATOES, SKINNED AND DICED

1 RIPE AVOCADO, FINELY DICED

4 TABLESPOONS EXTRA VIRGIN OLIVE OIL

2 TABLESPOONS ROUGHLY CHOPPED FRESH
    CORIANDER

SERVES 4

Trim the salmon of any brown meat and check for any bones, which should be removed with tweezers or small pliers. Using a long sharp knife, cut the salmon into 12 thin slices. Lay each slice in turn on some lightly oiled clingfilm or greaseproof paper, fold the paper over the fish and then, using a small rolling pin or cleaver, lightly flatten each slice so that it is very thin and even. Arrange the slices of salmon completely flat on four plates.

Reserving 1 tablespoon of the lime juice, whisk the remainder with the zest and 1 teaspoon salt, then add the chillies and chopped onion. Divide this lime mixture between the four plates, spreading it evenly over the salmon. Leave to marinate for 10–15 minutes.

When you are ready to serve, season the diced tomatoes and avocado with a little salt and pepper and toss in the reserved lime juice and olive oil. Divide between the four plates, sprinkle with the chopped coriander and serve at once.

Paul & Jeanne Rankin

COD WITH A PEANUT CRUST

1 ROUNDED TABLESPOON PEANUT BUTTER

1 EGG

1 TABLESPOON SOY SAUCE

1 TEASPOON GROUND GINGER

1 TABLESPOON FINELY CHOPPED ONION

50 G/2 OZ SALTED PEANUTS, CHOPPED

4 ROUNDED TABLESPOONS DRIED BREADCRUMBS

4 BONELESS COD FILLETS, ABOUT 175 G/6 OZ EACH

SALT AND WHITE PEPPER

1 TABLESPOON VEGETABLE OIL

1 TABLESPOON BUTTER

SAUCE

2 TABLESPOONS OYSTER SAUCE

1 TABLESPOON SOY SAUCE

1 TABLESPOON SWEET SHERRY

1 TABLESPOON RICE WINE VINEGAR

1 TEASPOON SUGAR

1 TEASPOON DRIED CHILLI FLAKES

TO SERVE

1 BUNCH OF BOK CHOY OR CHINESE CABBAGE

FRESH CORIANDER AND SLICED SPRING ONIONS

SERVES 4

In a shallow bowl, whisk together the peanut butter, egg, soy sauce, ginger and onion until very smooth. Mix the chopped peanuts and the breadcrumbs together on a plate. Season the cod fillets with salt and pepper. Dip one side of each fillet into the peanut paste and then into the crumb mixture.

Heat the oil and butter in a frying pan until the butter foams, then add the cod fillets, crumb side down. Cook over moderate heat for about 4 minutes or until the crumbs are golden brown. Carefully turn the fish over and cook for about another 5 minutes, depending on how thick it is.

Stir together all the ingredients for the sauce.

Cook the bok choy in boiling salted water for 30 seconds, then drain well.

To serve, divide the bok choy between four warmed plates and surround with a little of the sauce. Carefully place a cod fillet on each plate and sprinkle with the coriander and spring onions.

Jacki Passmore

FRIED FISH CAKES
(Tod Mun Pla)

2 SLICES OF FRESH GINGER

1–2 GARLIC CLOVES

1 SPRING ONION, CHOPPED

2 TABLESPOONS CHOPPED FRESH LEMON GRASS

325 G/12 OZ BONELESS, SKINLESS WHITE FISH
 (COD, LING), CUT INTO CUBES

1 TABLESPOON THAI FISH SAUCE

1 EGG

1 TEASPOON SALT

½ TEASPOON GROUND PEPPER

1½ SNAKE/LONG BEANS OR 4 GREEN BEANS

VEGETABLE OIL FOR DEEP-FRYING

CUCUMBER SAUCE (PAGE 377)

SERVES 4

Place the ginger, garlic, spring onion and lemon grass in a food processor and process to a paste.

Add the fish to the food processor. Using the pulse control, chop for about 1 minute, then add the fish sauce, egg, salt, pepper and 2 tablespoons of cold water and process until you have a smooth, thick purée.

Cut the beans into paper-thin slices and add to the fish purée. Process just long enough for them to be incorporated. (If the beans are not cut paper-thin, they should be briefly parboiled and well drained before adding to the fish.)

Heat the oil in a wok or deep frying pan to 180–190°C/350–375°F or until a cube of bread browns in 30 seconds. Drop heaped teaspoons of the fish purée into the oil, about eight at a time. Fry until they float to the surface, then turn and cook until golden brown on both sides, about 1–2 minutes. Drain on paper towels and serve at once, with the cucumber sauce for dipping.

Yon-Rit So

STIR-FRIED MONKFISH
with black bean sauce

500 G/1 LB 2 OZ MONKFISH FILLET

1½ TEASPOONS CORNFLOUR MIXED WITH ¼ TEASPOON
    SALT

2½ TABLESPOONS FERMENTED BLACK BEANS, RINSED

¼ TEASPOON SUGAR

2 TABLESPOONS SESAME OIL

3½–4 TABLESPOONS PEANUT OR CORN OIL

1 TABLESPOON FINELY CHOPPED GARLIC

1 LONG FRESH RED CHILLI, SEEDED AND CUT INTO
    ROUNDS (OPTIONAL)

1 TABLESPOON SHAOXING WINE OR MEDIUM-DRY
    SHERRY

¾ TEASPOON CORNFLOUR DISSOLVED IN 3
    TABLESPOONS CHICKEN STOCK (PAGE 374)

ABOUT 12 LETTUCE LEAVES

SERVES 4

Pat the fish dry and cut into pieces about 2
cm/¾ inch wide, removing any membrane.
Coat evenly with the seasoned cornflour. (This
will help to seal in the juices during stir-frying.)

Using a spoon, mash the fermented black
beans with the sugar and sesame oil to form a
coarse paste.

Heat a wok over high heat until smoke rises.
Add the peanut oil and swirl it around. Add the
garlic, chilli (if using) and black bean paste and
stir to mix. Add the fish, turn and toss for about
30 seconds or until browned on all sides. Splash
in the wine or sherry; as the sizzling subsides,
reduce the heat and continue to stir-fry for
about 2 minutes or until the fish is cooked.

Stir the cornflour in the chicken stock and
add to the wok, stirring as it thickens. Transfer
to a serving dish and arrange the lettuce leaves
around the edge. Serve at once.

BAKED HAKE
with a hot fennel and butter sauce

225 G/8 OZ UNSALTED BUTTER

2 FENNEL BULBS, TRIMMED AND SLICED INTO
ARC-SHAPED PIECES

1 ONION, CHOPPED

1 GARLIC CLOVE, CHOPPED

300 ML/½ PINT FISH OR LIGHT CHICKEN STOCK

2 TABLESPOONS DRY WHITE WINE

1 TEASPOON SALT

10 TURNS OF THE BLACK PEPPER MILL

1 BUNCH OF FENNEL HERB

4 HAKE STEAKS, ABOUT 225 G/8 OZ EACH

2 TABLESPOONS PERNOD OR RICARD

2 TEASPOONS FRESH LEMON JUICE

2 EGG YOLKS

SERVES 4

Preheat the oven to 200°C/400°F/Gas Mark 6.

Melt 25 g/1 oz of the butter in a shallow flameproof dish. Add the fennel, onion and garlic and fry for about 5 minutes or until the vegetables are soft but not browned. Add the stock, wine, salt and pepper and simmer gently for 15 minutes.

Set aside four sprigs of the fennel herb for the garnish. Remove any large stalks and roughly chop the remainder.

Season the hake on both sides, lay it on top of the fennel and onion mixture and bake in the oven for 15–20 minutes.

Lift the hake off the fennel mixture to a warmed plate and keep hot. Remove a quarter of the fennel and place in a liquidizer with the Pernod or Ricard, lemon juice and egg yolks.

Melt the remaining butter in a saucepan. When it begins to bubble, turn on the liquidizer and blend the contents for 1 minute. Then slowly pour the hot butter through the hole in the top of the liquidizer goblet. Pour the sauce into a bowl, stir in the chopped fennel herb and season to taste.

To serve, spoon the remaining baked fennel mixture on to four warmed plates. Rest the hake steaks partly on the fennel. Spoon some of the butter sauce over the hake and the rest of the plate. Garnish with the reserved fennel sprigs and serve at once.

Jacki Passmore

GINGER FISH
(Pla Prio Wan)

1 WHOLE SNAPPER OR SEA BREAM, ABOUT
  675 G/1½ LB, CLEANED AND SCALED
SALT AND WHITE PEPPER
2–3 TABLESPOONS CORNFLOUR
600 ML/1 PINT VEGETABLE OIL
8 DRIED CHINESE MUSHROOMS, SOAKED FOR
  25 MINUTES
2 SPRING ONIONS, SHREDDED
1 TABLESPOON THAI FISH SAUCE OR LIGHT SOY SAUCE
2 TABLESPOONS DARK SOY SAUCE
50 G/2 OZ SOFT BROWN SUGAR
85 G/3 OZ PICKLED GINGER, SHREDDED
4 TABLESPOONS LIQUID FROM THE PICKLED GINGER
175 ML/6 FL OZ WATER
1–2 TEASPOONS LIME JUICE
CORIANDER SPRIGS AND EXTRA PICKLED GINGER,
  TO GARNISH

SERVES 4

Using a sharp knife, make several deep slashes across each side of the fish. Season lightly with salt and pepper, then coat with cornflour, reserving 3 teaspoons.

Heat the oil in a wok or large frying pan to 180–190°C/350–375°F or until a cube of bread browns in 30 seconds. Carefully slide in the fish and fry for about 2½ minutes on each side. Remove and set aside on a plate, covered with foil.

Drain the mushrooms, cut off the stems and slice the caps finely. Heat 1 1/2 tablespoons oil in a small saucepan. Sauté the mushrooms and spring onions for 1 minute, then add the fish sauce and soy sauce, sugar, pickled ginger and its liquid, and bring back to the boil.

Blend the reserved cornflour with the water. Pour into the saucepan and stir over medium-high heat until the sauce thickens.

Place the fish on a platter and spoon the sauce over. Garnish with coriander sprigs and ginger. Serve with boiled or fried rice.

Yan-Kit So

SAUTÉED AND BRAISED COD

2 LARGE COD STEAKS, EACH ABOUT 275 G/10 OZ AND
  2.5 CM/1 INCH THICK
1–1½ TEASPOONS CORNFLOUR
4 TABLESPOONS PEANUT OR CORN OIL
2 LARGE GARLIC CLOVES, CRUSHED
1 TABLESPOON SHAOXING WINE OR MEDIUM-DRY
  SHERRY
2 TEASPOONS FINELY CHOPPED GARLIC
4 TEASPOONS FINELY CHOPPED FRESH GINGER
6–8 SPRING ONIONS, CUT INTO SMALL ROUNDS,
  WHITE AND GREEN PARTS SEPARATED

FOR THE SAUCE

½ TEASPOON SALT
2½ TABLESPOONS THIN OR LIGHT SOY SAUCE
1½ TEASPOONS SUGAR
8 TURNS OF THE PEPPERMILL
2½ TABLESPOONS UNSALTED CHICKEN STOCK
  (PAGE 374)

SERVES 2-4

Pat the cod steaks dry and sift the cornflour over them to coat both sides of the fish.

To make the sauce, stir all the ingredients together in a small bowl until the sugar dissolves.

Heat a wok over high heat until smoke rises. Add the oil and swirl it around. Add the crushed garlic, fry until lightly browned, then discard.

Add the cod steaks and brown for about 20 seconds on each side. Splash in the wine or sherry; as the sizzling subsides, remove the wok from the heat. Spread the chopped garlic, ginger and white spring onions on top of the fish. Pour in the sauce.

Place the wok over medium heat to bring the sauce to a simmer. Cover and cook for about 4 minutes or until the fish is just done – a fork or chopstick will easily pierce the flesh. Spread the green spring onions over the fish and spoon some hot sauce over them. Transfer to a serving dish and serve hot.

Rick Stein

CACCIUCCO

1 LOAF OF CIABATTA BREAD

150 ML/5 FL OZ OLIVE OIL

5 GARLIC CLOVES

3.2 KG/7 LB WHITE FISH (JOHN DORY, GURNARD, COD), FILLETED

1 COOKED LOBSTER

450 G/1 LB SQUID, CLEANED

1 LARGE ONION, CHOPPED

1 LARGE CARROT, FINELY CHOPPED

2 STICKS OF CELERY, FINELY CHOPPED

300 ML/10 FL OZ RED WINE

400 G/14 OZ CANNED TOMATOES

2 BAY LEAVES

2–3 FRESH RED CHILLIES, SLIT OPEN

6 FRESH SAGE LEAVES

900 G/2 LB MUSSELS, CLEANED AND OPENED WITH A LITTLE WHITE WINE FOR 3–4 MINUTES OVER MEDIUM–HIGH HEAT

SERVES 8–10

Preheat the oven to 200°C/400°F/Gas Mark 6.

Cut the ciabatta into 1 cm/½ inch thick slices, place on a baking sheet and drizzle with about 2 tablespoons olive oil. Bake for 20 minutes or until crisp. Rub a halved garlic clove over the bread.

Cut the fish into 4 cm/1½ inch thick slices. Remove the meat from the lobster and reserve the shell. Slice the squid into rings.

Heat half of the remaining oil in a large saucepan. Fry the onion, carrot and celery for 7–8 minutes, until beginning to brown. Add the wine, lobster shell, tomatoes, bay leaves, chillies and 2.3 litres/4 pints water. If you have any squid ink sacs, mash one with a little water and add. Bring to the boil and simmer for 45 minutes.

Pour the liquid through a sieve into another large pan and press with a ladle to extract as much flavour and liquid as possible.

Slice the remaining garlic. Heat the remaining oil in the cleaned pan, add the sage and garlic and fry for 1 minute. Add the squid and fry for 2 minutes, then remove and keep warm. Add the stock and fish, bring to the boil and simmer for 2 minutes. Add the lobster meat, the fried squid, the mussels and their strained cooking liquid and simmer for 1 minute.

To serve, lay two slices of the crisp bread in the bottom of each plate and ladle the soup on top.

FILLETS OF LEMON SOLE
with salsa verde mayonnaise

1 LOAF OF SLIGHTLY STALE BLACK OLIVE CIABATTA
  BREAD
50 G/2 OZ PLAIN FLOUR
2 LARGE EGGS, BEATEN
VEGETABLE OIL FOR DEEP-FRYING
12 LEMON SOLE FILLETS, ABOUT 65 G/2½ OZ EACH,
  SKINNED

SALSA VERDE MAYONNAISE
3 TABLESPOONS ROUGHLY CHOPPED FRESH PARSLEY
1 TABLESPOON ROUGHLY CHOPPED FRESH MINT
3 TABLESPOONS CAPERS
6 ANCHOVY FILLETS
1 GARLIC CLOVE, CRUSHED
1 TEASPOON DIJON MUSTARD
1 TABLESPOON FRESH LEMON JUICE
½ TEASPOON SALT
6 TABLESPOONS MAYONNAISE (PAGE 375)

TO SERVE
LEMON WEDGES

SERVES 4

For the salsa verde mayonnaise, put the parsley, mint, capers, anchovies, garlic, mustard, lemon juice and salt into a pestle and mortar or food processor and grind to a coarse paste. Stir into the mayonnaise and season with a little more salt if required. Set aside.

Break the ciabatta bread into small pieces. Place in a food processor and process into crumbs – they do not need to be too fine – then turn out on to a large plate. Spoon the flour on to another plate and pour the beaten eggs into a shallow dish.

Heat the oil for deep-frying to 190°C/375°F or until a cube of bread browns in 30 seconds. Preheat the oven to 150°C/300°F/Gas Mark 3. Line a large baking sheet with paper towels.

Season the lemon sole fillets with a little salt and pepper. Dip the fillets into the flour, then into the beaten egg and then the breadcrumbs, pressing them on well to give an even coating. Deep-fry, two pieces at a time, for 2 minutes or until crisp and golden. Remove to the baking sheet and keep hot in the oven while you cook the rest. Serve at once, with the salsa verde mayonnaise and lemon wedges.

CHARGRILLED SEA BASS

with roasted red pepper, tomato and basil salsa

4 SMALL SEA BASS, 400–450 G/14 OZ–1 LB EACH,
    CLEANED AND SCALED
2 TABLESPOONS OLIVE OIL
COARSE SEA SALT AND FRESHLY GROUND BLACK
    PEPPER

SALSA

1 RED PEPPER
1 TABLESPOON EXTRA VIRGIN OLIVE OIL
2 TOMATOES, SKINNED AND SEEDED
½ RED ONION, PEELED
2 FRESH RED CHILLIES, SEEDED AND FINELY CHOPPED
1 LARGE GARLIC CLOVE, VERY FINELY CHOPPED
2 TABLESPOONS CHOPPED FRESH PURPLE BASIL
1 TABLESPOON FRESH LEMON JUICE

SERVES 4

Preheat the oven to 220°C/425°F/Gas Mark 7.

For the salsa, rub the outside of the pepper with a little of the olive oil and roast for 15–20 minutes or until soft and slightly blackened. Place in a plastic bag, seal tightly and leave to cool. When cool, the skin should come off easily. Cut the pepper in half and discard the seeds. Cut the red pepper flesh, tomatoes and red onion into 1 cm/½ inch pieces. Place in a bowl and mix in the chillies, garlic, basil, lemon juice, the remaining olive oil, and salt and pepper to taste. Set aside while you cook the fish.

Make three diagonal slashes in both sides of each fish, then brush with olive oil and season with sea salt and black pepper. Brush a ridged cast-iron griddle with a little oil, place over a high heat and leave until very hot. Add the fish and cook for 4½–5 minutes on each side. Alternatively, preheat a grill to very hot and cook the fish on an oiled grill pan. Serve hot, with the salsa.

Rick Stein

POACHED MACKEREL FILLETS
with mint, sherry vinegar and butter sauce

1 TABLESPOON SALT

4 MACKEREL, ABOUT 175 G/6 OZ EACH, FILLETED

SAUCE

225 G/8 OZ UNSALTED BUTTER

2 EGG YOLKS

1 TEASPOON LEMON JUICE

A GOOD PINCH OF CAYENNE PEPPER

10 TURNS OF THE BLACK PEPPER MILL

½ TEASPOON SALT

2 TABLESPOONS SHERRY VINEGAR

1 SHALLOT, VERY FINELY CHOPPED

1 TABLESPOON CHOPPED FRESH MINT

TO GARNISH

SPRIGS OF MINT

SERVES 4

For the sauce, first clarify the butter by placing it in a small saucepan and heating it gently for a few minutes until it has melted and the solids have fallen to the bottom of the pan. Carefully pour off the clear butter and reserve. Discard the solids.

Half fill a saucepan with water and bring to the boil. Reduce to a simmer and rest a bowl over the pan. Add the egg yolks and 2 tablespoons water and whisk until voluminous and fluffy.

Remove the bowl from the heat and gradually whisk in the clarified butter, building up an emulsion as if making mayonnaise. Add the lemon juice, cayenne pepper, black pepper and salt.

Place the sherry vinegar and shallot in a small saucepan, bring to the boil and boil until reduced to 1 teaspoon. Stir into the warm butter sauce with the chopped mint. Keep warm in a bowl of warm water.

Bring 600 ml/1 pint water and 1 tablespoon salt to the boil in a large frying pan. Reduce to a simmer, add the mackerel fillets and poach for 3 minutes, turning them after 1½ minutes. Lift out with a slotted fish slice and serve on warmed plates, with the sauce spooned around. Garnish with sprigs of mint.

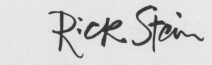

GRILLED FISH SAUSAGES
with Chambéry and sorrel sauce

325 G/12 OZ WHITE FISH FILLETS (LEMON SOLE,
    WHITING, POLLACK), SKINNED AND BONED
50 G/2 OZ FRESH CRAB MEAT
4 SCALLOPS, WITH THE CORALS
1 EGG WHITE
SALT AND FRESHLY GROUND BLACK PEPPER
150 ML/¼ PINT DOUBLE CREAM, CHILLED
PINCH OF CAYENNE PEPPER
1 TABLESPOON ROUGHLY CHOPPED FRESH CHERVIL
A LITTLE SUNFLOWER OIL

TO SERVE

CHAMBÉRY AND SORREL SAUCE (PAGE 376)

SERVES 4

Cut the white fish into small pieces and place in a food processor. Chill in the refrigerator for 30 minutes. Cut the crab meat, scallops and corals into about 1 cm/½ inch pieces and chill.

After 30 minutes, add the egg white and seasoning to the white fish and process until smooth. With the machine running, pour in the cream in a steady stream, making sure that you complete this stage within 10 seconds (if over-processed, the mixture tends to curdle). Season the crab and scallops with salt, pepper and cayenne, then fold into the fish mixture together with the chervil.

Divide the mixture into eight and spoon on to eight pieces of clingfilm, placing the mixture slightly to one side. Form the mixture into sausage shapes, about 12 cm/5 inches long, then carefully roll up in the clingfilm, twisting the ends firmly to seal.

Fill a large, deep frying pan with water and bring to a gentle simmer. Reduce the heat and poach the sausages for 8 minutes. Transfer the sausages to a bowl of cold water and leave for 2 minutes.

Lift the sausages out of the water, remove the clingfilm and brush each sausage with a little oil.

Preheat the grill to medium.

Grill the sausages for 8 minutes, turning occasionally, until golden. Serve on warmed plates, with a little of the Chambéry and sorrel sauce spooned around them.

Richard Olney

BRAISED STUFFED SQUID

3 TABLESPOONS OLIVE OIL

1 ONION, FINELY CHOPPED

2 MEDIUM-LARGE SQUID (POUCHES ABOUT 20 CM/8 INCHES LONG), CLEANED, WINGS AND TENTACLES CHOPPED

PINCH OF SAFFRON STIGMAS

SALT AND FRESHLY GROUND BLACK PEPPER

CAYENNE PEPPER

HANDFUL (ABOUT 85 G/3 OZ) OF LONG-GRAIN RICE, PARBOILED FOR 15 MINUTES, RINSED UNDER COLD WATER AND DRAINED WELL

450 G/1 LB MUSSELS, OPENED IN WHITE WINE (PAGE 30)

1 CLOVE GARLIC, FINELY CHOPPED

SMALL BUNCH OF FLAT-LEAF PARSLEY, FINELY CHOPPED

3 SALTED ANCHOVIES, SOAKED, FILLETED AND CHOPPED

ABOUT 2 TABLESPOONS COGNAC

SERVES 2

Heat 1 tablespoon of the oil in a small frying pan, add half the onion and cook until softened but not coloured. Add the chopped squid wings and tentacles, saffron, salt, pepper and cayenne, turn up the heat and cook, stirring, until the squid juices have been released and reduced to about 1 tablespoon. Mix with the rice and half the mussels. Fill the pouches (not too tightly) and close with a trussing needle and kitchen string.

In a small, heavy sauté pan over low heat, cook the rest of the onion in the remaining oil until softened. Increase the heat, add the garlic and parsley, anchovies and stuffed squid; roll the pouches around until the flesh has contracted. Add the brandy and cook, shaking the pan, until the liquid has almost disappeared. Add mussel broth to about 5 mm/¼ inch, cover tightly and simmer over very low heat for 50 minutes; add more mussel broth if necessary.

Add the remaining mussels to warm through. Remove the string from the pouches and serve on warmed plates.

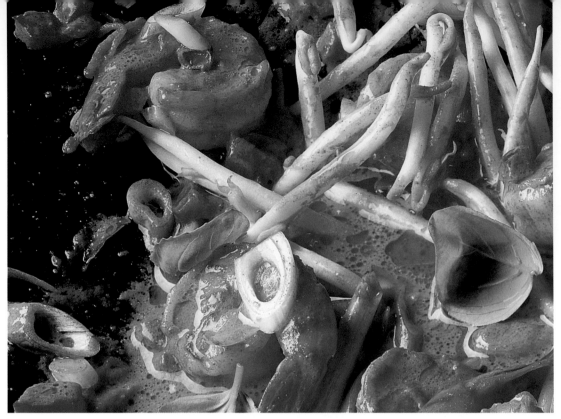

Pat Chapman

THAI KING PRAWN RED CURRY

2–3 LEMONGRASS STALKS

4 TABLESPOONS SUNFLOWER OIL

4 GARLIC CLOVES, SLICED

5 CM/2 INCH CUBE OF FRESH GINGER, SHREDDED

4–6 SPRING ONIONS, CHOPPED

600 G/1¼ LB UNCOOKED KING PRAWNS, SHELLED,
   DEVEINED AND WASHED

1 TABLESPOON TOMATO PURÉE

1 RED PEPPER, CHOPPED

1–3 FRESH RED CHILLIES, VERY FINELY CHOPPED

3–4 KAFFIR LIME LEAVES

200 ML/7 FL OZ COCONUT MILK

100 G/3½ OZ BEANSPROUTS

12–15 FRESH BASIL LEAVES, CHOPPED

1 TEASPOON FISH SAUCE OR SOY SAUCE

SALT

2 LIMES OR LEMONS, HALVED

SPICES

2 TEASPOONS PAPRIKA

½ TEASPOON EACH OF CHILLI POWDER AND CHINESE
   FIVE-SPICE POWDER

SERVES 4

Slit the lemongrass stalks lengthways, keeping each stalk in one piece.

Heat the oil in a wok or karahi and stir-fry over high heat for 10–15 minutes with the garlic, ginger, spices and spring onions, gradually lowering the heat.

Increase the heat and add the lemongrass, prawns, tomato purée, red pepper and chillies. Stir-fry for 5 minutes, adding just enough water to keep the prawns moist.

Add the lime leaves and the coconut milk, and reduce the heat to maintain a gentle simmer for 5 minutes, stirring occasionally.

Add the beansprouts, basil, fish or soy sauce and enough water to create a thin rather than creamy sauce. Stir to mix, and simmer for a further 1–2 minutes.

Discard the lemongrass stalks, season to taste, garnish and serve with the lime or lemon halves for squeezing over the curry.

Valentina Harris

SQUID AND MUSHROOM STEW

1.8 KG/4 LB SQUID, CLEANED

4 TABLESPOONS EXTRA VIRGIN OLIVE OIL

3 GARLIC CLOVES, THINLY SLICED

300 ML/½ PINT FISH STOCK (PAGE 374)

1 LARGE GLASS OF DRY WHITE WINE

50 G/2 OZ DRIED PORCINI MUSHROOMS, SOAKED FOR
    30 MINUTES IN WARM WATER

SALT AND FRESHLY GROUND BLACK PEPPER

2 TABLESPOONS CHOPPED FRESH FLAT-LEAF PARSLEY

SERVES 4

Cut the squid into finger-sized strips. Heat the oil and garlic in a large saucepan over a low heat for about 6 minutes, then add the squid. As soon as the squid is heated through, add the stock and the wine. Cover and simmer gently for about 1 hour or until the squid is tender.

Drain the mushrooms carefully. Strain their soaking liquid and reserve. Chop the mushrooms and add them to the squid, then add the strained liquid. Season with salt and pepper. Simmer, uncovered, for a further 20 minutes.

Pour the stew into a large bowl, sprinkle with parsley and serve with mashed potatoes or creamy soft polenta.

Yon-Rit So

STIR-FRIED PRAWNS
with pine nuts

450 G/1 LB UNCOOKED PRAWNS, IN THEIR SHELLS BUT
   WITHOUT HEADS (25–40 PRAWNS)

4 TABLESPOONS PEANUT OR CORN OIL

4–5 LARGE GARLIC CLOVES, FINELY CHOPPED

2–3 TEASPOONS CHILLI OIL OR CHILLI SAUCE
   (PAGE 377)

2–3 TEASPOONS THIN OR LIGHT SOY SAUCE

½ TEASPOON CORNFLOUR DISSOLVED IN 2½
   TABLESPOONS CHICKEN STOCK

25–50 G/1–2 OZ PINE NUTS

SMALL BUNCH OF CORIANDER LEAVES (WITHOUT MAIN
   STALKS)

FOR THE MARINADE

¼–⅓ TEASPOON SALT

1 TEASPOON CORNFLOUR

1 TABLESPOON EGG WHITE

SERVES 4

Shell the prawns and devein by slitting along the back with a small sharp knife.

To marinate, place the prawns in a bowl, add the salt, cornflour and egg white and stir vigorously in one direction for about 30 seconds. Leave in the refrigerator, covered, for 2–3 hours or overnight. (This will help to seal the prawns in a crisp coating during stir-frying.)

Heat a wok over high heat until smoke rises. Add the oil and swirl it around. Add the garlic, stir for a few seconds, then add the prawns. Using a wok spatula, turn and toss for about 20 seconds; the prawns will curl and turn opaque. Reduce the heat to medium, add the chilli oil or chilli sauce and soy sauce and stir for about 1 minute.

Stir the cornflour in the chicken stock and add to the wok, stirring as it thickens. The prawns should be cooked by now. Add the pine nuts and stir to mix. Transfer to a serving dish, scatter the coriander leaves on top and serve at once.

poultry
and
game

Alastair Little

ROAST MARINATED CHICKEN
with bitter leaves

2 SHALLOTS OR 1 RED ONION, COARSELY CHOPPED

6 TABLESPOONS DIJON MUSTARD

A LARGE HANDFUL OF FLAT-LEAF PARSLEY

2 GARLIC CLOVES

JUICE OF 1–2 LEMONS

6 TABLESPOONS OLIVE OIL

10 CHICKEN THIGHS (OR MORE)

A SELECTION OF BITTER SALAD LEAVES (CURLY ENDIVE,
    CHICORY/BELGIAN ENDIVE, TREVISO, RADICCHIO,
    ROCKET, PUNTARELLA, DANDELION)

2 LEMONS, HALVED

SALAD DRESSING

1 TABLESPOON SHERRY VINEGAR

SALT AND PEPPER

3 TABLESPOONS OLIVE OIL

1 TABLESPOON WALNUT OIL

SERVES 4

Begin making this dish the day before you want to serve it. Place the shallots or onion, mustard, parsley, peeled garlic, lemon juice and olive oil in a food processor and process until chopped and amalgamated. Marinate the chicken thighs in this mixture overnight.

The next day, preheat the oven to its highest setting. Place the chicken thighs, skin side up, on the rack in your roasting tin, having allowed any excess marinade to drop off. Roast for 40 minutes or until well browned and the thigh bones are starting to protrude, an indication that the meat is cooked.

Ten minutes before the chicken is ready, assemble the salad dressing ingredients in a large bowl and dress the salad.

Transfer the chicken to four serving plates and sprinkle generously with sea salt and coarsely ground black pepper. Add the salad and half a lemon. The ideal accompaniment would be a plate of French fries.

Bruno Loubet

COQ AU VIN

1 COCKEREL OR LARGE CHICKEN, ABOUT 2.5 KG/5½
    LB, CUT INTO EIGHT PIECES

2 CARROTS, THICKLY SLICED

2 STICKS OF CELERY, THICKLY SLICED

2 ONIONS, ROUGHLY CHOPPED

4 GARLIC CLOVES, CRUSHED

1 BAY LEAF

1 SPRIG OF THYME

1.5 LITRES/2½ PINTS RED WINE

6 TABLESPOONS SEASONED FLOUR

4 TABLESPOONS OLIVE OIL

1 SPRIG OF TARRAGON

ABOUT 1 LITRE/1¾ PINTS VEAL STOCK

SALT AND PEPPER

100 G/3½ OZ STREAKY BACON, CUT INTO THICK
    STRIPS (LARDONS)

20 BUTTON ONIONS

125 G/4 OZ BUTTON MUSHROOMS

SERVES 4–6

Begin 3 days before serving. Put the chicken in a large bowl, add the carrots, celery, onions, garlic, bay leaf, thyme and wine. Mix, cover and refrigerate overnight.

The next day, drain the chicken and vegetables in a colander over a bowl to reserve the wine marinade. Pat the chicken dry with paper towels, then toss in seasoned flour. Heat the oil in a frying pan and brown the chicken, then transfer to a flameproof casserole.

In the same frying pan, fry the carrots, onions and celery until well browned, then add the wine marinade and pour over the chicken, adding the garlic, bay leaf, thyme and tarragon. Bring to the boil and simmer for 10 minutes. Then add enough veal stock to cover the chicken. Cover with a lid and simmer very gently for 1 hour.

Drain in a colander over a bowl, then pour the sauce into a pan and boil to reduce and thicken. Strain through a fine sieve into a clean saucepan. Season to taste, add the chicken and set aside.

Fry the bacon strips gently until golden. Add the button onions and fry until lightly coloured, then add to the sauce. In the same pan, sauté the mushrooms for a few minutes, then add to the sauce. Simmer for 15 minutes. Leave to cool, then cover with clingfilm and refrigerate for 48 hours (see page 30).

To serve, reheat and simmer for 5 minutes.

Jacki Passmore

RED DUCK CURRY
(Gaeng Ped Bet)

1 DUCK, ABOUT 1.5 KG/3 LB
1 TABLESPOON VEGETABLE OR PEANUT OIL
1 ONION, CHOPPED
2 GARLIC CLOVES, CHOPPED
½ RECIPE THAI RED CURRY PASTE (PAGE 377)
375 ML/12 FL OZ COCONUT CREAM
250 ML/8 FL OZ WATER
2 FRESH RED CHILLIES, SEEDED
1 TEASPOON PAPRIKA
2 TEASPOONS SOFT BROWN SUGAR
SALT AND PEPPER
THAI FISH SAUCE
12 CHERRY TOMATOES
SMALL BUNCH OF BASIL LEAVES

SERVES 4–6

Cut the duck into small pieces. Heat the oil in a large, heavy frying pan over medium-high heat. Brown the duck in the oil, turning frequently so it colours evenly. Remove excess fat with a spoon and discard, or reserve for use when stir-frying another dish. Remove the duck and set aside.

In the same pan, brown the onion and garlic for 3–4 minutes, stirring frequently. Stir in the curry paste and fry for 1–2 minutes, then add the coconut cream and water, the chillies, paprika and brown sugar. Bring to the boil, then reduce the heat and simmer for 6–8 minutes.

Return the duck to the pan and simmer gently until the duck is tender, about 40 minutes.

Taste and adjust the seasoning, adding salt, pepper and fish sauce if necessary. Add the cherry tomatoes and basil and heat through. Serve with boiled or steamed white rice.

Bruno Loubet

CLAY POT SPICY CHICKEN

1 CINNAMON STICK
1 CHICKEN, ABOUT 1.8 KG/4 LB
½ A LEMON
SALT AND PEPPER
4 TABLESPOONS CLEAR HONEY
½ TABLESPOON CRUSHED CORIANDER SEEDS
4 GARLIC CLOVES, CRUSHED
½ TEASPOON CHOPPED, SEEDED FRESH RED CHILLI
1 TABLESPOON ROUGHLY CHOPPED FRESH MINT
½ A CHICKEN STOCK CUBE
4 TABLESPOONS RED WINE VINEGAR
2 TOMATOES, EACH CUT INTO FOUR
3 TABLESPOONS OLIVE OIL
1 TABLESPOON ROUGHLY CHOPPED FRESH FLAT-LEAF PARSLEY

SERVES 4

Soak the clay pot in water for 30 minutes. Preheat the oven to 180°C/350°F/Gas Mark 4.

Place the cinnamon stick inside the chicken. Rub the chicken all over with the lemon, season with salt and pepper, then place in the clay pot. Spread the chicken with the honey, then add all the other ingredients to the clay pot, except the parsley. Place the pot in the oven and bake for 45 minutes.

Open the pot and quickly sprinkle the parsley over the chicken, then close the pot again, re-opening at the table to release all the delightful spicy aromas.

Serve with mashed potato, to which you have added plenty of chopped spring onions.

Bruno Loubet

CHICKEN À LA KIEV

100 G/3½ OZ BUTTER, AT ROOM TEMPERATURE

50 G/2 OZ FRESH FLAT-LEAF PARSLEY, FINELY CHOPPED

50 G/2 OZ FRESH TARRAGON, FINELY CHOPPED

50 G/2 OZ FRESH CHERVIL, FINELY CHOPPED

1 GARLIC CLOVE, CRUSHED, THEN FINELY CHOPPED

1 TABLESPOON WHOLEGRAIN MUSTARD

GRATED ZEST AND JUICE OF 1 LEMON

1 TEASPOON PAPRIKA

SALT AND PEPPER

4 CHICKEN BREASTS, SKINNED

6 TABLESPOONS FLOUR

2 EGGS, BEATEN

10 TABLESPOONS FRESH WHITE BREADCRUMBS

VEGETABLE OIL FOR DEEP-FRYING

SERVES 4

Begin making this dish the day before you want to serve it. Place the butter in a bowl and mix in the parsley, tarragon, chervil, garlic, mustard, paprika, lemon zest and juice; season with salt and pepper and place in the refrigerator.

Cover the chicken breasts with clingfilm and, using a rolling pin, flatten each breast until it forms an escalope or 'supreme' about 5 mm/¼ inch thick. Season with salt and pepper, then place some of the herb butter in the centre of each breast. Roll up the breasts to completely enclose the butter, wrap each one separately in clingfilm and place in the refrigerator overnight.

To cook the chicken, place the flour in a shallow dish, the well-beaten eggs in a second dish and the breadcrumbs in a third dish. Heat the oil for deep-frying to 160°C/325°F.

Coat each chicken supreme first in the flour, then in the egg and finally in the breadcrumbs, gently shaking off any excess. Deep-fry the breasts for about 8 minutes, then drain on paper towels to absorb any fat.

Serve with boiled or steamed French beans, mangetout or asparagus; the butter from the chicken will act as a sauce.

Bruno Loubet

CHICKEN PASTILLA

4 CHICKEN THIGHS, SKINNED

5 TABLESPOONS OLIVE OIL

100 G/3½ OZ SHALLOTS, CHOPPED

1 SMALL AUBERGINE, FINELY DICED

¾ TEASPOON GROUND CORIANDER

3 PINCHES OF GROUND CINNAMON

LARGE PINCH OF SAFFRON STRANDS

85 G/3 OZ RAISINS, SOAKED OVERNIGHT IN WATER

1 GARLIC CLOVE, CHOPPED

1 TEASPOON CHOPPED FRESH THYME

1 TABLESPOON CHOPPED FRESH MINT

SALT AND PEPPER

16 ROUND SPRING ROLL WRAPPERS

1 EGG, BEATEN

SERVES 4

Fry the chicken in 1 tablespoon of the oil until cooked. Leave to cool.

Preheat the oven to 180°C/350°F/Gas Mark 4.

In a saucepan heat 3 tablespoons of the olive oil and cook the shallots until soft. Add the diced aubergine, stir well, then add the coriander, cinnamon, saffron, raisins, garlic and thyme. Cook over a very low heat for 10 minutes, then turn off the heat and add the chopped mint.

Cut the chicken into fine strips and add to the aubergine mixture. Stir to mix and season to taste with salt and pepper.

Brush eight of the spring roll wrappers with beaten egg, then lay the other eight wrappers on top of them. Divide the chicken mixture between four of the doubled wrappers. Brush the edges with beaten egg and cover with the four remaining doubled wrappers. Press around the edges to seal, making four 'flying saucer' shaped pastillas. Brush both sides of each pastilla with the remaining olive oil.

Place the pastillas on a baking sheet and bake for about 8 minutes or until golden brown and crisp.

Bruno Loubet

CHICKEN IN A SALT CRUST

1 CHICKEN, ABOUT 1.8 KG/4 LB
2 TABLESPOONS OLIVE OIL
FRESHLY GROUND BLACK PEPPER
FEW SPRIGS OF FRESH ROSEMARY
FEW SPRIGS OF FRESH MARJORAM (OPTIONAL)
1 EGG YOLK, BEATEN WITH 1 TABLESPOON WATER

SALT CRUST

1 KG/2¼ LB PLAIN FLOUR
6 EGG WHITES
500 G/1 LB 2 OZ SALT

SAUCE

100 G/3½ OZ BUTTER
4 TABLESPOONS WORCESTERSHIRE SAUCE
100 ML/3½ FL OZ CHICKEN STOCK OR WATER
1 TABLESPOON CHOPPED FRESH LOVAGE
½ A LEMON

SERVES 4–6

To make the crust, place the flour, egg whites and salt in a large bowl and beat with an electric mixer on medium speed for 1 minute. Add just enough water to bind to the consistency of a dough. Shape into a ball.

Preheat the oven to 150°C/300°F/Gas Mark 2. Brush the chicken with olive oil, and season with pepper.

On a lightly floured surface, roll out the salt dough to an oblong about 8 mm/⅜ inch thick; it should be large enough to wrap comfortably around the chicken.

Make a bed of herbs on one side of the salt dough and set the chicken on top. Brush the dough around the chicken with the egg wash. Place more herbs over the chicken, then roll it over to wrap it in the salt dough. Seal all the joins completely with the egg wash, pressing with your fingers. Place, seam down, on a baking sheet and bake for 1¼ hours.

Remove from the oven and leave to rest for 15 minutes.

Meanwhile, make the sauce: melt the butter in a saucepan and heat until it turns a hazelnut colour. Remove from the heat and stir in the Worcestershire sauce, stock or water and lovage. Add a squeeze of lemon juice. Keep warm.

Take the chicken to the table in its crust. Cut around the salt crust, lift off the top, and then lift out the chicken. Discard the herbs and carve the chicken.

Bruno Loubet

STUFFED CHICKEN LEG
with almond and lime pickle potatoes

4 TABLESPOONS OLIVE OIL

1 ONION, CHOPPED

85 G/3 OZ SUN-DRIED TOMATOES IN OIL, DRAINED
AND CHOPPED

2 GARLIC CLOVES, CHOPPED

1 TABLESPOON CHOPPED FRESH CORIANDER

4 CHICKEN LEG JOINTS, BONED), BONES RESERVED

12 THIN SLICES OF PANCETTA

SAUCE

2 TABLESPOONS OLIVE OIL

3 SHALLOTS, CHOPPED

2 SMALL CARROTS, CHOPPED

1 STICK OF CELERY, CHOPPED

200 G/7 OZ RIPE TOMATOES, SEEDED AND CHOPPED

100 ML/3½ FL OZ DRY WHITE WINE

1 GARLIC CLOVE, CHOPPED

500 ML/16 FL OZ CHICKEN STOCK (PAGE 374), BOILED
WITH 2–3 DROPS DARK SOY SAUCE TO REDUCE TO
200 ML/7 FL OZ

40 G/1½ OZ BUTTER, DICED

SALT AND PEPPER

SERVES 4

In a frying pan, heat 2 tablespoons of the olive oil and cook the onion until soft. Add the sun-dried tomatoes, garlic and coriander. Leave on a plate until cold.

Stuff the chicken legs with the tomato mixture. Wrap the legs in pancetta and tie with string. Refrigerate until ready to cook.

To make the sauce, heat the olive oil in a heavy-based saucepan, add the chicken bones and brown for a few minutes, then add the shallots, carrots and celery and cook, stirring, until the vegetables are turning golden. Add the tomatoes, wine and garlic and cook for a few minutes. Add the stock and simmer gently for 30 minutes.

Strain the sauce through a fine sieve into a clean saucepan. Bring back to the boil and whisk in the butter, a few pieces at a time. Season to taste. Keep warm.

Fry the chicken legs in the remaining oil in a covered pan for about 10 minutes, turning from time to time. Remove the string and cut each leg into three. Serve with the sauce, accompanied by new potatoes.

Bruno Loubet

BRUNO'S CHICKEN CURRY

3 TABLESPOONS VEGETABLE OIL

2 SMALL ONIONS

1 TABLESPOON CURRY MIX (PAGE 376)

12 CHICKEN THIGHS, SKINNED AND CUT INTO 2 CM/¾
INCH CUBES

4 GARLIC CLOVES, CHOPPED

¾ TEASPOON CHOPPED FRESH GINGER

1 STALK OF LEMONGRASS, OUTER PART REMOVED,
HEART CHOPPED

½ CHICKEN STOCK CUBE

125 ML/4 FL OZ CARROT JUICE

125 ML/4 FL OZ APPLE JUICE

50 G/2 OZ CREAMED COCONUT (FROM A BLOCK),
DISSOLVED IN A LITTLE BOILING WATER

SALT

SUGAR

2 RIPE TOMATOES, CUT INTO 1 CM/½ INCH CUBES

1 TABLESPOON CHOPPED FRESH CORIANDER

100 G/3½ OZ NATURAL YOGURT

SERVES 4

Heat the oil in a heavy saucepan, then add the onions and the curry mix. Fry for a few minutes, stirring, until the onions soften and the spices are fragrant.

Add the chicken, garlic, ginger and lemongrass and crumble in the stock cube. Fry and stir for 2 minutes, then pour in the carrot and apple juices and the coconut cream. Season with salt and 3 pinches of sugar. Leave to simmer gently for 20 minutes.

Remove from the heat and add the tomatoes, coriander and yogurt. Stir well and serve hot, with plain boiled rice.

Roger Vergé

GARLIC CHICKEN CASSEROLE

1 CHICKEN, ABOUT 1.8 KG/4 LB, CUT INTO 4 PIECES
SALT AND PEPPER
4 TABLESPOONS EXTRA VIRGIN OLIVE OIL
100 G/3½ OZ SHALLOTS, CHOPPED
1 SPRIG OF ROSEMARY
3 SAGE LEAVES
200 G/7 OZ GARLIC, PEELED
200 G/7 OZ TOMATOES, SKINNED, SEEDED AND DICED
85 G/3 OZ PITTED BLACK OLIVES
1 TABLESPOON CHOPPED FRESH PARSLEY

SERVES 4

Season the chicken pieces. Heat half the oil in a large casserole, add the chicken and brown on all sides. Add the shallots, rosemary and sage, cover the casserole and cook over low heat for 40–50 minutes, until the chicken is cooked.

Meanwhile, place the garlic in a saucepan with 1 litre/1¾ pints water and bring to the boil. Discard the water, replace with fresh water and bring to the boil again. Repeat five times. The garlic should be meltingly tender; if not, leave it to simmer for a few minutes. Drain well.

Remove the chicken from the casserole and keep warm. Add the tomatoes to the casserole and simmer for 5 minutes. Tip the contents of the casserole into a liquidizer, blend briefly, then rub through a fine sieve.

Return the sauce to the liquidizer and add the garlic and olives. Season to taste and slowly blend in the remaining olive oil.

Return the chicken to the casserole and pour over the sauce. Reheat gently, without boiling. Serve hot, sprinkled with parsley.

Bruno Loubet

PANCETTA-WRAPPED CHICKEN
with asparagus and hazelnut risotto

4 CHICKEN BREASTS, SKINNED

SALT AND PEPPER

12 THIN SLICES OF PANCETTA

1 TABLESPOON OLIVE OIL

50 G/2 OZ BUTTER

2 SMALL ONIONS, FINELY CHOPPED

2 GARLIC CLOVES, FINELY CHOPPED

350 G/13 OZ RISOTTO RICE

½ A GLASS OF DRY WHITE WINE

900 ML/1½ PINTS CHICKEN STOCK (PAGE 374), HOT

450 G/1 LB GREEN ASPARAGUS, PEELED

2 TABLESPOONS FRESHLY GRATED PARMESAN CHEESE

2 TABLESPOONS CHOPPED FRESH CHERVIL

85 G/3 OZ HAZELNUTS, TOASTED

SERVES 4

Season the chicken with salt and pepper and wrap each breast in three slices of pancetta. Heat the oil in a heavy-based frying pan, add the chicken and fry until lightly and evenly browned, then lower the heat and cook slowly for about 7–8 minutes on each side. When the chicken is cooked, cover the pan with foil and set aside.

Melt the butter in a wide, heavy saucepan, add the onions and garlic and cook until the onions are soft, stirring occasionally. Add the rice and stir well to coat the grains with the butter. Add the wine and simmer until absorbed by the rice, stirring constantly.

Add a small ladleful of hot stock and stir well all around the pan and across the bottom to ensure that the rice does not stick. Cook, stirring constantly, until the stock has been absorbed, then repeat the process until all the stock has been used and the rice is just tender to the bite, about 20 minutes. If the rice needs further cooking, add a little boiling water and keep stirring.

Meanwhile, blanch the asparagus in salted boiling water, drain and cut into 2.5 cm/1 inch pieces. Add the asparagus to the risotto and stir in the Parmesan. Season to taste, then add the chervil and the hazelnuts. Spoon on to deep plates and arrange the chicken on top. Sprinkle with a few drops of olive oil and some freshly ground pepper.

Pat Chapman

CHICKEN TIKKA MASALA CURRY

85 ML/3 FL OZ NATURAL YOGURT

2 TABLESPOONS TOMATO PURÉE

1 TABLESPOON PAPRIKA

½ TEASPOON CHILLI POWDER

675 G/1½ LB SKINLESS, BONELESS CHICKEN BREAST, CUBED

4 TABLESPOONS VEGETABLE OIL

4 GARLIC CLOVES, FINELY CHOPPED

3 TABLESPOONS RED TANDOORI PASTE

2 SMALL ONIONS, FINELY CHOPPED

½ RED PEPPER, FINELY CHOPPED

½ GREEN PEPPER, FINELY CHOPPED

4 CANNED PLUM TOMATOES, CHOPPED

200 ML/7 FL OZ CANNED CREAM OF TOMATO SOUP

85 ML/3 FL OZ SINGLE CREAM

2 TEASPOONS GARAM MASALA

2 TEASPOONS CHOPPED MANGO CHUTNEY

1 TABLESPOON COCONUT MILK POWDER

1 TABLESPOON FINELY CHOPPED FRESH MINT

2 TABLESPOONS CHOPPED FRESH CORIANDER LEAVES

SALT

SERVES 4

Mix the yogurt with the tomato purée, paprika and chilli powder. Mix in the chicken cubes to coat them evenly.

Heat the oil in a wok or karahi and stir-fry over high heat for 10–15 minutes with the garlic, tandoori paste and onions, gradually lowering the heat.

Increase the heat, add the peppers and stir briefly. Add the chicken and all the yogurt mixture and stir-fry for about 3 minutes.

Add the tomatoes and stir well. Gradually add the tomato soup, little by little over 5 minutes, stirring often.

Add the cream, garam masala, mango chutney, coconut powder, mint and coriander and stir-fry for a further 5–8 minutes or until the chicken is cooked through. Season to taste, garnish and serve.

Pat Chapman

BANGLADESHI CHICKEN REZALA

4 TABLESPOONS GHEE OR CLARIFIED BUTTER

4 GARLIC CLOVES, FINELY CHOPPED

2 ONIONS, FINELY CHOPPED

675 G/1½ LB SKINLESS, BONELESS CHICKEN BREAST, CUBED

2–3 GREEN CHILLIES, SLICED LENGTHWAYS (OPTIONAL)

200 ML/7 FL OZ EVAPORATED MILK

2 TABLESPOONS SULTANAS (OPTIONAL)

4 TEASPOONS GROUND ALMONDS

1 TABLESPOON COCONUT MILK POWDER

1 TEASPOON GRANULATED SUGAR

2 TABLESPOONS CHOPPED FRESH CORIANDER LEAVES

2 TEASPOONS CHOPPED FRESH MINT

20 SAFFRON STRANDS (OPTIONAL)

2 TEASPOONS GARAM MASALA

SALT

SPICES

1 TEASPOON CORIANDER SEEDS, CRUSHED

1 TEASPOON CUMIN SEEDS

½ TEASPOON EACH OF BLACK MUSTARD SEEDS, FENNEL SEEDS, SESAME SEEDS AND WILD ONION SEEDS (KALONJI)

⅛ TEASPOON FENUGREEK SEEDS

SERVES 4

Heat the ghee or clarified butter in a wok or karahi and stir-fry over high heat for 10–15 minutes with the garlic, spices and onions, gradually lowering the heat.

Increase the heat and add the chicken and chillies, if using. Stir-fry for about 3 minutes. As the ingredients start to sizzle, gradually add the evaporated milk, little by little over 5 minutes.

Reduce the heat to a simmer and add the sultanas, if using, ground almonds, coconut powder and sugar, and stir-fry for a further 5 minutes.

Add the coriander, mint, saffron, garam masala and just enough water to maintain a creamy consistency. Stir-fry for a further 5–8 minutes or until the chicken is cooked through. Season to taste, garnish and serve.

Yon-Rit So

STIR-FRIED CHICKEN
with mangetout

325 G/12 OZ SKINLESS, BONELESS CHICKEN BREAST
  FILLET, CUT CROSSWAYS INTO THIN SLIVERS
SALT
5 TABLESPOONS PEANUT OIL
175 G/6 OZ MANGETOUT OR SUGAR SNAP PEAS,
  TRIMMED
2 LARGE GARLIC CLOVES, CUT INTO THIN SLIVERS
4 LARGE SPRING ONIONS, CUT INTO 4 CM/1½ INCH
  SECTIONS, WHITE AND GREEN PARTS SEPARATED
1 TABLESPOON SHAOXING WINE OR MEDIUM-DRY
  SHERRY
1 TEASPOON CORNFLOUR DISSOLVED IN 4
  TABLESPOONS CHICKEN STOCK (PAGE 374)
2–3 TEASPOONS SESAME OIL

FOR THE MARINADE
½ TEASPOON SALT
¼ TEASPOON SUGAR
2–3 TEASPOONS THIN OR LIGHT SOY SAUCE
1 TEASPOON SHAOXING WINE
  OR MEDIUM-DRY SHERRY
8 TURNS OF THE PEPPERMILL
1 TEASPOON CORNFLOUR
1 TABLESPOON EGG WHITE
1 TABLESPOON PEANUT OIL

SERVES 4

Put the chicken in a bowl, add the marinade
ingredients and stir until coated. Leave for
15–20 minutes.

Bring a saucepan of salted water to the boil
and add 1 tablespoon of the oil. Blanch the
mangetout for 10 seconds or sugar snap peas for
1 minute after the water returns to the boil.
Drain in a colander, refresh with cold water and
leave to drain.

Heat a wok over high heat until smoke rises.
Add the remaining oil and swirl it around. Add
the garlic and white spring onions and stir to
mix. Add the marinated chicken and turn and
toss, using a wok spatula, for 30–40 seconds or
until the chicken is pale all over. Splash in the
wine or sherry, stirring as it sizzles; reduce the
heat.

Stir the cornflour in the stock and add to the
wok, stirring as it thickens. When the chicken is
cooked, add the mangetout or sugar snaps and
green spring onions, and stir until everything is
hot. Transfer to a serving dish, drizzle with
sesame oil, serve hot.

Jacki Passmore

GRILLED PEPPER CHICKEN WITH SPICED PEANUT SAUCE

(Kai Yang)

8 CHICKEN THIGHS (SKINNED IF PREFERRED)

2 TABLESPOONS PEANUT OR VEGETABLE OIL

2–3 GARLIC CLOVES, CRUSHED

1½ TABLESPOONS THAI FISH SAUCE OR LIGHT SOY
  SAUCE

1 TABLESPOON VERY FINELY CHOPPED FRESH
  CORIANDER (OPTIONAL)

1 TEASPOON SALT

1 TABLESPOON COARSELY GROUND WHITE PEPPER

275 G/10 OZ CHINESE CABBAGE, COARSELY CHOPPED

2 TEASPOONS FINELY GRATED FRESH GINGER

SPICED PEANUT SAUCE (PAGE 377)

SERVES 4

Using a fork, prick the skin of the chicken all over, to allow the flavours to penetrate. Brush with a little of the oil. Grind together the garlic, fish sauce or soy sauce, coriander, salt and pepper to form a paste. Spread over the chicken and set aside for at least 1 hour.

Heat the grill to moderate and cook the chicken, turning frequently, until golden brown and cooked through, about 25 minutes.

Meanwhile, heat 1 tablespoon of the oil in a wok or large frying pan and stir-fry the cabbage with the ginger for about 5 minutes, then cover and cook gently until it is tender. Season to taste with salt and pepper.

Serve the cabbage on a large platter or individual plates. Place the chicken on the cabbage and spoon the peanut sauce over.

Rowley Leigh

CHICKEN WITH MORELS

100 G/3½ OZ FRESH MORELS
1 CHICKEN, CUT INTO 8 PIECES
SALT AND PEPPER
50 G/2 OZ BUTTER
1 GLASS OF DRY WHITE WINE
4 SHALLOTS, VERY FINELY CHOPPED
200 ML/7 FL OZ DOUBLE CREAM

SERVES 4

Wash the morels well, drain on a clean tea towel and then cut in half or into strips.

Season the chicken pieces and brown in the butter in a heavy saucepan over a low heat, skin side down. Turn and continue to cook very gently. When nearly cooked, pour out any excess fat and add the wine, scraping up the juices, and then boil until the wine has almost completely evaporated.

Add a little more butter and the shallots, and cook until they are soft, but without colour.

Add the morels and cook gently for 2–3 minutes.

Add the cream, turn the chicken in the sauce and bring to the boil. Simmer gently until the sauce is well reduced. Serve with rice pilaff cooked in chicken stock.

Jameen Garlin

POMANDER CHICKEN

3 TANGERINES OR MINNEOLAS

12 WHOLE CLOVES

2 STICKS OF CELERY, CHOPPED

1 LARGE ROASTING CHICKEN (ABOUT 3.4–3.6 KG/7½–8 LB), WASHED AND PATTED DRY

1 LIME, CUT IN HALF

COARSE SALT

FRESHLY GROUND BLACK PEPPER

15 CM/6 INCH CINNAMON STICK, BROKEN IN HALF

85 G/3 OZ BUTTER, SOFTENED

ABOUT 125 ML/4 FL OZ CHICKEN STOCK (PAGE 374)

85 ML/3 FL OZ FRESH ORANGE JUICE

SERVES 6–8

Preheat the oven to 220°C/425°F/Gas Mark 7. Slice off the tops and bottoms of two of the tangerines and stud each with six cloves. Pare off the zest of the remaining tangerine and cut into fine strips.

Spread the celery in a roasting tin; set a rack over the celery. Rub the skin and inside the chicken with the lime; season with salt and pepper. Place the tangerines and the cinnamon inside the chicken.

Mix half the butter with the strips of zest. Gently lift the skin from the breast and thighs and push the tangerine butter under the skin. Rub the remaining butter over the chicken. Truss and place on the rack, breast down.

Roast for 35–45 minutes or until the skin is brown. Turn breast side up and continue roasting for about 35 minutes or until the breast skin is brown. Once the skin is crisp, baste with the juices.

Reduce the oven temperature to 180°C/350°F/Gas Mark 4 and roast the chicken for a further 1–1½ hours, basting occasionally, until the juices run clear when the thigh is pierced with a skewer. Leave to rest in a warm place for 20–25 minutes before carving.

Pour the roasting tin juices into a jug or fat strainer and leave for 5 minutes. Pour off the fat, then pour the juices into a saucepan and add enough stock to make up 125 ml/4 fl oz. Add the orange juice and simmer for a few minutes. Add the juices from the resting roast. Reheat the sauce and serve with the chicken.

Jameen Garlin

ROAST TURKEY BURGUNDY

2 CARROTS, CHOPPED

2 LARGE ONIONS, CHOPPED

4 STICKS OF CELERY, CHOPPED

6–6.4 KG/12–14 LB FRESH TURKEY, WASHED AND
WIPED DRY (GIBLETS MADE INTO STOCK)

1 LEMON, CUT IN HALF

COARSE SALT

FRESHLY GROUND BLACK PEPPER

3–4 LARGE FRESH SAGE LEAVES, CHOPPED

4 TABLESPOONS SOFTENED BUTTER

SAUSAGE STUFFING (PAGE 376), OPTIONAL

1 BOTTLE BURGUNDY WINE

SERVES 12

Preheat the oven to 220°C/425°F/Gas Mark 7. Strew the carrots, onions and celery in a roasting tin and set a rack over them.

Rub the skin and inside the turkey with the lemon, then season generously with salt and pepper. Mix the chopped sage with the butter. Using your fingers, carefully separate the skin from the breast and thighs. Push half the butter under the skin. Rub the remaining butter all over the turkey.

Either place a handful of the chopped vegetables inside the turkey or stuff with Sausage Stuffing. Truss the turkey and place on the rack, breast side down.

Roast breast side down for 20–30 minutes or until the skin is brown. Turn on to one side and roast for 20 minutes, then turn on to the other side for a further 20 minutes. Finally, turn the bird breast side up and continue roasting until the skin is brown. Once the skin is crisp, begin basting with some of the wine.

Reduce the oven temperature to 180°C/350°F/Gas Mark 4 and roast for a further 2½–3 hours, basting occasionally with the wine, until the juices run clear when the meat is pierced with a fork and the thighs move freely. Leave to rest for 20–25 minutes before carving.

Pour the roasting tin juices into a jug or fat strainer and leave for 5 minutes. Pour off the fat, then pour the juices into a saucepan. Simmer for a few minutes, skimming off any fat. Add the juices from the resting roast. Reheat the sauce and serve with the turkey.

Richard Olney

GRILLED SPLIT QUAIL
stuffed beneath the skin

2 QUAIL

OLIVE OIL

PINCH OF MIXED DRIED HERBS

SALT AND FRESHLY GROUND BLACK PEPPER

STUFFING

1 TABLESPOON OLIVE OIL

125 G/4 OZ MUSHROOMS, FINELY CHOPPED

1 CLOVE GARLIC, FINELY CHOPPED

SMALL HANDFUL OF FLAT-LEAF PARSLEY, FINELY
  CHOPPED

½ LEMON

SMALL HANDFUL OF FRESH BREADCRUMBS

15 G/½ OZ UNSALTED BUTTER, SOFTENED

SERVES 2

First make the stuffing. Heat the oil in a frying
pan, add the mushrooms, season and toss until
the liquid they render has reduced and the pan
is nearly dry. Add the garlic and parsley, toss
until its scent fills the room, then squeeze over a
few drops of lemon juice. Scrape the
mushrooms into a bowl and leave to cool.
Using a fork, mash together the mushrooms,
breadcrumbs and softened butter. Refrigerate
until firm.

Stuff the quail (page 374). Heat the grill or a
barbecue over wood embers. Drizzle olive oil
over the birds, gently rubbing it over surface.
Sprinkle herbs, salt and pepper over the birds,
then grill them, underside first, for 7–8 minutes.
Turn them to grill the skin side for 5 minutes
(take care, as skin burns easily), then turn over
to finish grilling – about 18 minutes in all. Serve
accompanied by sautéed or fried potatoes.

Rowley Leigh

WILD RABBIT
with nettles, onions and cider

85 G/3 OZ BUTTER

6 ONIONS, THINLY SLICED

1 WILD RABBIT, JOINTED

SALT AND PEPPER

4 TABLESPOONS FLOUR

2 TABLESPOONS OLIVE OIL

500 ML/16 FL OZ CIDER

2 SPRIGS OF THYME

1 BAY LEAF

A LARGE HANDFUL OF NETTLES, WASHED, LEAVES
   PICKED OFF

1 TEASPOON ENGLISH MUSTARD

SERVES 4

Melt 25 g/1 oz of the butter in a casserole over a low heat and cook the onions until soft.

Season the rabbit pieces, dredge in a little flour and shake off any excess. Heat the oil and another 25 g/1 oz butter in a frying pan; add the rabbit pieces and brown all over.

Add the rabbit to the casserole with the onions. Pour out the fat from the frying pan and add some of the cider; stir over a fairly high heat to deglaze, then add to the rabbit together with the remaining cider. Add the thyme and bay leaf, bring to a gentle boil and simmer very gently for 1¼ hours.

Add the washed nettle leaves and simmer for another 15 minutes. The rabbit should now be very tender. Transfer the rabbit pieces to warmed plates. Add the mustard and the remaining butter to the sauce, taste and adjust the seasoning and pour over the rabbit.

Roger Vergé

STUFFED SADDLE OF RABBIT

2 YOUNG RABBITS, ABOUT 1.5 KG/3 LB EACH

4 TABLESPOONS OLIVE OIL

4 SHALLOTS, CHOPPED

400 ML/14 FL OZ DRY WHITE WINE

1 SPRIG OF THYME

2 BAY LEAVES

1 GARLIC CLOVE

200 G/7 OZ BUTTER

2 LEEKS, WHITE PART ONLY, CUT IN JULIENNE STRIPS

2 CARROTS, CUT IN JULIENNE STRIPS

2 COURGETTES, CUT IN JULIENNE STRIPS

1 SMALL STICK OF CELERY, CUT IN JULIENNE STRIPS

½ BUNCH OF PARSLEY, FINELY CHOPPED

10 BASIL LEAVES, FINELY CHOPPED

2 EGG YOLKS

SALT AND PEPPER

SERVES 6–8

Cut the legs off the rabbits above the thighs and at shoulders. Bone the saddles from the inside, running a small sharp knife around the bones to free them from the flesh and removing them carefully. Set aside. Chop the bones and front legs and brown in a large saucepan with half the oil. When well browned, pour off the fat, add the shallots and cook for about 5 minutes or until softened. Deglaze the pan with half of the wine and boil to reduce by half. Add the thyme, bay leaves, garlic and water to cover; simmer gently for 1 hour.

Melt 25 g/1 oz of the butter in a saucepan and cook the vegetables until just tender. Stir in the parsley, basil, egg yolks, salt and pepper.

Place the boned saddles on a board, season and spread each with about 4 tablespoons of the vegetable mixture. Tie to form neat shapes. Preheat the oven to 220°C/ 425°F/Gas Mark 7.

Strain the stock through a sieve, pressing on the bones to extract all the liquid. Strain again, through a muslin-lined sieve, then return to the cleaned saucepan and boil to reduce to 250 ml/8 fl oz.

Heat the remaining oil and 25 g/1 oz butter in a roasting pan over high heat and brown the saddles all over, then cover with foil and roast in the hot oven for 10 minutes. Keep the rabbits warm while you make the sauce.

Dice the remaining butter. Pour off the fat from the roasting pan and deglaze with the remaining wine. Add the stock, bring back to the boil, then, over low heat, whisk in the butter. Slice the rabbits and serve with the sauce.

BAKED RABBIT,
sorrel cream sauce

½ RABBIT, CUT INTO SERVING PIECES (2 LEGS, 2
    SADDLE SECTIONS)
275 G/10 OZ SMALL, FIRM-FLESHED POTATOES, PEELED
1 HEAD OF NEW GARLIC, CLOVES PEELED (ELIMINATE IF
    OUT OF SEASON)
LARGE HANDFUL OF SORREL, SHREDDED
COARSE SEA SALT
JUICE OF ½ LEMON
1 TABLESPOON DIJON MUSTARD
125 ML/4 FL OZ DOUBLE CREAM

MARINADE

1 TEASPOON MIXED DRIED HERBS
1 BAY LEAF
1 ONION, SLICED
1 TABLESPOON OLIVE OIL
SMALL GLASS OF DRY WHITE WINE

SERVES 2

First marinate the rabbit. Sprinkle the rabbit pieces with the herbs and place in a bowl with the bay leaf, onion, oil and wine. Leave to marinate for about 3 hours, turning twice.

Preheat the oven to 200°C/400°F/Gas Mark 6. Fit the rabbit pieces, potatoes and garlic cloves into an ovenproof dish just large enough to hold them in a single layer. Strain the marinade and add the onion and bay leaf to the dish. Scatter the shredded sorrel over the surface and sprinkle with salt.

Mix together the strained marinade, lemon juice, mustard and cream, spoon about half over the rabbit and bake for 1 hour, basting with the remaining cream mixture two or three times after the first 30 minutes. When the surface begins to colour, reduce the oven temperature to 180°C/350°F/Gas Mark 4 and cover the dish with foil. Serve hot, on warmed plates.

Rowley Leigh

WILD DUCK WITH BLACKBERRIES

1 WILD DUCK

2 SHALLOTS, ROUGHLY CHOPPED

1 CARROT, ROUGHLY CHOPPED

1 STICK OF CELERY, ROUGHLY CHOPPED

A SPRIG OF THYME

25 G/1 OZ BUTTER

2 TEASPOONS SUGAR

225 G/8 OZ BLACKBERRIES

1 TEASPOON RED WINE VINEGAR

1 GLASS OF RED WINE

SALT AND PEPPER

SERVES 2

Preheat the oven to 230°C/450°F/Gas Mark 8.

Put the duck in a small, flameproof roasting pan and roast for 10 minutes. Add the vegetables and thyme to the roasting pan and cook for a further 10 minutes.

Remove the duck from the pan and leave to rest in a warm place for 10 minutes.

Add the butter and sugar to the vegetables in the roasting pan and brown over a fairly high heat.

Add half the blackberries and continue cooking over a high heat until their liquid has evaporated. Add the vinegar and cook until it has reduced away. Add the wine.

Remove the legs from the duck, add to the sauce and simmer gently for 15 minutes.

Carve the duck breast and serve on warmed plates with a few blackberries. Arrange the duck legs on the plates, strain over the sauce and serve at once.

Paul & Jeanne Rankin

BREAST OF DUCK WITH HONEY
and Chinese five-spice

4 BARBARY DUCK BREASTS, ABOUT 175 G/6 OZ EACH

SALT

1 TEASPOON CHINESE FIVE-SPICE POWDER

2 TABLESPOONS HONEY

4 TABLESPOONS JAPANESE SOY SAUCE

2 TABLESPOONS BALSAMIC VINEGAR

A GOOD PINCH OF DRIED CHILLI FLAKES

2 TABLESPOONS PICKLED GINGER, CUT INTO THIN
    STRIPS

ABOUT 225 G/8 OZ EACH OF CARROTS AND PARSNIPS,
    CUT INTO STRIPS AND STEAMED OR LIGHTLY BOILED

TO GARNISH
3–4 SPRING ONIONS, SLICED

SERVES 4

Trim the duck breasts and lightly score the skin
side with a sharp knife. Season each breast
lightly with salt. Heat a large frying pan over
moderate heat and add the duck breasts, skin
side down. Cook for about 5 minutes or until
the skin is an even golden colour. Turn the
breasts over and cook for about another 2–3
minutes for medium-rare duck.

In a small bowl, mix together the five-spice
powder, honey, soy sauce, vinegar, chilli flakes
and pickled ginger.

Turn the duck breasts back to their skin side
down and pour off any excess fat. Turn the heat
up to high and add the carrot and parsnip strips.
Sear for about 1 minute, then add the soy and
honey mixture. Let it bubble furiously until it
glazes the vegetables and the duck.

Serve at once, on individual warmed plates,
sprinkled with spring onions.

Yan-Rit So

BRAISED DUCK
in spiced soy sauce

1 DUCKLING, ABOUT 2 KG/4½ LB, OIL SACS DISCARDED,
    SKIN PRICKED ALL OVER

85 G/3 FL OZ PERNOD OR CHINESE MEI KUEI LIEW
    WINE

SPICED SOY SAUCE

375 ML/12 FL OZ THICK OR DARK SOY SAUCE

2 LITRES/3½ PINTS WATER

125 G/4 OZ CHINESE CRYSTAL OR DEMERARA SUGAR

1 TABLESPOON SEA SALT

25 G/1 OZ FRESH GINGER, BRUISED

1 WHOLE OR 3 PIECES DRIED TANGERINE PEEL

2½ STAR ANISE PODS

5 CM/2 INCH CINNAMON STICK, BROKEN UP

1 TEASPOON BLACK PEPPERCORNS

2 TEASPOONS SICHUAN PEPPERCORNS

1 TABLESPOON FENNEL SEEDS

1 TEASPOON CLOVES

GARLIC DIPPING SAUCE

4 TEASPOONS VERY FINELY CHOPPED GARLIC

6 TABLESPOONS WINE VINEGAR OR CHINESE RICE
    VINEGAR

SERVES 6

Preheat the oven to 240°C/475°F/Gas Mark 9.

Put the soy sauce, water, sugar, salt, ginger and tangerine peel in a large, heavy-bottomed saucepan. Tie the star anise, cinnamon, peppercorns, fennel seeds and cloves in a large piece of muslin and add to the pan. Slowly bring to the boil, then cover and simmer gently for 30 minutes.

Meanwhile, fill a roasting pan with about 2.5 cm/1 inch of water and place the duck on a rack over the water. Roast in the hot oven for 20–25 minutes; this will rid the skin of much of its fat.

Bring the spiced sauce to the boil, add the Pernod or wine and let it bubble for a few seconds. Add the duck, breast side up, cover and simmer very gently for 30 minutes. Remove from the heat, turn the duck breast side down and leave in the sauce, covered, for 1 hour.

For the dipping sauce, mix together the garlic and vinegar.

Carve the duck. Strain the spiced soy sauce and serve as an alternative dipping sauce.

Roger Vergé

DUCK COOKED IN WINE
with apples and prunes

1 DUCK, 2–2.5 KG/4½–5½ LB, CUT INTO SERVING
  PIECES, BONES RESERVED
1 SMALL STICK OF CELERY, SLICED
1 CARROT, SLICED
1 ONION, SLICED
3 GARLIC CLOVES, SLICED
1 BOUQUET GARNI
1 BOTTLE FULL-BODIED RED WINE
10 STONED PRUNES
10 WALNUT HALVES
25 G/1 OZ BUTTER
SALT AND PEPPER
2 TABLESPOONS PLAIN FLOUR
1 GOLDEN DELICIOUS APPLE

SERVES 2

Place the duck pieces in a large bowl with the vegetables, bouquet garni and wine. Cover and leave in a cool place to marinate for 10–12 hours. Soak the prunes.

Strain the duck and vegetables in a colander over a large saucepan. Add the prunes to the marinade, with the bouquet garni and walnuts. Simmer for 15 minutes.

Meanwhile, heat half the butter in a large flameproof casserole. Pat dry the duck legs and breasts and season. Brown the duck in the butter over low heat, skin side down, then turn and brown the flesh side. Remove and set aside.

Brown the reserved bones and the vegetables in the casserole. Pour off the fat, add the flour and cook, stirring, for 2–3 minutes. Return the legs and breasts to the pan and pour the marinade through a sieve over the duck. Reserve the prunes and walnuts. If necessary, add a little water to cover the duck and simmer gently for 45 minutes.

When the duck is cooked, remove and keep warm. Tilt the casserole and leave for a few minutes for the fat to rise.

Peel and cube the apple and fry in the remaining butter until golden. Drain and add to the duck.

Spoon off the fat from the casserole, then return to the heat and boil to reduce to about 150 ml/5 fl oz. Strain into a jug and discard the bones and vegetables.

Clean the casserole and add the duck, prunes, walnuts and apples. Pour the sauce over the duck, bring to the boil and simmer for 5–10 minutes.

Pat Chapman

SRI LANKAN DUCK CURRY

675 G/1½ LB SKINLESS, BONELESS DUCK, CUBED

50 G/2 OZ CORNFLOUR

4 TABLESPOONS VEGETABLE OIL

3 GARLIC CLOVES, FINELY CHOPPED

2.5 CM/1 INCH CUBE OF FRESH GINGER, FINELY
   CHOPPED

2 ONIONS, FINELY CHOPPED

300 ML/10 FL OZ COCONUT MILK

1 TABLESPOON VINEGAR

1 TEASPOON WORCESTERSHIRE SAUCE

1 TABLESPOON MOLASSES OR MUSCOVADO SUGAR

1 TABLESPOON EACH OF CHOPPED FRESH BASIL AND
   CORIANDER LEAVES

1 TEASPOON GARAM MASALA

1–3 FRESH RED CHILLIES, SLICED

SALT

WHOLE SPICES

3 TEASPOONS CORIANDER SEEDS

1 TEASPOON EACH OF CUMIN SEEDS, FENNEL SEEDS
   AND BLACK MUSTARD SEEDS

6 WHOLE GREEN CARDAMOM PODS

GROUND SPICES

1 TEASPOON CINNAMON

½ TEASPOON CLOVES

⅓ TEASPOON CHILLI POWDER

SERVES 4

Heat a wok or karahi over fairly high heat. Add
the whole spices and dry-fry, stirring constantly,
for about 30 seconds. Leave to cool, then grind
in a coffee grinder. Add the ground spices and
mix well.

Toss the duck in the cornflour until evenly
coated.

Heat the oil in a wok or karahi and stir-fry
over high heat for 10–15 minutes with the
garlic, ginger, spices and onions, gradually
lowering the heat.

Increase the heat and add the duck. Stir-fry
for about 5 minutes, adding just enough water
to keep the duck moist.

Cook for a further 10 minutes, stirring and
adding a little water from time to time.

Add the coconut milk, vinegar,
Worcestershire sauce and sugar and mix well.
Cook for a further 5 minutes, stirring from time
to time.

Add the basil, coriander, garam masala and
chillies and cook for a final 5–8 minutes or until
the duck is tender. The curry should be creamy
and not too thin. Season to taste, garnish and
serve.

PEPPER DUCK
with brandy sauce

2 DUCKS, ABOUT 1.6–1.8 KG/3½–4 LB EACH, EXCESS
 FAT REMOVED, WASHED, PATTED DRY

1 LEMON, CUT IN HALF

COARSE SALT

2–2½ TABLESPOONS MIXED BLACK AND WHITE
 PEPPERCORNS, CRUSHED

ZEST OF 1 LARGE ORANGE AND ½ LARGE GRAPEFRUIT

2 STICKS OF CELERY, CHOPPED

125 ML/4 FL OZ BRANDY

SERVES 8

Rub the skin and inside the ducks with the lemon and season with salt and a generous pinch of the crushed peppercorns. Cut the orange and grapefruit zest into fine strips and blanch in boiling water for 2 minutes, then pat dry. Place half of the celery, orange and grapefruit zest in the cavity of each duck and truss the ducks. Using a two-pronged fork, prick the ducks all over, making more holes in fatty areas. Rub the remaining peppercorns all over the ducks, then leave to stand at room temperature for 30 minutes.

Preheat the oven to 230°C/450°F/Gas Mark 8. Set a rack in a roasting tin.

Roast the ducks on the rack, breast side down, for 15–20 minutes or until the skin is brown. Turn breast side up and continue roasting for 15–20 minutes or until the breast skin is brown and crisp. Pour out the fat from the tin.

Reduce the oven temperature to 200°C/400°F/Gas Mark 6 and roast the ducks for a further 1–1½ hours, piercing the skin several times to release the excess fat. Occasionally you will need to pour out more fat from the bottom of the tin. The ducks are done when the drumsticks move up and down easily and the inside juices are no longer red. Leave to rest for 15–20 minutes before carving.

Pour out all but 1 tablespoon of the fat and peppercorns from the tin. Place the tin over medium heat and add the brandy. Stir well to deglaze and simmer until syrupy.

Using poultry shears, cut on either side of the backbone and discard. Cut each duck half into two and serve with the sauce.

Bruno Loubet

GRILLED CHICKEN ESCALOPES
and raw artichoke salad

2 GLOBE ARTICHOKES

½ A LEMON

85 G/3 OZ PARMESAN CHEESE

2 CHICKEN BREASTS, SKINNED AND EACH OPENED OUT
    FLAT ('BUTTERFLIED') TO FORM FOUR ESCALOPES

100 ML/3½ FL OZ VIRGIN OLIVE OIL

SALT AND PEPPER

2 TABLESPOONS FINELY CHOPPED FRESH PARSLEY

25 G/1 OZ PINE KERNELS, TOASTED

SERVES 4

Snap off all the coarse outside leaves from the artichokes. Using a stainless steel knife, gently remove all the green leaves, the cone of pointed violet leaves and finally the hairy choke. Put 300 ml/½ pint water in a small bowl. Squeeze the lemon into the water, add the squeezed half lemon and immerse the artichokes in the lemon water. Cover with clingfilm.

With a vegetable peeler, 'shave' the Parmesan on to a plate.

Brush the chicken escalopes with olive oil, season with salt and pepper then char-grill on a hot cast-iron ridged grill pan or under a very hot grill; it will take only a few minutes to cook the chicken.

To serve, drain the artichokes, pat dry, slice finely and arrange on four plates. Place the grilled chicken on top of the artichokes. Sprinkle with the shaved Parmesan and the parsley. Grind over some black pepper, drizzle with olive oil and scatter on the pine kernels.

ONE-POT DUCK
with noodles and greens

4 DUCK LEGS, WELL SEASONED WITH COARSELY
    GROUND PEPPER AND SEA SALT

4 TEASPOONS SUNFLOWER OIL

2 LITRES/3½ PINTS CHICKEN STOCK (STOCK CUBES
    DILUTED WITH TWICE AS MUCH WATER AS STATED
    ON PACKET)

2 GARLIC CLOVES

2 CM/¾ INCH PIECE OF FRESH GINGER, SLICED

8 SPRING ONIONS, CUT INTO 1 CM/½ INCH LENGTHS
    (SAVE TRIMMINGS FOR THE STOCK)

400 G/14 OZ WINTER OR SPRING GREENS, TRIMMED
    AND DESTALKED

8 TABLESPOONS SOY SAUCE, PLUS EXTRA, TO TASTE

200 G/7 OZ CHINESE WHEAT NOODLES (CHOW MEIN)

A LITTLE SESAME OIL

SOY SAUCE AND CHINESE CHILLI OIL TO SERVE AS DIPS

SERVES 4

Sauté the duck legs, skin side down, in a little
sunflower oil over a medium heat; cook for 30
minutes, then turn and cook on the other side
for 20 minutes. Pour off any excess fat. (The fat
can be saved and used for sautéing potatoes.)
Bring the stock to the boil, adding the garlic,
ginger and spring onion trimmings. Bring a
large saucepan of salted water to the boil and
blanch the greens for 3 minutes. Drain and
refresh in cold water. When cool, drain again,
squeeze dry and chop coarsely.

Preheat the oven to its highest setting. Strain
the stock into a large saucepan and bring to the
boil. Add the duck legs and soy sauce, reduce
the heat and simmer the duck for 10 minutes.

Take a casserole or four individual lidded
claypots (available from Oriental shops) and
place the noodles in the bottom. Scatter with
the spring onions and the greens. Sprinkle with
sesame oil and a little soy sauce. Add the duck
legs and pour over the boiling stock. Cover and
bake in the very hot oven for 15 minutes. Serve
from the casserole or claypot, removing the hot
lids carefully.

Soy and chilli oil can be served in dipping
bowls.

chapter ten

meat

Janeen Garlin

GARLIC-STUDDED ROAST BEEF

3.2–3.4 KG/7–7¼ LB FORERIB OF BEEF, ON THE BONE,
   CHINED
2 WHOLE GARLIC CLOVES, CUT INTO SLIVERS
½ TEASPOON DRIED CHILLI FLAKES
1 TEASPOON FRESHLY GROUND BLACK PEPPER
½ TEASPOON COARSE SALT
2 CARROTS, CHOPPED
2 ONIONS, CHOPPED
ABOUT 125 ML/4 FL OZ BEEF STOCK

★ *Buy the beef up to 5 days in advance. Trim off any excess fat and leave in the refrigerator, uncovered, to dry-age for at least 24 hours (or up to 5 days). Before roasting, shave off the dried ends with a sharp knife. Tie between the ribs with kitchen string.*

SERVES 6–8

Using the point of a small knife, cut slits in the meat and stud with slivers of garlic. Crush the chilli flakes together with the black pepper. Rub the salt and the pepper mixture into the meat. Leave to stand at room temperature for 30 minutes.

Preheat the oven to 240°C/475°F/Gas Mark 9. Strew the carrots and onions in a roasting tin and set a rack over the vegetables. Place the beef on the rack and roast for 30 minutes.

Reduce the oven temperature to 180°C/350°F/Gas Mark 4 and continue roasting the beef for a further 1–1½ hours, until the meat is done to your liking. Leave to rest for 20–25 minutes before carving.

Pour the roasting tin juices into a jug or fat strainer and leave for 5 minutes. Pour off the fat, then pour the juices into a saucepan and add enough stock to make up 125 ml/4 fl oz. Simmer for a few minutes, skimming off any fat. Add the juices from the resting roast. Reheat the sauce and serve with the beef.

Jameen Garlin

TENDERLOIN OF BEEF

1 WHOLE FILLET OF BEEF, WELL TRIMMED (ABOUT 1.8
  KG/4 LB AFTER TRIMMING)
1 TABLESPOON COARSELY GROUND BLACK PEPPER
1½ TEASPOONS DRIED TARRAGON
1 TEASPOON HERBES DE PROVENCE
3 TABLESPOONS COGNAC
ABOUT 1 TABLESPOON EXTRA VIRGIN OLIVE OIL
175 ML/6 FL OZ BEEF STOCK

SERVES 6–8

Rub the meat with pepper, tarragon and herbes de Provence. Fold the thin tail-end under and tie with kitchen string every 5 cm/2 inches. Place the beef in a roasting tin. Drizzle 2 tablespoons of the Cognac over the meat. Leave to stand at room temperature for 30 minutes.

Preheat the oven to 240°C/475°F/Gas Mark 9. Rub olive oil all over the meat and roast for exactly 30 minutes for rare, 35 minutes for medium rare.

Remove the roast from the oven and wrap in nonstick baking paper, folding the edges of the paper together to make a sealed parcel. Then roll up the parcel in several thicknesses of newspaper and leave to rest for 20–25 minutes before slicing.

Place the roasting tin over medium-high heat, pour in the beef stock and stir well to deglaze while bringing to the boil. Pour into a jug or fat strainer and leave to stand for 5 minutes. Pour off the fat, then pour the juices into a saucepan. Add the remaining Cognac and simmer for a few minutes, skimming off any fat, to reduce and enrich the flavour of the sauce. Add the juices from the resting beef. Reheat the sauce and serve with the sliced beef. Garnish with watercress.

Antony Worrall Thompson

LEBANESE STEAK TARTARE

1 SMALL ONION, FINELY DICED

1 GARLIC CLOVE, FINELY DICED

450 G/1 LB LEAN LEG OF LAMB, MINCED

1 TABLESPOON GOOD OLIVE OIL

3 TABLESPOONS CHOPPED FRESH MINT

½ TEASPOON GROUND CINNAMON

½ TEASPOON GROUND ALLSPICE

½ TEASPOON GROUND BLACK PEPPER

TO SERVE

MINT LEAVES

TOASTED ALMONDS

WHOLE TRIMMED SPRING ONIONS

LIME WEDGES

SERVES 4

Put the onion, garlic, lamb, olive oil, mint, cinnamon, allspice and black pepper in a food processor and blend until smooth.

Transfer to a mixing bowl. With wet hands, work the meat until you have a smooth purée, removing any sinew or fat that you may have missed when trimming the meat.

Shape the meat into flat patties and scatter with mint leaves and almonds. Serve with spring onions and lime wedges, and a warm flatbread such as pitta.

Paul & Jeanne Rankin

RUMP STEAK WITH SOY AND GINGER
and chilli onion rings

4 WELL-AGED RUMP STEAKS, EACH 175–225 G/6–8 OZ
  AND ABOUT 2 CM/¾ INCH THICK
3 TABLESPOONS VEGETABLE OIL

MARINADE
4 TABLESPOONS JAPANESE SOY SAUCE
4 TABLESPOONS MUSHROOM SOY SAUCE
1 TABLESPOON GRATED FRESH GINGER
2 TABLESPOONS SESAME OIL
1 TABLESPOON CURRY POWDER

CHILLI ONION RINGS
2–3 ONIONS
SALT
VEGETABLE OIL FOR DEEP-FRYING
300 G/11 OZ PLAIN FLOUR
2 TABLESPOONS CHILLI POWDER
2 TABLESPOONS PAPRIKA
2 TABLESPOONS CUMIN

SERVES 4

Combine all the marinade ingredients in a ceramic dish. Add the steaks and leave to marinate for at least 30 minutes, preferably 2 hours, turning occasionally.

Using a very sharp knife or a vegetable slicer, slice the onions about 2 mm/1⁄16 inch thick. Sprinkle lightly with salt and leave to stand for 2–3 minutes.

Remove the steaks from the marinade and pat dry, reserving the marinade. Heat the oil in a large frying pan and, when it is smoking, add the steaks. Cook for 2 minutes on each side for rare and about 4 minutes for medium. When the steaks are cooked, transfer them to a warmed plate and add the reserved marinade to the pan. Boil until it reduces to form a thickish sauce. Keep warm.

To cook the onions, heat the oil for deep-frying to about 170°C/340°F. Mix together the flour, chilli powder, paprika and cumin. Toss the onion slices in the spiced flour and ensure that they are evenly coated. Shake off excess flour and deep-fry until brown and crisp. Drain thoroughly on paper towels and season with a little salt.

Arrange the steaks on four warmed plates and spoon the sauce over. Top with the chilli onion rings and serve at once.

Yan-Rit So

BEEF WITH OYSTER SAUCE

225 G/8 OZ TRIMMED BEEF (RIBEYE, RUMP, SKIRT OR
    FILLET STEAK), CUT INTO SLIVERS ABOUT 4 X 1
    CM/1½ X ½ INCH AND 5 MM/¼ INCH THICK
4½ TABLESPOONS PEANUT OR CORN OIL
125 G/4 OZ SHIITAKE MUSHROOMS, TRIMMED AND
    CUT INTO STRIPS
SALT
2 LARGE GARLIC CLOVES, FINELY CHOPPED
4–6 THIN SLICES OF FRESH GINGER
3 LARGE SPRING ONIONS, CUT INTO 4 CM/1½ INCH
    SECTIONS, WHITE AND GREEN PARTS SEPARATED
1 TABLESPOON SHAOXING WINE OR MEDIUM-DRY
    SHERRY
1–1½ TABLESPOONS OYSTER SAUCE

FOR THE MARINADE
¼ TEASPOON SALT
1 TEASPOON THICK OR DARK SOY SAUCE
6 TURNS OF THE PEPPERMILL
1 TEASPOON SHAOXING WINE OR MEDIUM-DRY
    SHERRY
1 TEASPOON POTATO OR TAPIOCA FLOUR
2 TEASPOONS SESAME OIL

SERVES 2

To marinate, place the beef in a bowl, add the
salt, soy sauce, pepper, wine and flour and stir
in one direction until well coated. (This coating
will help to seal in the juices during stir-frying.)
Gradually add 1–1½ tablespoons water, stirring
vigorously until absorbed. Stir in the sesame oil.

Heat 1½ tablespoons of the oil in a frying pan
over medium heat and fry the mushrooms for
2–3 minutes, adding a good pinch of salt. Set
aside.

Heat a wok over high heat until smoke rises.
Add the remaining oil and swirl it around. Add
the garlic, ginger and white spring onions and
stir to mix. Add the beef and, using a wok
spatula, turn and toss for about 20 seconds or
until the beef is partially cooked. Splash in the
wine or sherry, stirring as it sizzles. Add 2
tablespoons water and reduce the heat, stirring
as the water is incorporated. Add the
mushrooms, green spring onions and oyster
sauce, stir to mix, then transfer to a serving dish
and serve at once.

Jacki Passmore

MUSSAMAN BEEF CURRY
(Gaeng Mussaman)

600 G/1¼ LB BEEF SHIN OR OTHER BRAISING STEAK

2½ TABLESPOONS VEGETABLE OR PEANUT OIL

3 ONIONS, CHOPPED

3 GARLIC CLOVES, CHOPPED

2 CM/¾ INCH PIECE OF FRESH GINGER, GRATED OR CHOPPED

1 LEMON GRASS STALK, SLIT LENGTHWAYS

1 SMALL FRESH RED CHILLI, SEEDED

2 TABLESPOONS GROUND CORIANDER

2 TEASPOONS GROUND CUMIN

2 WHOLE CLOVES

1 SMALL CINNAMON STICK

2 POINTS STAR ANISE (OPTIONAL)

2½ TEASPOONS SOFT BROWN SUGAR

500 ML/16 FL OZ COCONUT CREAM

125 ML/4 FL OZ WATER

3 POTATOES, CUBED

SALT AND PEPPER

THAI FISH SAUCE (OPTIONAL)

LIME JUICE (OPTIONAL)

50 G/2 OZ ROASTED PEANUTS, ROUGHLY CHOPPED

SERVES 4–6

Cut the beef into 4 cm/1½ inch cubes. Heat the oil in a saucepan over medium heat and brown the onions for about 6 minutes.

Add the garlic, ginger and lemon grass and cook for 2 minutes. Add the chilli, all the spices and the sugar, with 375 ml/12 fl oz of the coconut cream and the water, and bring to just below boiling point.

Add the beef and cover the pan. Cook for about 55 minutes, stirring the meat occasionally.

Pour in the remaining coconut cream and add the potatoes, salt and pepper. Cook for a further 20 minutes or until the potatoes are tender. Taste and adjust the seasoning, adding more salt and pepper and a splash of Thai fish sauce or lime juice if you like. Stir in the peanuts and serve accompanied by boiled or steamed white rice.

Jameen Garlin

ROAST VEAL DIJON

1.6–1.8 KG/3½–4 LB BONELESS TOP RUMP OF VEAL,
   TRIMMED AND TIED

1 TEASPOON MUSTARD SEEDS

1 TEASPOON WHOLE BLACK PEPPERCORNS

500 ML/16 FL OZ MILK

2 TEASPOONS DRIED TARRAGON

FRESHLY GROUND BLACK PEPPER

225 G/8 OZ DIJON MUSTARD

5 TABLESPOONS BUTTER, MELTED

85 ML/3 FL OZ DRY SHERRY

85 ML/3 FL OZ CHICKEN STOCK (PAGE 374)

2 SHALLOTS, CHOPPED

1 TART GREEN APPLE, PEELED, CORED AND SLICED

FLAT LEAF PARSLEY, TO GARNISH

SERVES 6

Soak the veal, mustard seeds and peppercorns in the milk overnight in the refrigerator.

Discard the marinade, rinse the veal and pat dry with paper towels. Rub the meat with the tarragon and freshly ground black pepper.

Preheat the oven to 160°C/325°/Gas Mark 3. Place the meat in a roasting tin. Beat the Dijon mustard with 4 tablespoons of the melted butter and pour over the meat, to cover on all sides. Roast for 2½ hours.

Reduce the oven temperature to 150°C/300°F/Gas Mark 2 and continue to roast the veal for about 1 hour, basting every 15 minutes with sherry and chicken stock. Leave to rest for 15–20 minutes before slicing.

While the veal is roasting, heat the remaining 1 tablespoon butter in a small saucepan and sauté the chopped shallots until soft. Add the apple slices and sauté until just tender but still holding their shape. Set aside.

Add the juices from the roasting tin to the shallot and apple mixture and simmer for a few minutes to reduce and enrich the flavour of the sauce.

Garnish the carved veal with parsley. Serve the sauce separately.

Roger Vergé

MEDALLIONS OF VEAL
with lemon

1 RIPE JUICY LEMON

1 TEASPOON SUGAR

600 G/1¼ LB VEAL FILLET, CUT INTO PIECES AND
  TRIMMED OF FAT AND SINEWS, OR 4 VEAL CUTLETS,
  TRIMMED OF FAT

SALT AND PEPPER

125 G/4 OZ BUTTER

8 TABLESPOONS DRY WHITE WINE

2 TABLESPOONS CHOPPED FRESH PARSLEY

SERVES 4

Pare off the lemon zest as thinly as possible and cut into very thin strips. Place the strips in a small saucepan with a little cold water and bring to the boil. Drain and refresh in cold water. Return to the pan with the sugar and 2 tablespoons water and cook until the water has evaporated and the zest has become a beautiful bright yellow. Set aside. Cut off the lemon peel and all the pith, and cut out the lemon segments. Set aside.

Season the veal on both sides. Heat one-third of the butter in a frying pan over moderate heat; when it begins to sizzle, add the veal and cook for about 5 minutes on each side. Remove from the pan and keep warm.

Pour off the cooking butter, then deglaze the pan with the wine, scraping up the caramelized residue from the bottom of the pan. Keeping the pan over a moderate heat, let the wine reduce to 2 tablespoons of syrupy sauce. Cut the remaining butter into small cubes and beat into the sauce. Add the parsley and season to taste.

Serve the veal on warmed plates. Add any meat juices to the sauce and pour over the veal. Garnish with the lemon segments and strips of zest and serve with a selection of vegetables.

Richard Olney

BRAISED SWEETBREADS
with little peas

2 LOBES OF VEAL SWEETBREADS, ABOUT 450 G/1 LB

25 G/1 OZ UNSALTED BUTTER

BOUQUET GARNI

HANDFUL OF SMALL WHITE ONIONS, PEELED

COARSE SEA SALT

450 G/1 LB FRESHLY PICKED LITTLE PEAS, SHELLED

PINCH OF SUGAR

HANDFUL OF LETTUCE, SHREDDED

1 TABLESPOON WATER

SERVES 2

Soak the sweetbreads in cold water for 4–5 hours.

Place them in a large saucepan, cover with cold water, bring slowly to boiling point and keep them barely simmering over low heat for 15 minutes. Drain, refresh in cold water and peel them, removing superficial membranes and fat.

Butter a flameproof earthenware casserole and add the sweetbreads, bouquet garni and onions. Sprinkle with a little salt, add the peas, the remaining butter, cut into tiny dice, a little more salt and the sugar. Spread the shredded lettuce over the surface, sprinkle over a little water, cover tightly and cook over low heat for 45–50 minutes, shaking the casserole occasionally. Discard the bouquet garni and serve directly from the casserole.

Janeen Garlin

LEG OF LAMB
with mint and watercress

2 BUNCHES OF WATERCRESS LEAVES, COARSELY
   CHOPPED

2 SMALL BUNCHES OF FRESH SPEARMINT LEAVES,
   COARSELY CHOPPED

1 LARGE BUNCH OF FLAT LEAF PARSLEY LEAVES,
   COARSELY CHOPPED

3 GARLIC CLOVES, CHOPPED

125–150 ML/4–5 FL OZ OLIVE OIL

COARSE SALT

FRESHLY GROUND BLACK PEPPER

2 ONIONS, SLICED

3–3.2 KG/6–7 LB LEG OF LAMB, TRIMMED OF ALL
   EXCESS FAT

250 ML/8 FL OZ CHICKEN STOCK (PAGE 374)

SPRIGS OF WATERCRESS, TO GARNISH

SERVES 6–8

Place the watercress, mint, parsley and garlic in a food processor and pulse briefly. With the machine running, pour the olive oil through the feeder tube to make a stiff, spreadable paste. Season with salt and pepper to taste.

Preheat the oven to 230°/450°F/Gas Mark 8. Strew the onions in a roasting tin and set a rack over them.

Season the lamb, then, using a spatula, spread the herb mixture all over the meat. Place the lamb on the rack and roast for 30 minutes.

Reduce the oven temperature to 180°C/350°F/Gas Mark 4 and continue roasting for a further 30 minutes–1 hour. Leave to rest for 15–20 minutes before carving.

Pour the stock into the hot roasting tin and stir well to deglaze. Pour into a jug or fat strainer and leave for 5 minutes. Pour off the fat, then pour the juices into a saucepan and simmer for a few minutes, skimming off any fat. Add the juices from the resting roast. Reheat the sauce and serve with the lamb. Garnish with watercress.

Paul & Jeanne Rankin

ROAST LEG OF LAMB
with cumin, lemon and mint

1 BONELESS LAMB JOINT, ABOUT 800 G/1¾ LB

SALT

2 TABLESPOONS LIGHT OLIVE OIL

1 TEASPOON TOMATO PURÉE

1 TABLESPOON MINT SAUCE

1½ TABLESPOONS COLD BUTTER, CUT INTO SMALL
PIECES

MARINADE

2 TEASPOONS GROUND CUMIN

1 TEASPOON GROUND BLACK PEPPER

1 TEASPOON HARISSA OR CHILLI AND GARLIC SAUCE

½ TEASPOON GROUND CORIANDER SEEDS

½ TEASPOON OREGANO

1 GARLIC CLOVE, CHOPPED, OR ¼ TEASPOON GARLIC
POWDER

GRATED ZEST OF 1 LEMON

JUICE OF ½ LEMON

SERVES 4

Season the lamb generously with salt. Combine all the marinade ingredients in a shallow bowl. Dip the lamb into the marinade and rub the mixture into the meat. Leave to marinate for at least 30 minutes, preferably 2–3 hours, turning the meat occasionally.

Preheat the oven to 180°C/350°F/Gas Mark 4. Heat the olive oil in a large frying pan over medium-high heat. Brown the lamb on all sides, then transfer to a warmed casserole dish. Add 2 tablespoons water and any remaining marinade and roast for about 20 minutes for medium-rare, 35 minutes for well-done lamb.

Transfer the roast to a warmed plate and cover with foil. Leave to rest in a warm place for 10 minutes. Pour the juices from the casserole into a small saucepan. Add the tomato purée and the mint sauce. Bring to the boil, then remove from the heat and whisk in the butter. Carve the roast and add any juices to the sauce. Serve with grilled Mediterranean vegetables: tomatoes, courgettes, aubergine.

Antony Worrall Thompson

MOROCCAN LAMB STEW
with pumpkin and pickled lemon

450 G/1 LB LEAN SHOULDER OF LAMB, CUT INTO 2.5
   CM/1 INCH CUBES

1½ TEASPOONS FRESHLY GROUND BLACK PEPPER

3 TABLESPOONS OLIVE OIL

1 ONION, ROUGHLY DICED

4 GARLIC CLOVES, CRUSHED WITH A LITTLE SALT

4 TOMATOES, SKINNED AND DICED

1 TABLESPOON HARISSA (PAGE 376) OR HOT PEPPER
   PASTE

400 G/14 OZ CANNED CHICKPEAS, DRAINED

325 G/12 OZ TRIMMED AND PEELED PUMPKIN, CUT
   INTO 2.5 CM/1 INCH CUBES

1 TEASPOON SALT

1 PICKLED LEMON, FINELY DICED

2 TABLESPOONS CHOPPED FRESH MINT

1 TABLESPOON CHOPPED FRESH CORIANDER

SERVES 4

Coat the lamb in the black pepper. Heat the oil in a large saucepan, add the lamb and cook until it has browned all over.

Add the onion and garlic and cook until the onion has softened and is slightly browned.

Add the tomatoes, harissa and 450 ml/¾ pint water. Bring to the boil, cover and cook over a medium heat for 1½ hours, topping up with water as necessary. Add the chickpeas and pumpkin and cook for a further 15 minutes or until the pumpkin is tender. Add the salt, lemon, mint and coriander and serve immediately.

Pat Chapman

BOMBAY LAMB DHANSAK

125 G/4 OZ SPLIT RED LENTILS, SOAKED FOR
   20 MINUTES
4 TABLESPOONS VEGETABLE OIL
4 GARLIC CLOVES, FINELY CHOPPED
2 SMALL ONIONS, SLICED
450 G/1 LB LEG OF LAMB, CUBED
1 LARGE POTATO, QUARTERED
2–3 BAY LEAVES
400 G/14 OZ CANNED RATATOUILLE
1 TEASPOON DRIED FENUGREEK LEAVES
1 TABLESPOON COCONUT MILK POWDER
1 TEASPOON GARAM MASALA
1 TABLESPOON CLEAR HONEY
1 TABLESPOON CHOPPED FRESH MINT
1 TABLESPOON CHOPPED FRESH CORIANDER LEAVES
SALT

WHOLE SPICES

1 TABLESPOON CORIANDER SEEDS
½ TEASPOON CUMIN SEEDS
3 WHOLE BROWN CARDAMOM PODS
4 WHOLE GREEN CARDAMOM PODS
2 WHOLE STAR ANISE PODS

GROUND SPICES

½ TEASPOON EACH OF CINNAMON, NUTMEG,
   TURMERIC AND CHILLI POWDER

SERVES 4

Heat a wok or karahi over fairly high heat. Add the whole spices and dry-fry, stirring constantly, for about 30 seconds. Leave to cool, then grind in a coffee grinder. Add the ground spices and mix well.

Bring 300 ml/½ pint water to the boil. Rinse the lentils, add to the water; simmer for 20 minutes.

Preheat the oven to 190°C/ 375°F/Gas Mark 5; warm a 2.3–2.8 litre/4–5 pint casserole dish.

Heat the oil in a wok or karahi and stir-fry over high heat for 10–15 minutes with the garlic, spices and onions, gradually lowering the heat.

Increase the heat, add the lamb and potato and stir-fry until mixed. Transfer to the casserole dish, cover and place in the hot oven.

After 20 minutes, stir in the bay leaves, ratatouille and lentils.

After a further 20 minutes, stir in all the remaining ingredients, except the salt. Add a little water if the mixture looks dry.

Cook for a final 20 minutes, then test the lamb for tenderness (if necessary, return to the oven until the lamb is tender). Season to taste, garnish and serve.

Pat Chapman

NORTH INDIAN KEEMA CURRY

4 TABLESPOONS CORN OIL

2–3 GARLIC CLOVES, FINELY
CHOPPED

2.5 CM/1 INCH CUBE OF FRESH GINGER, CHOPPED

2 ONIONS, SLICED

600 G/1¼ LB LEAN MINCED BEEF, LAMB OR PORK

½ RED PEPPER, SLICED

1–2 GREEN CHILLIES, SLICED (OPTIONAL)

3–4 BAY LEAVES

300 ML/10 FL OZ CANNED CREAM OF TOMATO SOUP

6 CHERRY TOMATOES, HALVED

2 TEASPOONS GARAM MASALA

100 G/3½ OZ CANNED SWEETCORN AND ITS LIQUID

1 TEASPOON SUGAR

1 TABLESPOON CHOPPED FRESH CORIANDER LEAVES

SALT

GROUND SPICES

1 TEASPOON EACH OF CORIANDER AND CUMIN

½ TEASPOON EACH OF PAPRIKA, HOT CURRY POWDER
  AND TURMERIC

⅓ TEASPOON EACH OF CINNAMON, CLOVES AND
  MANGO POWDER (AMCHOOR)

SERVES 4

Preheat the oven to 190°C/375°F/ Gas Mark 5 and warm a 2.3–2.8 litre/4–5 pint casserole dish.

Heat the oil in a wok or karahi stir-fry over high heat for 10–15 minutes with the garlic, ginger, ground spices and onions, gradually lowering the heat.

Increase the heat and add the mince, pepper, chillies, if using, and bay leaves. Stir-fry until thoroughly mixed, then transfer to the casserole dish, cover and place in the hot oven.

After 20 minutes, stir in half the tomato soup.

After a further 20 minutes, stir in all the remaining ingredients, except the salt, and cook for a final 20 minutes. Season to taste, garnish and serve.

ROAST FILLETS OF LAMB
with a gâteau of ratatouille

2½ TABLESPOONS BUTTER

2 TABLESPOONS OLIVE OIL

1 SMALL ONION, DICED

2 COURGETTES, DICED

1 AUBERGINE, DICED

1 RED PEPPER, DICED

1 GREEN PEPPER, DICED

2 TOMATOES, SKINNED, SEEDED AND DICED

1 TABLESPOON CHOPPED FRESH THYME

SALT AND PEPPER

2 EGGS

1 GARLIC CLOVE, CHOPPED

6 FRESH BASIL LEAVES, CHOPPED

1–2 TABLESPOONS CRÈME FRAÎCHE (OPTIONAL)

1 SADDLE OF LAMB, 1.5–1.8 KG/3–4 LB, BONED, BONES RESERVED

SERVES 4

Preheat the oven to 180°C/350°F/Gas Mark 4. Use 1 tablespoon of the butter to grease four round moulds, about 10 cm/4 inches in diameter.

Heat the oil in a frying pan and sauté the vegetables until just tender, adding the thyme, salt and pepper. Beat the eggs in a large bowl and mix in the vegetables, garlic and basil, and the cream, if using. Spoon into the buttered moulds and cook in the preheated oven for about 20 minutes or until just set. Remove from the oven and keep warm.

Increase the oven temperature to 240°C/ 475°F/Gas Mark 9.

Brown the bones, with a little olive oil, in a roasting pan over high heat. Add ½ tablespoon butter and the lamb fillets and brown well all over. Roast in the hot oven for 10 minutes; they should still be pink in the centre. Keep the lamb warm while you make the sauce.

Pour off the fat and add 200 ml/7 fl oz water to the bones in the roasting pan. Place over medium-high heat and boil to reduce by half. Strain into a small jug. Heat the remaining 1 tablespoon butter in a small saucepan until it foams and turns light brown, then add this to the sauce.

Unmould the vegetable cakes on to warmed serving plates. Slice the lamb thinly and arrange around the vegetables, with a little sauce poured over. Serve immediately.

BRAISED PORK
with aubergine

675 G/1½ LB AUBERGINES, TOPPED AND TAILED

SALT

4 TABLESPOONS PEANUT OR CORN OIL

2–3 LARGE GARLIC CLOVES, ROUGHLY CHOPPED

4 SPRING ONIONS, CUT INTO 5 CM/2 INCH SECTIONS,
   WHITE AND GREEN PARTS SEPARATED

125 G/4 OZ PORK, MINCED

1 TABLESPOON SHAOXING WINE OR MEDIUM-DRY
   SHERRY

½ TEASPOON POTATO OR TAPIOCA
   FLOUR

1 TABLESPOON THICK OR DARK SOY SAUCE

¼ TEASPOON SUGAR

85 ML/3 FL OZ CHICKEN STOCK (PAGE 374)

SERVES 6

Cut the aubergines into pieces about 5 cm/2 inches long and 2.5 cm/1 inch wide and thick. Sprinkle 1 teaspoon salt over the flesh and leave for 1 hour. Rinse and dry thoroughly.

In a large, heavy-bottomed saucepan, heat 2 tablespoons of the oil. Add half the aubergine pieces and brown over medium heat for about 2 minutes. Remove to a dish. Add 1 more tablespoon of the oil and brown the remaining aubergine. Remove to the dish.

Add the remaining oil to the pan. Add the garlic and white spring onions, stir, then add the pork and stir vigorously until it turns opaque. Splash in the wine or sherry, stirring as it sizzles. Sprinkle over the flour and stir to coat. Reduce the heat slightly, add the soy sauce, sugar and stock and bring to a simmer. Return the aubergine to the pan, cover and simmer gently for 10–15 minutes or until meltingly tender.

Add the green spring onions, then taste and season. Transfer to a serving dish and serve hot.

Jacki Passmore

HOT AND SPICY PORK
WITH BEANS
(Pad Prik King Tua Fak Yaeow)

400 G/14 OZ LEAN PORK

1½ TABLESPOONS VEGETABLE OIL

2 SPRING ONIONS, SHREDDED

1 TABLESPOON FINELY SHREDDED FRESH GINGER

1 TABLESPOON CHOPPED GARLIC

2 FRESH RED CHILLIES, SEEDED

½ RECIPE THAI RED CURRY PASTE (PAGE 377)

1 TEASPOON SHRIMP PASTE

1 TEASPOON PAPRIKA

125 ML/4 FL OZ COCONUT CREAM

1 TEASPOON SUGAR

125 ML/4 FL OZ WATER

4–5 SNAKE/LONG BEANS OR 12 GREEN BEANS, CUT
    INTO 5 CM/2 INCH PIECES

½ RED PEPPER, CUT INTO STRIPS

SALT

SERVES 4

Cut the pork into thin strips and set aside.

Heat the oil in a wok or large heavy frying pan and stir-fry the spring onions, ginger, garlic and chillies for about 1½ minutes. Add the curry paste, shrimp paste and paprika and stir-fry for 1 minute.

Add the strips of pork, coconut cream and sugar and stir-fry over high heat until the liquid has been absorbed. Add the water and the beans and continue to cook, stirring frequently, until the beans are tender.

Add the strips of pepper and salt to taste. Cook, stirring frequently, until the liquid has been absorbed and the meat and vegetables are tender. Serve with boiled rice or rice noodles.

Alastair Little

PORK DIJONNAISE

800 G/1¾ LB PORK FILLET

SALT AND PEPPER

SUNFLOWER OIL

UNSALTED BUTTER

1 GLASS OF DRY WHITE WINE

200 ML/7 FL OZ DOUBLE CREAM

4 TABLESPOONS DIJON MUSTARD

A SMALL HANDFUL OF FLAT-LEAF PARSLEY, CHOPPED

A FEW CAPERS OR CHOPPED GHERKINS (OPTIONAL)

SERVES 4

Cut the pork into 1 cm/½ inch slices, then flatten out into escalopes using a meat bat or rolling pin. Season with a little salt and pepper.

Heat a large frying pan over a medium heat. Add a little oil and a generous knob of butter and cook the escalopes for 4–5 minutes on each side. Do not overcrowd the pan; you will almost certainly need to cook the pork in two batches. When it is done, remove from the pan to a plate and keep warm in a very low oven.

Add the wine to the pan and increase the heat. Boil until the wine has reduced by at least half, then add the cream and bring back to the boil until lightly thickened. Stir in the mustard and parsley, and a few capers or chopped gherkins if you like, then taste and adjust the seasoning. Return the pork escalopes and any collected meat juices to the sauce and swirl until coated. Do not boil the pork in the sauce or it will toughen. Serve at once, with garlicky green beans.

Pat Chapman

CARIBBEAN PEPPER POT

4 TABLESPOONS VEGETABLE OIL

6 GARLIC CLOVES, CHOPPED

3 ONIONS, SLICED

500 G/1 LB 2 OZ LAMB, CUBED

1 SWEET POTATO, CUBED

300 ML/½ PINT STOCK OR WATER

3–4 BAY LEAVES

1–3 FRESH RED CHILLIES, SLICED

1 GREEN PEPPER, SLICED

1 TEASPOON EACH OF BLACK AND GREEN
  PEPPERCORNS

3 TABLESPOONS CHOPPED SUN-DRIED TOMATOES IN
  OIL

125 G/4 OZ CANNED PINEAPPLE
  CHUNKS IN NATURAL JUICE

2 TEASPOONS MOLASSES OR
  MUSCOVADO SUGAR

1 TABLESPOON RED WINE VINEGAR

50 ML/2 FL OZ RUM

SALT

WHOLE SPICES

6 WHOLE GREEN CARDAMOM PODS

2 TEASPOONS FENNEL SEEDS

10 WHOLE CLOVES

5 CM/2 INCH PIECE OF CASSIA BARK

4 WHOLE STAR ANISE PODS

GROUND SPICES

½ TEASPOON EACH OF CORIANDER, TURMERIC,
  PAPRIKA, GINGER, CUMIN AND GARAM MASALA

SERVES 4

Preheat the oven to 190°C/375°F/Gas Mark 5 and warm a 2.3–2.8 litre/4–5 pint casserole dish.

Heat the oil in a wok or karahi and stir-fry over high heat for 10–15 minutes with the whole spices, garlic, ground spices and onions, gradually lowering the heat.

Increase the heat and add the meat, sweet potato and the stock or water. Mix well, then transfer to the casserole dish, cover and place in the hot oven.

After 20 minutes, stir in the bay leaves, chillies, pepper, peppercorns and tomatoes.

After a further 20 minutes, stir in all the remaining ingredients, except the salt. Cook for a final 20 minutes, then test the meat for tenderness (if necessary, return to the oven until tender). Season to taste, garnish and serve.

Janeen Garlin

CALIFORNIA LOIN OF PORK
with mango, date and apple salsa

2.4–3 KG/5½–6 LB BONELESS LOIN OF PORK, WELL
    TRIMMED AND TIED EVERY 5 CM/2 INCHES
3 PIECES OF CRYSTALLIZED GINGER, CUT INTO SLIVERS
ZEST OF 1 LIME, CUT INTO FINE STRIPS
1 SMALL ONION, SLICED
1 BOTTLE FULL-BODIED RED WINE
1 TABLESPOON FRESH ROSEMARY OR 1½ TEASPOONS
    DRIED
1½ TEASPOONS FRESHLY GROUND BLACK PEPPER
½ TEASPOON COARSE SALT

MANGO, DATE AND APPLE SALSA

2 LARGE MANGOES, DICED
12 LARGE FRESH DATES, PITTED AND CHOPPED
2 LARGE, FIRM, TART APPLES (GRANNY SMITH),
    PEELED, CORED AND CHOPPED
3 TABLESPOONS SNIPPED CHIVES
2 TABLESPOONS CHOPPED CRYSTALLIZED GINGER
JUICE OF 3 LARGE LIMES
ABOUT 4 TABLESPOONS EXTRA VIRGIN OLIVE OIL

SERVES 10–12

Using the point of a small knife, cut slits in the meat and stud with slivers of ginger. Place in a shallow, non-reactive dish, add the lime zest and onion and pour over the wine. Cover and marinate for 2 hours at room temperature or overnight in the refrigerator. Bring back to room temperature before roasting.

Preheat the oven to 220°C/425°F/Gas Mark 8. Set a rack in a roasting tin.

Remove the meat from the marinade and pat dry. Chop the rosemary together with the pepper and salt. Rub the seasonings all over the pork, then place on the rack, fat side up.

Roast for 45 minutes or until the meat begins to brown. Reduce the oven temperature to 180°C/350°F/Gas Mark 4 and continue roasting for a further 1½ hours.

Meanwhile, make the salsa: mix all the ingredients together, add pepper to taste, and add enough olive oil to bind the mixture.

Leave the pork to rest for 15–20 minutes before carving, then serve with the salsa.

Pat Chapman

CHINESE PORK CURRY

600 G/1¼ LB LEAN PORK, CUBED

50 G/2 OZ CORNFLOUR

4 TABLESPOONS GHEE OR CLARIFIED BUTTER

4 GARLIC CLOVES, SLICED

4 CM/1½ INCH CUBE OF FRESH GINGER, SLICED

1 TABLESPOON HOT CURRY POWDER

2 TEASPOONS CHINESE FIVE-SPICE POWDER

2 ONIONS, SLICED

300 ML/½ PINT CHICKEN STOCK OR WATER

4 BAY LEAVES

225 G/8 OZ CANNED PINEAPPLE CHUNKS IN NATURAL
   JUICE

125 G/4 OZ OYSTER MUSHROOMS, SLICED

125 ML/4 FL OZ CRÈME FRAÎCHE

SALT

SERVES 4

Preheat the oven to 190°C/375°F/Gas Mark 5 and warm a 2.3–2.8 litre/4–5 pint casserole dish.

Toss the pork in the cornflour until evenly coated.

Heat the ghee or butter in a wok or karahi and stir-fry over high heat for 10–15 minutes with the garlic, ginger, curry and five-spice powders and onions, gradually lowering the heat.

Increase the heat and add the pork. Stir-fry for about 5 minutes, adding just enough of the stock or water to keep the pork moist.

Add the bay leaves and the remaining stock or water, then transfer the mixture to the casserole dish, cover and place in the hot oven.

After 20 minutes, stir in the pineapple and juice.

After a further 20 minutes, stir in the mushrooms and crème fraîche. Cook for a final 20 minutes, then test the pork for tenderness (if necessary, return to the oven until the pork is

Alastair Little

SAUSAGE AND BEAN CASSEROLE

2 x 400 G/14 OZ CANS OF CANNELLINI BEANS,
  DRAINED AND RINSED
1 x 400 G/14 OZ CAN OF CHOPPED TOMATOES
EXTRA VIRGIN OLIVE OIL
250 ML/8 FL OZ CHICKEN STOCK (PAGE 374, OR MADE
  WITH A STOCK CUBE)
2 SPRIGS OF ROSEMARY
3 GARLIC CLOVES, FINELY CHOPPED
2 BAY LEAVES
600 G/1¼ LB SPICY ITALIAN-STYLE SAUSAGES (OR
  TOULOUSE SAUSAGES)
100 G/3½ OZ STREAKY BACON, CUT INTO THICK
  STRIPS (LARDONS)
400 G/14 OZ MORTADELLA SAUSAGE, SKINNED AND
  CUT INTO 1 CM/½ INCH CUBES
200 G/7 OZ FRESH BREADCRUMBS

SERVES 4

Preheat the oven to 160°C/325°F/Gas Mark 3.

Put the beans and tomatoes in a saucepan with a good dash of olive oil and place over a medium heat. Add the stock, rosemary, garlic and bay leaves and simmer for 10–15 minutes.

Place a large frying pan over a medium heat, add a little oil and brown the sausages for a few minutes, then add the bacon and mortadella and cook for 2 minutes.

Tip the bean mixture into the frying pan and return to a simmer. Taste and adjust the seasoning and transfer to a wide casserole. Cover with a thin crust of breadcrumbs, moisten with olive oil and bake for 1 hour, occasionally adding a few breadcrumbs or a drizzle of oil as the crust develops. Serve straight from the casserole.

desserts

Antony Worrall Thompson

POACHED FIGS
with blackberries in red wine

675 G/1½ LB RIPE, UNDAMAGED BLACKBERRIES,
    WASHED
JUICE OF 2 LEMONS
JUICE OF 1 ORANGE
175 G/6 OZ CASTER SUGAR
1 BOTTLE ZINFANDEL RED WINE
16 FIRM FRESH FIGS
85 ML/3 FL OZ CRÈME DE MÛRE (BLACKBERRY
    LIQUEUR) OR CRÈME DE CASSIS (BLACKCURRANT
    LIQUEUR)
1 TABLESPOON FINELY CHOPPED FRESH MINT

SERVES 4–6

Put the blackberries in a food processor or liquidizer with the lemon and orange juice and blend until smooth.

Strain the resulting purée through a fine sieve into a non-reactive saucepan. Add the sugar and red wine and bring to the boil over a medium heat. Reduce the heat to a simmer and skim off any scum that may have risen to the surface.

When the sugar has dissolved, add the figs, in batches of four, and poach for 4–5 minutes, depending on their ripeness, until just tender. Remove the cooked figs to a glass serving bowl.

When all the figs are cooked, increase the heat and allow the blackberry purée to boil and reduce to about 450 ml/15 fl oz. Leave to cool, then stir in the liqueur and chopped mint and pour over the figs.

This dish is best prepared 24 hours in advance, turning the figs in the liquid from time to time.

Richard Olney

GLAZED APPLE CRÊPE ROULADES

50 G/2 OZ UNSALTED BUTTER

3 NON-ACIDIC APPLES (FOR EXAMPLE, RUSSET OR
COX'S PIPPINS), PEELED, QUARTERED, SEEDED AND
SLICED

6 CRÊPES (PAGE 378)

SUGAR

SERVES 2

Melt half the butter in a large frying pan, add
the apples and sauté, tossing often, until they are
soft and tender, but still intact.

Butter a gratin dish large enough to hold the
rolled crêpes, side by side, without crowding.
Roll a couple of tablespoons of sautéed apples in
each crêpe and place it, seam-side down, in the
dish. Place a strip of butter on each crêpe and
sprinkle with sugar. The crêpes may be prepared
up to this point 1–2 hours in advance.

Preheat the oven to 230°C/450°F/Gas Mark
8. Put the dish into the hot oven for about 10
minutes or until a light caramel glaze has formed
on the surface of the crêpes. Serve hot, with a
glass of fine Sauternes.

Paul Gayler

MAPLE-GLAZED PUMPKIN TATIN
with sweet spices

25 G/1 OZ BUTTER

450 G/1 LB PUMPKIN FLESH

2 TABLESPOONS MAPLE SYRUP

2 TABLESPOONS SHERRY VINEGAR OR RED WINE
VINEGAR

15 G/½ OZ FRESH GINGER, FINELY CHOPPED

1 TEASPOON GROUND CINNAMON

½ TEASPOON GROUND CUMIN

250 G/9 OZ PUFF PASTRY, THAWED IF FROZEN

1 EGG YOLK, BEATEN WITH 1 TABLESPOON WATER,
TO GLAZE

SERVES 6–8

Preheat the oven to 200°C/400°F/Gas Mark 6.
Smear the butter over the base of a 22 cm/9
inch cast-iron frying pan with an ovenproof
handle or a flameproof cake tin.

Cut the pumpkin into wedges, 1 cm/½ inch
thick. Mix the maple syrup with the vinegar,
ginger, cinnamon and cumin and pour into the
buttered pan. Arrange the pumpkin wedges
neatly on top, to cover the base of the pan.

Place the pan over a high heat and cook for
10 minutes or until the syrup and butter are
lightly caramelized and golden. Leave to cool
for 10 minutes.

Roll out the pastry 5 mm/¼ inch thick and
cut out a 22 cm/9 inch diameter circle. Cover
the pumpkin with the pastry, tucking it down at
the edges. Brush the pastry with the beaten egg
and bake for 12–15 minutes or until risen and
golden (after 10 minutes, press the pastry down
with a plate).

Carefully turn out on to a serving plate and
pour any caramelized juices over the pumpkin.
Serve hot.

Rowley Leigh

WILD STRAWBERRY PUDDING

250 ML/8 FL OZ MILK

1 VANILLA POD, SPLIT IN HALF

3 GELATINE LEAVES

4 EGG YOLKS

100 G/3½ OZ CASTER SUGAR

225–250 G/8–9 OZ WILD STRAWBERRIES

250 ML/8 FL OZ DOUBLE OR WHIPPING CREAM

SERVES 4

Bring the milk to the boil with the vanilla pod, then leave to infuse for 20 minutes. Soak the gelatine leaves in some tepid water.

Whisk the egg yolks and sugar together until thick and pale, pour over the hot milk and return to the heat. Cook slowly, stirring constantly with a wooden spoon until the mixture begins to thicken. Remove from the heat, add the drained gelatine, whisk well and leave to cool.

Add the wild strawberries to the custard. Whip the cream to a soft ribbon consistency and fold into the custard. Pour into one large mould or four small moulds. Place in the refrigerator and leave until set.

If you have some more strawberries and some are a little soft, purée them in a liquidizer with a little caster sugar to make a coulis to serve with the pudding.

Jill Dupleix

TROPICAL FRUIT SOUP
with lemongrass

RIND OF 1 ORANGE, CUT INTO TINY STRIPS

RIND OF 1 LEMON, CUT INTO TINY STRIPS

1 BOTTLE (75 CL) WHITE DESSERT WINE

2 TABLESPOONS CASTER SUGAR

1 VANILLA POD, SPLIT LENGTHWAYS

1 TABLESPOON GRATED FRESH GINGER

2 STALKS OF FRESH LEMONGRASS

5 CLOVES

SMALL BUNCH OF FRESH MINT LEAVES

4 PASSIONFRUIT

450 G/1 LB (PEELED WEIGHT) MIXED TROPICAL FRUIT (PINEAPPLE, MANGO, PEACH, PAPAYA, KIWI FRUIT, LYCHEES, BANANA), PEELED AND CUBED

150 G/5 OZ STRAWBERRIES AND OTHER BERRIES IN SEASON

FRESH MINT LEAVES, TO DECORATE

SERVES 4

Place the orange and lemon rind, wine, sugar, vanilla pod, ginger, lemongrass, cloves and mint leaves in a saucepan and add 500 ml/16 fl oz cold water. Bring to the boil and simmer for 30 minutes.

Cover the pan, leave to cool, then chill overnight.

The next day, strain the syrup through a fine sieve, reserving the lemongrass and the orange and lemon rind.

Cut the passionfruit in half, scoop out the pulp and push it through a sieve. Add the passionfruit juice to the syrup.

Prepare the fruit and berries and arrange in four chilled soup plates, tucking extra mint leaves among the fruit. Spoon the syrup over the fruit until it just starts to float. Serve sprinkled with a few pieces of the reserved lemongrass and orange and lemon rind.

Michel Roux

BLACKBERRY CLAFOUTIS

250 G/9 OZ QUICK PUFF PASTRY (PAGE 378)
4 EGGS
200 G/7 OZ CASTER SUGAR
25 G/1 OZ FLOUR
125 ML/4 FL OZ MILK
125 ML/4 FL OZ DOUBLE CREAM
2 TABLESPOONS KIRSCH (OPTIONAL)
250 G/9 OZ BLACKBERRIES
2 TABLESPOONS GRANULATED SUGAR

SERVES 8

On a lightly floured work surface, roll out the pastry to form a circle, 2 mm/¹⁄₁₆ inch thick. Use to line a greased, loose-bottomed 24 cm/ 9½ inch diameter tart tin and cut off any excess pastry around the rim. Chill for 20 minutes.

Preheat the oven to 220°C/425°F/Gas Mark 7. Prick the pastry with a fork, line it with greaseproof paper and fill with baking beans. Bake blind for 20 minutes, then remove from the oven; remove the beans and paper. Reduce the oven temperature to 200°C/400°F/Gas Mark 6.

Put the eggs and caster sugar in a bowl, whisk together for 2 minutes, then add the flour and whisk for a further 2 minutes. Still whisking, add the milk, cream and kirsch, if using. Spread the blackberries over the pastry, pour in the cream mixture and bake for 30 minutes or until just set. As soon as the clafoutis is cooked, remove the outside of the tart tin, leaving the clafoutis on the base.

Just before serving, sprinkle the granulated sugar over the barely warm clafoutis.

Michel Roux

PEAR AND GINGER SABAYON

4 EGG YOLKS
50 G/2 OZ CASTER SUGAR
3 TABLESPOONS COLD WATER
100 ML/3½ FL OZ PEAR EAU-DE-VIE
50 G/2 OZ PRESERVED GINGER IN SYRUP, DRAINED
  AND FINELY CHOPPED

SERVES 6

First prepare a bain-marie: half-fill with cold water a saucepan large enough to hold the base of a mixing bowl.

Place all the ingredients in the mixing bowl and start whisking with a balloon whisk. Set the base of the bowl in the bain-marie and place over medium heat. Whisk continuously for 10–12 minutes; the temperature of the water in the bain-marie should not exceed 90°C/195°F or the sabayon will start to coagulate. If necessary, turn off or reduce the heat under the pan. Keep whisking until the sabayon becomes glossy and has the consistency of half-risen egg whites. The texture should be unctuous, frothy and light (the temperature should not exceed 55°C/130°F). As soon as the sabayon is ready, stop whisking, spoon it into bowls or large glasses and serve immediately.

Michel Roux

BANANA RAMEKINS
with caramel topping

5–6 BANANAS, NOT TOO RIPE
JUICE OF 2 LEMONS
150 G/5 OZ BUTTER
150 G/5 OZ CASTER SUGAR
600 G/1¼ LB PASTRY CREAM
  (PAGE 378)
150 ML/¼ PINT DOUBLE CREAM
6 TABLESPOONS DARK RUM

SERVES 4–8 (1 OR 2 RAMEKINS EACH)

Peel the bananas, cut them into 1 cm/½ inch rounds and mix them with the lemon juice in a bowl.

Heat the butter in a frying pan, sprinkle on 85 g/3 oz of the caster sugar, add the banana rounds and lightly brown them over high heat for 2 minutes. Transfer to a plate and set aside.

In a bowl, whisk together the pastry cream, double cream and rum. Place a spoonful of this cream into each of eight small ramekins, about 9 cm/3½ inches in diameter.

Reserve the eight best banana rounds for decoration, then divide the rest between the ramekins. Fill up the ramekins with the cream, smooth the surface with a palette knife and sprinkle the tops with the remaining caster sugar. Caramelize the sugar with a blowtorch or under a very hot salamander or grill. Place two ramekins on each plate and garnish each ramekin with a reserved banana round. Serve at once.

Michel Roux

WARM PEACH FEUILLETÉS

350 G/13 OZ QUICK PUFF PASTRY (PAGE 378)
150 G/5 OZ GRANULATED SUGAR
500 ML/16 FL OZ WATER
4 VERY RIPE PEACHES, SKINNED
EGGWASH (1 EGG WHITE MIXED WITH 1 TABLESPOON
   MILK)
40 G/1½ OZ ICING SUGAR
1 TABLESPOON GRENADINE SYRUP

SERVES 4

On a lightly floured work surface, roll out the pastry to about 5 mm/¼ inch thick. Using a 9 cm/3½ inch pastry cutter, cut out four circles and place them on a baking sheet lightly moistened with cold water. Chill for 20 minutes.

Place the granulated sugar and the water in a saucepan and bring to the boil over low heat, stirring occasionally until the sugar has dissolved. Add the peaches and poach until just tender. Using a slotted spoon, lift the peaches out of the syrup; reserve the syrup.

Preheat the oven to 220°C/425°F/Gas Mark 7. Brush the tops of the pastry circles with eggwash. Lightly press a 7 cm/2¾ inch pastry cutter on to the circles to mark out the lids. With the tip of a knife, score criss-crosses on the lids.

Bake the pastry circles in the oven for 10 minutes, then sprinkle them with the icing sugar and bake for another 2–3 minutes, until the sugar forms an attractive glaze.

Slide the pastry circles on to a wire rack. Run the tip of a knife around the marked lids and detach them carefully, lifting them off with the knife.

Put 85 ml/3 fl oz of the poaching syrup and the grenadine in a small saucepan and simmer over low heat until reduced by half.

Place a peach in each pastry case and put them on individual plates. Lightly coat the peaches with the reduced syrup and arrange the lids aslant at the edge of the pastry cases. Serve at once.

Carole Walter

GOLDEN APPLE CHEESECAKE

2 TABLESPOONS UNSALTED BUTTER

1.1 KG/2½ LB GOLDEN DELICIOUS
    APPLES, PEELED, CORED AND
    THINLY SLICED

2 TEASPOONS LEMON JUICE

275 G/10 OZ CASTER SUGAR

3 TABLESPOONS CALVADOS

675 G/1½ LB CREAM CHEESE, AT
    ROOM TEMPERATURE

2 TEASPOONS GRATED LEMON ZEST

1 TEASPOON VANILLA ESSENCE

250 ML/8 FL OZ SOUR CREAM

4 LARGE EGGS

2–3 TABLESPOONS APRICOT JAM,
    HEATED GENTLY WITH A LITTLE
    WATER, THEN RUBBED THROUGH
    A FINE SIEVE

CRUST

125 G/4 OZ GINGERNUT BISCUITS, FINELY GROUND

50 G/2 OZ FLAKED ALMONDS, LIGHTLY TOASTED

2 TABLESPOONS SUGAR

85 G/3 OZ UNSALTED BUTTER, MELTED AND COOLED

SERVES 10–12

For the crust, generously butter a 22 cm/9 inch springform tin. Place the gingernut crumbs, almonds and sugar in a food processor and chop finely. Blend in the melted butter. Press the crumbs on to the sides and base of the tin. Chill.

For the cake, melt the butter in a large frying pan. Add the apples, lemon juice and 125 g/4 oz of the sugar. Sauté the apples until tender. Add the Calvados and sauté for 1 minute. Leave to cool. Spread half of the apples over the crust.

Preheat the oven to 180°C/350°F/Gas Mark 4. Press a double thickness of foil around the bottom of the springform tin.

Using an electric mixer at low speed, combine the cream cheese, remaining sugar, lemon zest and vanilla. Add the sour cream, then the eggs, one at a time. Mix until smooth, then pour into the tin.

Bake for 55–60 minutes or until the centre is set. Leave on a rack to cool for 10 minutes. Spread the remaining apples on top and glaze with the warm apricot jam. Leave to cool completely before serving.

Michel Roux

TUTTI FRUTTI CHOUX PUFFS

100 G/3½ OZ WILD OR SMALL STRAWBERRIES
100 G/3½ OZ BILBERRIES
100 G/3½OZ REDCURRANTS
250 G/9 OZ CHOUX PASTE (½ QUANTITY, PAGE 379)
250 ML/8 FL OZ WHIPPING CREAM, CHILLED
40 G/1½ OZ ICING SUGAR, PLUS EXTRA FOR DUSTING
1 TEASPOON VANILLA ESSENCE

SERVES 4

Preheat the oven to 220°C/425°F/Gas Mark 7. If necessary, delicately wash and drain the fruit, then hull or top and tail.

Using a piping bag fitted with a plain nozzle, pipe four large choux puffs on to a baking sheet. Dip a fork into cold water and mark the tops lightly with the back of the fork, dipping it into cold water each time. This will help the pastry to develop evenly as it cooks. Bake the puffs for 20 minutes, reducing the oven temperature to 200°C/400°F/Gas Mark 6 after 10 minutes.

When the puffs are cooked, transfer them to a wire rack. Using a serrated knife, cut off a 'hat' four-fifths of the way up each puff.

In a bowl, whip the cream with the icing sugar and vanilla essence until it forms soft peaks. Fill a piping bag fitted with a fluted nozzle with this cream and pipe a small rosette into each puff. Pile a mixture of the fruits into the puffs, then pipe a band of cream around the puffs. Serve at once, or place in the refrigerator for no more than 1 hour before serving, dusted with icing sugar.

Michel Roux

HOT GRAND MARNIER SOUFFLÉS
with orange segments

25 G/1 OZ BUTTER, SOFTENED

175 G/6 OZ CASTER SUGAR

3 ORANGES, PEELED AND DIVIDED INTO SEGMENTS, ALL
   PITH AND MEMBRANE REMOVED

300 G/11 OZ PASTRY CREAM (PAGE 378)

3 TABLESPOONS GRAND MARNIER

8 EGG WHITES

4 SPRIGS OF MINT

2 TABLESPOONS ICING SUGAR

SERVES 4

Brush the insides of four small soufflé dishes, about 10 cm/4 inches in diameter, with the softened butter. Tip 25 g/1 oz of the caster sugar into one of the dishes and rotate it so that the interior is well coated with sugar. Tip the excess sugar into the next dish and repeat the process with all the dishes.

Preheat the oven to 190°C/375°F/Gas Mark 5 and put in a baking sheet to heat.

Reserve the eight best orange segments for the garnish and cut the remaining segments lengthways into three.

Put the pastry cream into a bowl, stand this in a bain-marie and warm gently. Whisk in the Grand Marnier.

Beat the egg whites with an electric mixer or by hand until half-risen, then add the remaining 150 g/5 oz of caster sugar and beat until the mixture forms soft peaks. Still using the whisk, fold one-third of the egg whites into the pastry cream, then very delicately fold in the rest of the whites, using a spatula.

Half-fill the soufflé dishes with the mixture, divide the cut orange segments between the dishes, then fill them up with soufflé mixture and smooth the surface with a palette knife. Using the tip of a knife, ease the mixture away from the edges of the dishes.

Stand the soufflé dishes on the heated baking sheet and cook in the oven for 7–8 minutes. As soon as they come out of the oven, arrange two of the reserved orange segments and a mint sprig on each soufflé and dust with icing sugar. Place each soufflé dish on a plate and serve immediately.

Jacki Passmore

BAKED COCONUT CUSTARD
(Songkaya)

375 ML/12 FL OZ COCONUT
   CREAM
5 LARGE EGGS
125 G/4 OZ SOFT BROWN SUGAR
40 G/1½ OZ DESICCATED
   COCONUT

SERVES 6–8

Preheat the oven to 180°C/350°F/Gas Mark 4.
Butter a 1.2 litre/2 pint ovenproof dish.

Combine the coconut cream, eggs, sugar and
coconut in a large bowl and place over a
saucepan of simmering water. Cook over
medium heat, whisking constantly, for about 10
minutes or until the custard has begun to
thicken.

Pour the custard into the buttered dish and
place the dish in a bain-marie or deep roasting
tin. Pour in warm water to come halfway up
the sides of the dish. Place in the preheated
oven for about 45 minutes or until the custard is
set.

To serve warm, sprinkle the surface with
brown sugar and glaze under a hot grill. Serve
with whipped cream. To serve cold, accompany
the custard with poached fruit or a fruit
compote.

Michel Roux

CHOCOLATE CRÈME BRÛLÉE

300 G/11 OZ BITTER COUVERTURE OR BEST-QUALITY
    PLAIN DARK CHOCOLATE (ABOUT 64% COCOA
    SOLIDS)
500 ML/16 FL OZ MILK
500 ML/16 FL OZ DOUBLE CREAM
3 TABLESPOONS LIQUID GLUCOSE
8 EGG YOLKS
150 G/5 OZ CASTER SUGAR

SERVES 8

Break the chocolate into a large bowl and sit the bowl over a saucepan half-filled with hot water. Leave to melt, stirring occasionally until smooth.

Place the milk, cream and liquid glucose in a saucepan and bring to the boil over low heat, whisking occasionally.

In a bowl, whisk the egg yolks with 50 g/2 oz of the sugar until just pale.

Whisking continuously, pour the boiling milk mixture on to the melted chocolate. When it is thoroughly combined, pour the mixture on to the egg yolk mixture, whisking all the time.

Preheat the oven to 90°C/195°F/Gas Mark ¼. Divide the chocolate cream mixture between eight gratin dishes, about 15 cm/6 inches in diameter, and cook for 40 minutes or until just set. Slide the dishes on to a wire rack and leave to cool at room temperature. Place in the refrigerator for a very short time.

Just before serving, sprinkle 2 teaspoons caster sugar evenly over each crème brûlée and caramelize with a blowtorch or under a very hot salamander or grill. Place each one on a plate and serve at once.

The contrast between the warm, crunchy topping and the lightly chilled cream is delicious. To reach the cream you will need to tap the top sharply with a spoon to crack it open, as shown in the picture.

Michel Roux

SURPRISE ORANGE PANCAKES

150 G/5 OZ FLOUR

25 G/1 OZ CASTER SUGAR

PINCH OF SALT

2 EGGS

300 ML/½ PINT MILK

6 TABLESPOONS DOUBLE CREAM

CLARIFIED BUTTER FOR COOKING THE PANCAKES

400 G/14 OZ PASTRY CREAM (PAGE 378)

GRATED ZEST AND JUICE OF 2 ORANGES, JUICE
   SIMMERED UNTIL REDUCED BY HALF

40 G/1½ OZ ICING SUGAR

SERVES 6

Sift the flour into a bowl and mix in the caster sugar and salt. Lightly whisk in the eggs, then the milk, a little at a time. When the mixture is thoroughly combined, stir in the cream, cover with clingfilm and leave the batter to rest for at least 1 hour.

Heat a frying pan, about 30 cm/12 inches in diameter, and brush it with a little clarified butter. Add a ladleful of batter, quickly swirl it around to cover the base of the pan, and cook the pancake for 30 seconds, then turn it over with a palette knife and cook on the other side for 30 seconds. Make more pancakes in this way until all the batter is used; there should be 12 pancakes in all.

Using a whisk, mix the pastry cream with the orange zest and juice. Spread a spoonful of this mixture over each pancake and roll them up. Arrange the filled pancakes on a baking sheet and sprinkle with icing sugar. Glaze them under a very hot salamander or grill, then place two pancakes on each plate, lifting them with a palette knife. Serve at once.

Michel Roux

APPLE HEDGEHOG

600 ML/1 PINT APPLE JUICE

8 EGG YOLKS

70 G/2½ OZ CASTER SUGAR

6 GELATINE LEAVES, SOAKED IN COLD WATER, THEN
  WELL DRAINED

4 TABLESPOONS CALVADOS

12 TABLESPOONS APPLE PURÉE

300 ML/½ PINT WHIPPING CREAM AND 85 G/3 OZ
  ICING SUGAR, WHIPPED TO SOFT PEAKS

APPLE CRISPS

4 DESSERT APPLES, NOT TOO RIPE

40 G/1½ OZ CASTER SUGAR

40 G/1½ OZ ICING SUGAR

SERVES 6

Pour the apple juice into a saucepan and simmer to reduce by one-third.

In a bowl, whisk the egg yolks with the caster sugar to a light ribbon consistency. Still whisking, pour the boiling apple juice on to the mixture. Return this to the saucepan and cook over very low heat, without boiling, stirring continuously with a wooden spoon until the custard is thick enough to coat the back of the spoon. Off the heat, stir in the drained gelatine, then pass the custard through a sieve into a bowl. Set aside, stirring from time to time. When almost cold, use a whisk to fold in the Calvados, apple purée and whipped cream. Divide between six moulds, about 10 cm/4 inches in diameter, and place in the freezer for 1 hour, or in the refrigerator for 4 hours, until the mousses are set but not too firm.

Preheat the oven to 180°C/350°F/Gas Mark 4. For the apple crisps, halve the apples horizontally and use a plain 3 cm/1¼ inch diameter pastry cutter to cut around the core to make cylinders of apple, leaving behind the core and pips. Cut the cylinders into the thinnest possible discs. Spread the discs over a greased baking sheet and sprinkle each with a pinch of caster sugar. Cook for 8 minutes, then turn them over one at a time and cook for a further 4 minutes. Transfer to a wire rack.

Briefly dip the base of each mould into very hot water. With your fingertips, lightly push one side of the mousse and invert the mould on to a serving plate. Poke the apple crisps into the mousses to resemble hedgehog spines and dust with a little icing sugar. Serve at once.

Jill Dupleix

MACADAMIA NUT TART

SHORTCRUST PASTRY
300 G/11 OZ MACADAMIA NUTS

4 EGGS

225 G/8 OZ SOFT BROWN SUGAR

175 ML/6 FL OZ LIGHT CORN SYRUP (LIQUID GLUCOSE)

3 TABLESPOONS MELTED BUTTER

1 TEASPOON VANILLA ESSENCE

SERVES 8

Roll out the pastry to about 3 mm/⅛ inch thick and use to line a buttered 25 cm/10 inch round flan tin. Place in the refrigerator and chill for 30 minutes.

Preheat the oven to 180°C/350°F/Gas Mark 4. Prick the base of the pastry, line with a circle of greaseproof paper and fill with baking beans. Bake for about 12–15 minutes or until the pastry is almost cooked but not browned.

Discard the paper and baking beans and fill the pastry case with macadamia nuts. Increase the oven temperature to 200°C /400°F/Gas Mark 6.

Beat the eggs and add the sugar, corn syrup, butter and vanilla. Mix well, then pour over the nuts and bake for 10 minutes.

Reduce the oven temperature to 180°C/350°F/Gas Mark 4 and bake for 40 minutes or until completely set. If the edge of the pastry edge is browning too quickly, cover it with foil. Leave in the oven to cool completely before serving, which will help it to become firm.

Michel Roux

RASPBERRY ICE CREAM

400 G/14 OZ FRESH OR FROZEN RASPBERRIES

100 ML/3½ FL OZ COLD WATER

200 G/7 OZ CASTER SUGAR

JUICE OF 2 LEMONS

3 TABLESPOONS RASPBERRY EAU-DE-VIE OR KIRSCH
  (OPTIONAL)

300 ML/½ PINT DOUBLE CREAM, WHIPPED TO A
  RIBBON CONSISTENCY

SERVES 6

Purée the raspberries with the water in a liquidizer for 2 minutes. Pass the purée through a wire-mesh conical sieve into a large bowl, rubbing and pushing it through with the back of a ladle.

Add the sugar to the resulting raspberry juice, then add the lemon juice and eau-de-vie or kirsch, if using, and whisk together. Fold in the cream, transfer the mixture to an ice-cream maker and churn for about 15 minutes or until the ice cream is velvety and half-frozen. Transfer to a bowl and freeze, or serve immediately.

Blackberries can be substituted for the raspberries.

cakes
and
cookies

Carole Walter

DOUBLE CHOCOLATE CAKE
with dates and walnuts

175 G/6 OZ DATES, COARSELY CHOPPED

250 ML/8 FL OZ BOILING WATER

1 TEASPOON BICARBONATE OF SODA

200 G/7 OZ PLAIN FLOUR

1½ TABLESPOONS UNSWEETENED COCOA POWDER, SIFTED

½ TEASPOON SALT

225 G/8 OZ UNSALTED BUTTER, AT ROOM TEMPERATURE

200 G/7 OZ CASTER SUGAR

2 LARGE EGGS

1 TEASPOON VANILLA ESSENCE

125 G/4 OZ WALNUTS, CHOPPED INTO APPROXIMATELY 5 MM/¼ INCH PIECES

125 G/4 OZ PLAIN CHOCOLATE DROPS

SERVES 12–16

Preheat the oven to 180°C/350°F/Gas Mark 4. Butter a 33 x 22 cm/13 x 9 inch baking tin, 5 cm/2 inches deep.

Place the dates, boiling water and bicarbonate of soda in a food processor and process for about 5–10 seconds or until fairly smooth and thick.

Sift the flour, cocoa powder and salt together.

Using an electric mixer, cream the butter until very light, then add the sugar, 1 tablespoon at a time, beating until pale and fluffy. Add the eggs, one at a time, beating well after each addition, then beat in the vanilla essence.

Fold in the flour mixture alternately with the puréed dates, beginning and ending with flour. Spoon the mixture into the prepared tin and spread evenly. Sprinkle the walnuts and chocolate drops over the top.

Bake for 40–45 minutes or until a small skewer inserted into the centre comes out clean. Leave the cake to cool in the tin. Serve cut into squares.

Carole Walter

BUTTERMILK POUND CAKE

250 G/9 OZ PLAIN FLOUR

1 TEASPOON BAKING POWDER

½ TEASPOON BICARBONATE OF SODA

¼ TEASPOON GROUND MACE

¼ TEASPOON SALT

175 G/6 OZ UNSALTED BUTTER, AT ROOM
　　TEMPERATURE

1 TEASPOON GRATED ORANGE ZEST

250 G/9 OZ CASTER SUGAR

3 LARGE EGGS, SEPARATED

1 TEASPOON VANILLA ESSENCE

250 ML/8 FL OZ BUTTERMILK

¼ TEASPOON CREAM OF TARTAR

ICING SUGAR, FOR DUSTING

SERVES 8–10

Preheat the oven to 180°C/350°F/Gas Mark 4.
Butter a 24 cm/9½ inch kugelhopf tin or a 24
cm/9½ inch round, 8 cm/3 inch deep cake tin
(a kugelhopf tin will mean the cake cooks more
evenly). Dust the tin with flour; shake out any
excess flour.

Sift the flour, baking powder, bicarbonate of
soda, mace and salt together three times.

Using an electric mixer on medium speed,
cream the butter with the orange zest. Beating
continuously, gradually add 175 g/6 oz of the
sugar, taking 4–6 minutes to incorporate it. Add
the egg yolks, one at a time, beating well after
each addition, then beat in the vanilla essence.

Fold in the flour mixture alternately with the
buttermilk, beginning and ending with flour.

In a clean bowl, whisk the egg whites until
frothy. Add the cream of tartar and beat until
soft peaks form. Gradually add the remaining
sugar, beating well to form a soft meringue.
Fold a quarter of the meringue into the cake
mixture, then gently fold in the remaining
meringue. Spoon into the cake tin and smooth
the top.

Bake for 55–60 minutes or until golden
brown and coming away from the sides of the
tin. Leave the tin on a cooling rack for about 20
minutes, then turn out the cake. Serve dusted
with icing sugar.

Elinor Klivans
COCONUT BUTTER BALLS

125 G/4 OZ UNSALTED BUTTER, SOFTENED

50 G/2 OZ CASTER SUGAR

1 LARGE EGG, SEPARATED

1 TEASPOON VANILLA ESSENCE

¼ TEASPOON ALMOND ESSENCE

1 TEASPOON GRATED LEMON ZEST

2 TEASPOONS LEMON JUICE

125 G/4 OZ PLAIN FLOUR

85 G/3 OZ DESICCATED COCONUT

24 GLACÉ CHERRY HALVES

MAKES ABOUT 24 COOKIES

Preheat the oven to 150°C/300°F/Gas Mark 2. Butter a baking sheet.

Using an electric mixer, cream the butter with the sugar until very light and smooth. Add the egg yolk, vanilla and almond essence, lemon zest and lemon juice and beat until smooth. Add the flour and mix until a dough forms.

Roll a rounded teaspoon of dough between the palms of your hands to form a 2.5 cm/1 inch ball, and repeat until all the dough is used.

Beat the egg white with a fork until foamy. Dip the balls of dough in egg white to coat evenly. Roll the balls in the coconut and place 4 cm/1½ inches apart on the baking sheet. Press a cherry half into the centre of each ball. Bake for about 35 minutes or until the coconut is golden brown.

Leave to cool on the baking sheet for 5 minutes, then transfer to a wire rack to cool completely.

Carole Walter

LEMON SPIRAL
with cream filling

5 LARGE EGGS, SEPARATED

150 G/5 OZ CASTER SUGAR

2 TABLESPOONS LEMON JUICE

1½ TEASPOONS GRATED LEMON ZEST

70 G/2½ OZ PLAIN FLOUR, SIFTED

½ TEASPOON CREAM OF TARTAR

⅛ TEASPOON SALT

3 TABLESPOONS ICING SUGAR, PLUS EXTRA FOR
   DUSTING

FILLING

150 G/5 OZ CASTER SUGAR

25 G/1 OZ PLAIN FLOUR

4 TABLESPOONS LEMON JUICE

1 EGG, LIGHTLY BEATEN

1 TABLESPOON GRATED LEMON ZEST

300 ML/1⁄2 PINT DOUBLE CREAM, WHIPPED UNTIL
   THICK

SERVES 10–12

Preheat the oven to 180°C/350°F/Gas Mark 4.
Butter the base of a 43 x 28 cm/17 x 11 inch
baking tin, 2.5 cm/1 inch deep. Line with
nonstick baking paper.

Using an electric mixer on medium speed,
beat the egg yolks until very pale. Gradually add
the caster sugar, beat until thick, then add the
lemon juice and zest. Fold in the flour.

In a separate bowl, beat the egg whites until
frothy. Add the cream of tartar and beat until
firm peaks form. Fold a quarter of the whites
into the cake mixture, then gently fold in the
remaining whites. Pour into the prepared tin.

Bake for 15 minutes or until golden brown.
Release the edges with a knife. Invert on to a
large sheet of nonstick baking paper dusted with
the icing sugar. Peel off the lining paper and roll
up the warm cake in the fresh paper. Leave to
cool on a cooling rack, seam side down.

For the filling, combine all the ingredients,
except the cream, in a bowl. Place over a
saucepan of simmering water and cook, stirring
occasionally, for 15 minutes or until thick.Cool.
Fold in the whipped cream in three additions.
Unroll the cake, spread with two-thirds of the
lemon cream and re-roll. To serve, decorate
with the remaining lemon cream and dust with
icing sugar.

Carole Walter

FUDGE-NUT CANDY CAKE

125 G/4 OZ GOOD-QUALITY PLAIN CHOCOLATE,
FINELY CHOPPED

375 ML/12 FL OZ MILK

1 TABLESPOON INSTANT ESPRESSO COFFEE POWDER,
DISSOLVED IN 1 TEASPOON BOILING WATER

275 G/10 OZ PLAIN FLOUR

2 TEASPOONS BAKING POWDER

½ TEASPOON BICARBONATE OF SODA

½ TEASPOON SALT

175 G/6 OZ UNSALTED BUTTER, AT ROOM
TEMPERATURE

425 G/15 OZ CASTER SUGAR

3 LARGE EGGS

1 TEASPOON VANILLA ESSENCE

FUDGE-NUT CANDY ICING (PAGE 379)

SERVES 12–14

Preheat the oven to 180°C/350°F/Gas Mark 4.
Butter two 22 cm/9 inch round cake tins and
line the bases with nonstick baking paper.

In a saucepan over low heat, melt the
chocolate in half of the milk, stirring until
smooth. Cool to tepid. Add the dissolved coffee
to the remaining milk. Sift the flour, baking
powder, bicarbonate of soda and salt together
three times.

Using an electric mixer, cream the butter
until very light. Gradually add the sugar, taking
6–8 minutes to incorporate it. Add the eggs,
one at a time, beating well, then add the
chocolate mixture and the vanilla essence.

Fold in the flour mixture alternately with the
coffee flavoured milk, beginning and ending
with flour. Divide the mixture between the two
tins.

Bake for 35–40 minutes or until firm to the
touch and coming away from the sides of the
tins. Leave the tins on a cooling rack for 15
minutes, then turn out, remove the baking
paper and leave to cool completely before filling
and icing.

Carole Walter

CHOCOLATE RASPBERRY TORTE

85 G/3 OZ PLAIN FLOUR

3 TABLESPOONS UNSWEETENED COCOA POWDER

3 TABLESPOONS CORNFLOUR

5 LARGE EGGS

200 G/7 OZ CASTER SUGAR

1 TEASPOON VANILLA ESSENCE

3 TABLESPOONS VEGETABLE OIL

300 ML/10 FL OZ WATER

2 TABLESPOONS CREME DE FRAMBOISE (RASPBERRY
LIQUEUR)

RASPBERRY VELVET BUTTERCREAM (PAGE 379)

CHOCOLATE SHAVINGS (PAGE 379)

FRESH RASPBERRIES (OPTIONAL)

SERVES 12–14

Preheat the oven to 180°C/350°F/Gas Mark 4. Generously butter a 25 cm/10 inch round, 5 cm/2 inch deep cake tin and dust with flour. Shake out any excess flour.

Sift the flour, cocoa and cornflour together three times.

In a mixer bowl, mix the eggs with 150 g/5 oz of the sugar. Heat over a saucepan of gently simmering water, then remove from the heat and beat with an electric mixer on high speed for 5 minutes or until thick. Reduce the speed to medium, add the vanilla essence and beat for a further 3 minutes.

Sift the flour mixture over the egg foam in six additions, folding in lightly with a large spatula.

Transfer a quarter of the mixture to a separate bowl. Drizzle in the oil while folding quickly. Fold the two mixtures together and pour into the prepared tin.

Bake for 30–35 minutes or until coming away from the sides of the tin. Invert on to a rack, remove the tin and leave to cool.

In a small saucepan, bring the water and remaining sugar to the boil; simmer briefly. Remove from the heat and add the liqueur.

Split the cake into three layers. Place the bottom layer on a cardboard circle. Brush generously with warm syrup, then spread with the raspberry buttercream. Repeat the layering twice, then coat the sides and top of the cake with the remaining buttercream. Decorate with chocolate shavings and fresh raspberries, if these are available.

Carole Walter

BANANA HAZELNUT TEA LOAF

200 G/7 OZ PLAIN FLOUR

1 TEASPOON BAKING POWDER

½ TEASPOON BICARBONATE OF SODA

½ TEASPOON SALT

100 G/3½ OZ HAZELNUTS, LIGHTLY TOASTED, THEN
  LEFT UNTIL COLD

2–3 SMALL RIPE BANANAS

4 TABLESPOONS ORANGE JUICE

1 TEASPOON VANILLA ESSENCE

2 LARGE EGGS

150 G/5 OZ CASTER SUGAR

125 ML/4 FL OZ SUNFLOWER OIL

85 G/3 OZ ICING SUGAR, SIFTED

¼ TEASPOON VANILLA ESSENCE

SERVES 8–10

Preheat the oven to 180°C/350°F/Gas Mark 4. Butter a 22 x 12 x 8 cm/9 x 5 x 3 inch loaf tin and line the base with nonstick baking paper.

Process the flour, baking powder, bicarbonate of soda, salt and hazelnuts for 15–20 seconds or until the nuts are chopped into small pieces.

Purée the bananas in the food processor, then measure the purée; you need 150 ml/5 fl oz. Stir in the orange juice and vanilla.

Using an electric mixer on medium-high speed, beat the eggs until foamy. Add the sugar, 1 tablespoon at a time. Still beating, slowly pour in the oil. Fold in the dry ingredients alternately with the banana mixture, beginning and ending with flour. Spoon the mixture into the loaf tin.

Bake for 50–55 minutes or until a small skewer inserted into the centre comes out clean. Leave the cake in the tin for 15 minutes, then turn out and remove the baking paper.

Meanwhile, in a small bowl, beat the icing sugar with 1 tablespoon boiling water and the vanilla essence until smooth. Drizzle this over the warm cake.

Carole Walter

MARBLE KUGELHOPF

40 G/1½ OZ FLAKED ALMONDS
285 G/10½ OZ PLAIN FLOUR
2 TEASPOONS BAKING POWDER
½ TEASPOON SALT
285 G/10½ OZ UNSALTED BUTTER, AT ROOM
   TEMPERATURE
¼ TEASPOON GRATED LEMON ZEST
¼ TEASPOON GRATED ORANGE ZEST
135 G/4½ OZ ICING SUGAR, SIFTED
6 LARGE EGGS, SEPARATED
2 TEASPOONS VANILLA ESSENCE
200 G/7 OZ CASTER SUGAR
2 TABLESPOONS UNSWEETENED COCOA POWDER
2 TABLESPOONS VEGETABLE OIL
85 G/3 OZ ICING SUGAR, SIFTED
¼ TEASPOON VANILLA ESSENCE

SERVES 8–10

Preheat the oven to 180°C/350°F/Gas Mark 4. Generously butter a 24 cm/9½ inch kugelhopf tin and sprinkle with the almonds. Sift the flour, baking powder and salt together three times.

Using an electric mixer, cream the butter with the lemon and orange zests. Add the icing sugar in four additions, beating well. Beat in the egg yolks, two at a time. Beat in the vanilla essence.

In a separate bowl, beat the egg whites until soft peaks form. Beat in the caster sugar, 2 tablespoons at a time, to form a soft meringue. Fold the meringue and flour alternately into the creamed mixture, beginning and ending with the meringue.

Place just over one third of the mixture in a separate bowl. Combine the cocoa and oil and fold into the mixture.

Place alternate layers of the vanilla and chocolate mixture in the tin, beginning and ending with vanilla, and smooth the top.

Bake for 60–65 minutes or until golden brown and coming away from the sides of the tin. Leave to cool in the tin for 15 minutes, then turn out on to a cooling rack.

Meanwhile, in a small bowl, beat the icing sugar with 1 tablespoon boiling water and the vanilla essence until smooth. Drizzle this over the warm cake.

Carole Walter
SNOWFLAKE LAYER CAKE

325 G/12 OZ PLAIN FLOUR

4 TEASPOONS BAKING POWDER

½ TEASPOON SALT

175 ML/6 FL OZ MILK

125 ML/4 FL OZ WATER

225 G/8 OZ UNSALTED BUTTER, AT ROOM
  TEMPERATURE

325 G/12 OZ CASTER SUGAR

1 LARGE EGG

1½ TEASPOONS VANILLA ESSENCE

1 TEASPOON COCONUT ESSENCE

5 LARGE EGG WHITES

½ TEASPOON CREAM OF TARTAR

VELVET BUTTERCREAM (PAGE 379)

200 G/7 OZ DESICCATED COCONUT

SERVES 12–14

Preheat the oven to 180°C/350°F/Gas Mark 4.
Butter two 22 cm/9 inch round, 5 cm/2 inch
deep cake tins and line the bases of the tins with
nonstick baking paper. Sift the flour, baking
power and salt together three times. Mix the
milk with the water.

Using an electric mixer on medium speed,
cream the butter until very light. Gradually add
225 g/8 oz of the sugar, taking 6–8 minutes to
incorporate it. Beat in the egg, then the vanilla
and coconut essences.

Fold in the flour mixture alternately with the
milk and water, beginning and ending with
flour mixture.

Whisk the egg whites until frothy. Add the
cream of tartar and beat until soft peaks form.
Add the remaining sugar, 1 tablespoon at a
time, beating to form a soft meringue. Fold into
the cake mixture and divide the mixture
between the prepared tins.

Bake for 30–35 minutes or until golden
brown and coming away from the sides of the
tins. Leave in the tins on a cooling rack for 15
minutes, then turn out and remove the nonstick
baking paper.

Leave to cool completely, then fill and coat
with velvet buttercream and cover with the
desiccated coconut.

Elinor Klivans

MOCHA SHORTBREAD FINGERS
dipped in chocolate

200 G/7 OZ PLAIN FLOUR

25 G/1 OZ CORNFLOUR

½ TEASPOON BAKING POWDER

¼ TEASPOON SALT

225 G/8 OZ UNSALTED BUTTER, SOFTENED

1 TABLESPOON INSTANT COFFEE GRANULES DISSOLVED
    IN 2 TEASPOONS WATER

150 G/5 OZ ICING SUGAR

225 G/8 OZ GOOD-QUALITY PLAIN CHOCOLATE,
    MELTED (PAGE 379)

MAKES 30–40 COOKIES

Preheat the oven to 150°C/300°F/Gas Mark 2. Sift the flour, cornflour, baking powder and salt together. Set aside.

Using an electric mixer, cream the butter with the dissolved coffee. Add the icing sugar and beat until smooth. Add the flour mixture and mix until a dough forms.

Transfer the dough to greaseproof paper and press out to a 20 x 30 cm/8 x 12 inch rectangle, about 1 cm/½ inch thick. Cut into strips about 2 x 6 cm/¾ x 2½ inches. Lift the strips from the paper and place them 2.5 cm/1 inch apart on two ungreased baking sheets. Bake for 30 minutes.

Leave to cool on the baking sheets for 10 minutes, then transfer to wire racks to cool completely.

Dip the shortbread ends in melted chocolate and remove excess chocolate by dragging the bottoms over the edge of a bowl. Leave on wire racks until the chocolate sets.

Elinor Klivans

TOASTED ALMOND CRESCENTS

125 G/4 OZ PLAIN FLOUR

½ TEASPOON SALT

125 G/4 OZ UNSALTED BUTTER, SOFTENED

85 G/3 OZ ICING SUGAR, SIFTED

½ TEASPOON VANILLA ESSENCE

½ TEASPOON ALMOND ESSENCE

50 G/2 OZ TOASTED ALMONDS, FINELY CHOPPED

MAKES 24 COOKIES

Preheat the oven to 160°C/325°F/Gas Mark 3. Sift the flour and salt together. Set aside.

Using an electric mixer, cream the butter with 25 g/1 oz of the icing sugar until smooth. Mix in the vanilla and almond essence and the toasted almonds, then add the flour mixture and mix until a dough forms.

Taking about 2 teaspoons of dough at a time, form into 6 cm/2½ inch long cylinders. Taper the ends and curve into crescent shapes. Place the crescents 2.5 cm/1 inch apart on an ungreased baking sheet. Bake for about 25 minutes or until the ends and bottoms of the cookies are golden.

Transfer to a wire rack and leave to cool for 15 minutes.

Sift the remaining icing sugar into a bowl. Roll the cookies in the sugar until they are evenly coated (you will not use all of the sugar). Return the cookies to the wire rack to cool completely.

Elinor Klivans

ORANGE CHOCOLATE PINWHEELS

125 G/4 OZ PLAIN FLOUR

¼ TEASPOON BAKING POWDER

⅛ TEASPOON SALT

125 G/4 OZ UNSALTED BUTTER, SOFTENED

125 G/4 OZ CASTER SUGAR

1 LARGE EGG, SEPARATED

1 TEASPOON VANILLA ESSENCE

1 TEASPOON GRATED ORANGE ZEST

50 G/2 OZ GOOD-QUALITY PLAIN CHOCOLATE,
    MELTED (PAGE 379)

2 TEASPOONS UNSWEETENED COCOA POWDER, SIFTED

MAKES 40 COOKIES

Sift the flour, baking powder and salt together. Set aside.

Using an electric mixer, cream the butter and sugar. Mix in the egg yolk and vanilla. Add the flour mixture and mix until a dough forms. Cut the dough in half; flavour half with the orange zest, half with the chocolate and cocoa. Form each piece into a 12 cm/5 inch disc, wrap and refrigerate until firm, about 2 hours.

Roll out each piece of dough on greaseproof paper to form a 12 x 25 cm/5 x 10 inch rectangle. Beat the egg white until foamy, then brush over the orange dough. Press the chocolate dough on top. Trim the edges, then roll up the two layers to form a tight cylinder. Refrigerate until firm.

Preheat the oven to 190°C/ 375°F/Gas Mark 5. Butter two baking sheets. Cut the cylinder into 5 mm/¼ inch rounds and place 2.5 cm/1 inch apart on the baking sheets. Bake for about 13 minutes or until the edges are light golden, then transfer to wire racks to cool.

Elinor Klivans

OATMEAL RAISIN CRISPS

125 G/4 OZ PLAIN FLOUR
½ TEASPOON BAKING POWDER
½ TEASPOON BICARBONATE OF SODA
½ TEASPOON SALT
1 TEASPOON GROUND CINNAMON
125 G/4 OZ UNSALTED BUTTER, SOFTENED
125 G/4 OZ CASTER SUGAR
125 G/4 OZ LIGHT BROWN SUGAR
1 LARGE EGG
2 TABLESPOONS GOLDEN SYRUP
1 TEASPOON VANILLA ESSENCE
150 G/5 OZ MEDIUM OATMEAL
150 G/5 OZ RAISINS

MAKES 24 COOKIES

Preheat the oven to 180°C/350°F/Gas Mark 4. Butter two baking sheets. Sift the flour, baking powder, bicarbonate of soda, salt and cinnamon together. Set aside.

Using an electric mixer, cream the butter with the caster sugar and brown sugar until very light and smooth. Beat in the egg, golden syrup and vanilla essence, then the flour mixture. Stir in the oatmeal and raisins.

Drop rounded tablespoons of the mixture, 5 cm/2 inches apart, on the prepared baking sheets. Bake for about 15 minutes or until the cookies are golden brown.

Leave to cool on the baking sheets for 5 minutes, then transfer to wire racks to cool completely.

Elinor Klivans

LACE COOKIES

with pistachio and white chocolate

85 G/3 OZ UNSALTED BUTTER

65 G/2½ OZ CASTER SUGAR

3 TABLESPOONS GOLDEN SYRUP

40 G/1½ OZ PLAIN FLOUR

125 G/4 OZ SHELLED, UNSALTED PISTACHIO NUTS,
  COARSELY CHOPPED

¼ TEASPOON GROUND CINNAMON

1 TEASPOON VANILLA ESSENCE

½ TEASPOON ALMOND ESSENCE

1 TABLESPOON VEGETABLE OIL

175 G/6 OZ WHITE CHOCOLATE, MELTED (PAGE 379)

MAKES 36 COOKIES

Preheat the oven to 180°C/350°F/Gas Mark 4. Line three baking sheets with strong foil and butter the foil.

Put the butter, sugar and golden syrup into a saucepan and heat until the butter melts and the sugar dissolves. Bring to the boil, stirring constantly, and boil for 30 seconds. Remove from the heat and stir in the flour, then the chopped pistachio nuts, cinnamon, vanilla and almond essence.

Drop teaspoons of the mixture, 8 cm/3 inches apart, on to the prepared baking sheets. Bake for about 10 minutes or until the cookies are evenly golden (reverse the baking sheets after 5 minutes to ensure even browning).

Leave to cool on the baking sheets for 10 minutes, then lift the cookies from the foil on to wire racks to cool completely.

Stir the oil into the melted chocolate. Drizzle the chocolate over the cookies.

Elinor Klivans

STRAWBERRY SANDWICH HEARTS

175 G/6 OZ PLAIN FLOUR

175 G/6 OZ COLD, UNSALTED BUTTER, CUT INTO
  SMALL PIECES

4–5 TABLESPOONS ICED WATER

1 LARGE EGG WHITE

2 TABLESPOONS CASTER SUGAR

3 TABLESPOONS STRAWBERRY JAM

MAKES 18 HEARTS

Preheat the oven to 200°C/400°F/Gas Mark 6. Line two baking sheets with nonstick baking paper.

Using an electric mixer on low speed, mix the flour and butter until pea-sized pieces form. Gradually add the water, until the dough holds together and comes away from the sides of the bowl. Form the dough into two discs, about 10 cm/4 inches in diameter. Wrap and refrigerate until firm, about 15 minutes.

Roll out the dough to about 3 mm/⅛ inch thick. Cut out hearts using a 6 cm/2½ inch heart-shaped cutter. Press the scraps together, roll out and cut out further hearts – you should have 36 hearts. Place 2 cm/¾ inch apart on the baking sheets. Brush with egg white and sprinkle with sugar. Bake for about 15 minutes, reversing the sheets after 6 minutes, until the bottoms of the cookies are golden. Transfer to wire racks to cool.

Spread jam on the bottom of 18 cookies and press the remaining cookies on top, bottom side down.

Elinor Klivans

BUTTERSCOTCH BROWNIES
with marble topping

175 G/6 OZ PLAIN FLOUR

1 TEASPOON BAKING POWDER

¼ TEASPOON SALT

150 G/5 OZ UNSALTED BUTTER, SOFTENED

250 G/9 OZ LIGHT BROWN SUGAR

1 TEASPOON VANILLA ESSENCE

2 LARGE EGGS

85 G/3 OZ GOOD-QUALITY PLAIN CHOCOLATE,
   MELTED (PAGE 379)

MAKES 16 BROWNIES

Preheat the oven to 180°C/350°F/Gas Mark 4. Butter a 22 cm/9 inch square cake tin, 5 cm/2 inches deep.

Sift the flour, baking powder and salt together. Set aside.

Using an electric mixer, cream the butter with the brown sugar and vanilla essence until smooth. Mix in the eggs, then the flour mixture. Spread the mixture in the prepared tin.

Drizzle the melted chocolate over the top. Run a knife through the chocolate to create a marbled effect. Bake for 30–35 minutes or until a small skewer inserted into the centre comes out clean.

Leave to cool in the tin. Cut into 16 brownies.

Elinor Klivans

LEMON CRUMBLE BARS

225 G/8 OZ PLAIN FLOUR
25 G/1 OZ ICING SUGAR, PLUS EXTRA, FOR DUSTING
175 G/6 OZ LIGHT BROWN SUGAR
175 G/6 OZ COLD, UNSALTED BUTTER, CUT INTO
   SMALL PIECES

LEMON FILLING

3 LARGE EGGS
200 G/7 OZ CASTER SUGAR
85 ML/3 FL OZ LEMON JUICE
2 TEASPOONS GRATED LEMON ZEST
25 G/1 OZ PLAIN FLOUR

MAKES 20–30 BARS

Preheat the oven to 180°C/350°F/Gas Mark 4.
Butter and flour a 22 cm/9 inch square cake tin,
5 cm/2 inches deep.

Using an electric mixer, mix the flour, icing
sugar, brown sugar and butter until pea-sized
crumbs form. Press half of the crumbs into the
bottom of the prepared tin and bake for 15
minutes.

To make the lemon filling, whisk the eggs,
sugar, lemon juice and lemon zest until smooth.
Add the flour and whisk again until smooth.
Pour the lemon filling over the partly baked
crust and bake for 20 minutes.

Sprinkle the reserved crumble mixture over
the filling and bake for a further 20 minutes.

Leave to cool in the tin. Dust with icing
sugar and cut into 20–30 bars.

Carole Walter

CINNAMON ANGEL CAKE
with almond crust

70 G/2½ OZ PLAIN FLOUR

1½ TEASPOONS GROUND CINNAMON

¼ TEASPOON BAKING POWDER

200 G/7 OZ CASTER SUGAR

8 LARGE EGG WHITES, AT ROOM TEMPERATURE

1 TEASPOON CREAM OF TARTAR

¼ TEASPOON SALT

1 TEASPOON VANILLA ESSENCE

¼ TEASPOON ALMOND ESSENCE

ALMOND CRUST

2 SMALL EGG WHITES

2½ TABLESPOONS CASTER SUGAR

125 G/4 OZ FLAKED ALMONDS (PREFERABLY
　　UNBLANCHED), CRUMBLED

½ TEASPOON GROUND CINNAMON

SERVES 12–14

Preheat the oven to 180°C/350°F/Gas Mark 4. Use an ungreased 22 cm/9 inch angel food (funnelled) tin or a 22 cm/9 inch round, 8 cm/3 inch deep cake tin. Line the base with nonstick baking paper.

Sift the flour, cinnamon, baking powder and 85 g/3 oz of the sugar together four times.

Using an electric mixer, beat the egg whites until frothy. Add the cream of tartar, salt, vanilla and almond essences and beat until soft peaks form. Gradually beat in the remaining sugar, taking 2 minutes to incorporate it.

Sift the flour mixture over the egg whites in five or six additions, folding in quickly. Turn the mixture into the tin. Circle the mixture twice with a knife to remove air pockets. Smooth the top.

Bake for 40–45 minutes or until the top feels dry. Invert on to four ramekins to support the rim of the tin, allowing air to circulate underneath; do not remove the tin until the cake is cool.

Turn the tin right-side up; shake gently to unmould the cake. Place the cake top side up on a lightly greased baking sheet. Preheat the oven to 160°C/325°F/Gas Mark 3.

For the crust, whisk the egg whites until foamy. Gradually add 1½ tablespoons of the sugar. Stir in the almonds. Spread over the cake. Sprinkle with the cinnamon mixed with the remaining sugar. Bake for 20 minutes or until light brown.

Elinor Klivans

GINGER SQUARES
with cream cheese frosting

225 G/8 OZ PLAIN FLOUR

1 TEASPOON BAKING POWDER

½ TEASPOON BICARBONATE OF SODA

½ TEASPOON SALT

2 TEASPOONS GROUND GINGER

1 TEASPOON GROUND CINNAMON

¼ TEASPOON GROUND CLOVES

125 G/4 OZ UNSALTED BUTTER, SOFTENED

325 G/12 OZ LIGHT BROWN SUGAR

2 LARGE EGGS

4 TABLESPOONS GOLDEN SYRUP

175 G/6 OZ CHOPPED DATES

CREAM CHEESE FROSTING

175 G/6 OZ SOFT CREAM CHEESE

85 G/3 OZ UNSALTED BUTTER, SOFTENED

1 TEASPOON VANILLA ESSENCE

325 G/12 OZ ICING SUGAR

2 TABLESPOONS CHOPPED CRYSTALLIZED GINGER

MAKES 36 SQUARES

Preheat the oven to 180°C/350°F/Gas Mark 4. Butter a 22 cm/9 inch square cake tin, 5 cm/2 inches deep. Sift the flour, baking powder, bicarbonate of soda, salt, ginger, cinnamon and cloves together. Set aside.

Using an electric mixer, cream the butter with the brown sugar. Mix in the eggs, golden syrup and dates, then the flour mixture. Spread the mixture in the prepared tin. Bake for about 35 minutes or until a small skewer inserted into the centre comes out clean.

Leave to cool in the tin. Cut into 36 squares.

To make the frosting, beat together the cream cheese, butter and vanilla essence until smooth. Add the icing sugar and beat until smooth. Put the frosting in a pastry bag fitted with a star tip. Pipe a swirl of frosting on each square. Top the frosting with a piece of crystallized ginger.

the basics

VEGETABLE STOCK

3 ONIONS
1 LEEK
2 STICKS OF CELERY
6 CARROTS
1 WHOLE HEAD OF GARLIC, SLIT IN HALF
1 LEMON, SLICED
¼ TEASPOON WHITE PEPPERCORNS
1 SMALL BAY LEAF
4 STAR ANISE
SPRIG EACH OF TARRAGON, BASIL, CORIANDER, THYME,
   PARSLEY AND CHERVIL
200 ML/7 FL OZ DRY WHITE WINE

Makes 1.5 litres/2½ pints
Put all the ingredients, except the herbs and wine, into a
stockpot with 2 litres/3½ pints cold water. Bring to the boil,
then simmer gently for 10 minutes.

   Remove from the heat, add the herbs and wine and leave
to infuse until cool.

   Chill in the refrigerator for 24 hours, with all the
vegetables, then strain through a muslin-lined sieve into a large
bowl before use.

CHICKEN STOCK

675 G/1½ LB CHICKEN WINGS, OR 1 CHICKEN CARCASS
1 LARGE ONION, QUARTERED
2 LEEKS, ROUGHLY CHOPPED
2 CARROTS, ROUGHLY CHOPPED
2 STICKS OF CELERY, ROUGHLY CHOPPED
1 BAY LEAF
½ TABLESPOON SEA SALT
12 BLACK PEPPERCORNS

Makes 900 ml/1½ pints
Put all the ingredients into a pressure cooker or deep saucepan.
Add 1 litre/2¼ pints water. Bring slowly to the boil, then cook
for 1 hour under pressure, or 3 hours in an ordinary pan. Strain
and cool, then chill overnight.

   The next day, remove all fat from the surface.

FISH STOCK

1 KG/2¼ LB FISH BONES – NOT FROM OILY FISH
1 ONION, CHOPPED
1 STICK OF CELERY, CHOPPED
2 SMALL CARROTS, CHOPPED
25 G/1 OZ BUTTON MUSHROOMS, SLICED
1 TEASPOON CHOPPED FRESH THYME

Makes 1.2 litres/2 pints
Place the fish bones in a large saucepan with 2.3 litres/4 pints

water, bring to the boil and simmer gently for 20 minutes.
Strain through a muslin-lined sieve into a clean pan, add the
vegetables and thyme and bring back to the boil. Simmer for
35 minutes, and strain once more.

STUFFING A SMALL BIRD UNDER THE SKIN

Cut off the bird's head, wingtips and feet. Slit the skin at the
back of the neck, pull it free from the neck and loosen the
trachea and oesophagus from the skin. Using poultry shears,
split along the back, from tail to neck, and remove the neck.
Discard any innards. Open out the bird, inside facing down,
and press hard on the breast with the heel of your hand to
rupture the breastbone and ribcage.

   Using your index and middle fingers, reach through the
neck opening to separate the breast skin from the flesh.
Introduce the stuffing, a teaspoonful at a time, moulding the
surface with your other hand. Fold the neck skin over the back
to close the opening. With the tip of a knife, make a slit in the
abdominal skin between the legs. Draw the legs up over the
lower breast and tuck through the slit to pull the bird together
in a neat, rounded form.

PREPARING WILD MUSHROOMS

Never leave mushrooms to soak. Simply wipe with a damp
cloth, or brush or scrape away any dirt. Cut away any spongy
or rotten parts. Larger mushrooms such as ceps need to have
their stems peeled. If you do have to wash mushrooms, drop
them gently into a bowl of cold salted water and immediately
lift them out again. This will get rid of the dirt and free them
of any strands of vegetation. Gently dry them in a colander.
Morels, with their honeycombed caps, need to be well washed.

   When cooking wild mushrooms, those with a high water
content will first need to be 'blanched'. Heat a little olive oil in
a frying pan until very hot, throw in the mushrooms, leave
them for 1 minute, then toss them in the pan and drain in a
colander over a bowl to collect the liquid. This is a kind of
mushroom stock, and is very good in soups, sauces and risottos.
Some mushrooms, such as morels and the smaller ceps, are best
cooked from raw, and their juices reduced with the
mushrooms themselves.

PREPARING ARTICHOKES

Artichokes discolour readily. To prevent this, rub them
frequently with a halved lemon while you are preparing them,
and have ready a bowl of cold water into which you have
squeezed the other half of the lemon, adding the squeezed
lemon half to the water.

   Snap off the stalks and slice off the top 4 cm/1½ inches of
leaves, using a serrated knife. Pull off the outer layers of leaves,
then trim the base and stalk with a sharp knife. As you prepare

the artichokes, drop them into the bowl of lemon water.

For artichoke hearts, take the artichokes out of the water one at a time and remove the dark, outer leaves until you reach the tender, yellowish green inner leaves. Cut off one- to two-thirds from the top of the artichoke, leaving about 2.5 cm/1 inch of leaves above the base. With a small knife, trim the base and pare away the remaining tough, dark green outer leaves to expose the tightly packed central leaves that conceal the hairy choke. Scoop out the raw choke with a teaspoon and replace in the lemon water until ready to cook.

CHOOSING FRESH FISH

The eyes should be bright with no red flushes, the skin should be bright, the gills should be a fresh pink or red, not brown. The smell should be welcoming, not fishy. If choosing fillets they should be white, not yellowing. Use the freshest-looking fish on the slab as a yardstick to judge the others.

Ask your fishmonger to prepare the fish, but remember to ask for the bones to make a good, simple fish stock. It is worth asking the fishmonger to scale the fish, as scales tend to fly all over the kitchen. You should check that all the scales have been removed, by scraping from the tail to the head with a blunt knife, holding the fish under running cold water.

ROUILLE

50 G/2 OZ DAY-OLD WHITE BREAD, CRUSTS REMOVED
6 TABLESPOONS MILK
¼ TEASPOON SAFFRON STRANDS
1 TABLESPOON FISH STOCK, HOT
3 RED CHILLIES, FRESH OR DRIED, SPLIT, SEEDED AND CHOPPED
3 GARLIC CLOVES, FINELY CHOPPED
¼ TEASPOON SEA SALT
4 TABLESPOONS EXTRA VIRGIN OLIVE OIL
2 TABLESPOONS FISH SOUP (PAGE 16)

Soak the bread in the milk for 10 minutes, then squeeze dry. Warm the saffron in a metal spoon over a low heat for about 30 seconds, then pound it in a mortar. Pour over the hot fish stock and leave to infuse. Pound the chillies, garlic and salt in a mortar, then add the soaked bread and continue pounding. When all is amalgamated, start to pour in the olive oil very slowly, as if making mayonnaise, continuing to pound until all is blended. Finally, stir in 2 tablespoons of fish soup. Serve the rouille spread on bread croütons, with the fish soup, or separately, in a small bowl.

CHERVIL DUMPLINGS

40 G/1½ OZ BUTTER, SOFTENED
1 EGG, BEATEN
PINCH OF SALT
50 G/2 OZ SOFT WHITE BREADCRUMBS
2 TABLESPOONS FINELY CHOPPED CHERVIL

Beat the softened butter with a wooden spoon, then gradually add the beaten egg, beating constantly. Add the salt, breadcrumbs and chopped chervil, beating until thoroughly blended. Cover and leave for 30 minutes.

Form the mixture into tiny balls, not much bigger than your thumbnail; you should make about 18 dumplings. Drop them into a wide pan of lightly salted simmering water and cook gently for 5 minutes. Have the hot soup already in bowls, then put 2–3 dumplings into each bowl.

SALSA FRESCA

4 RIPE TOMATOES, CUT INTO CHUNKS
1 LARGE GARLIC CLOVE, FINELY CHOPPED
1 FRESH RED CHILLI, SEEDED AND FINELY CHOPPED
1½ TABLESPOONS FRESH LIME JUICE
1½ TABLESPOONS CHOPPED FRESH CORIANDER

Put the tomato chunks into a food processor with the garlic and chilli. Process to a rough purée, then add the lime juice and coriander and process again briefly so you have a slightly smoother purée.

VINAIGRETTE

(French dressing)
250 ML/8 FL OZ OLIVE OR SUNFLOWER OIL
4 TABLESPOONS WINE VINEGAR, OR LEMON OR LIME JUICE
1–2 TEASPOONS SALT
½ TEASPOON FRESHLY GROUND BLACK PEPPER

Makes about 300 ml/½ pint
Place all the ingredients in a screw-topped jar and shake vigorously until emulsified and slightly thickened.

Larger quantities of vinaigrette can be made in a food processor. However, this should be done with care, as the vinaigrette can very easily become too thick, like mayonnaise.

Different combinations of oils and vinegars can be used as the basis for vinaigrette. Choose from oils such as soya bean, peanut, almond, hazelnut, walnut and sesame, and vinegars including cider, sherry, balsamic and those flavoured with herbs and fruit. Whichever you choose, remember to taste the dressing and adjust the proportions if necessary: it should be well balanced and delicate, to complement the food and not mask or overpower it. When using strongly flavoured oils such as sesame or walnut, use only a small amount and make up the volume with a blander-flavoured oil such as sunflower or corn.

Other ingredients such as mustard, garlic, herbs and spices can be added to this basic vinaigrette to give it individuality.

SESAME AND GINGER VINAIGRETTE

1 TABLESPOON FINELY CHOPPED PICKLED GINGER
4 TABLESPOONS RICE WINE VINEGAR
4 TABLESPOONS DARK SOY SAUCE
2 TEASPOONS CHILLI SAUCE
4 TABLESPOONS SESAME OIL
6 TABLESPOONS SUNFLOWER OIL

This vinaigrette has a slight piquancy, and makes a pleasant alternative to the usual salad dressing. Place all the ingredients in a small bowl and whisk together.

The vinaigrette can be stored in an airtight container in the refrigerator for up to 1 week. Whisk again before serving.

MAYONNAISE

2 EGG YOLKS
½ TEASPOON ENGLISH MUSTARD POWDER
300 ML/10 FL OZ OLIVE OR SUNFLOWER OIL
1–2 TABLESPOONS LEMON JUICE OR WINE VINEGAR
SALT
PINCH OF WHITE PEPPER

Makes about 300 ml/½ pint
Put the egg yolks and mustard in a bowl and beat with a whisk – preferably electric – for 1–2 minutes or until pale and thick.

Begin adding the oil, drop by drop at first, whisking constantly so that the oil is absorbed. After a while the oil can be added in a thin steady stream – keep whisking as you add the oil.

When all the oil has been added and the mixture is very thick, taste and adjust the flavour with lemon juice or vinegar, salt and pepper. If it is too thick, stir in a little extra lemon juice or vinegar, or add a little warm water amd stir gently until well incorporated.

Mayonnaise is really at its best when it is freshly made, but if you have some left over, it can be covered and stored in the refrigerator for up to 3–4 days.

HARISSA

50 G/2 OZ DRIED RED CHILLIES
2 GARLIC CLOVES, PEELED
SALT
OLIVE OIL

Soak the chillies in hot water for 1 hour.

Drain the chillies and cut into small pieces. Place in a mortar with the garlic and pound to form a coarse purée.

Sprinkle with a little salt, then transfer to a small, sterilized jar and cover with a layer of olive oil. The harissa keeps very well and can be stored in the refrigerator for as long as 2–3 months.

CURRY MIX

3 TABLESPOONS CORIANDER SEEDS
8 GREEN CARDAMOM PODS, CRUSHED AND BITS OF PODS REMOVED
1 BLACK CARDAMOM POD, CRUSHED AND BITS OF POD REMOVED
1 TEASPOON CUMIN SEEDS
1 TEASPOON FENUGREEK SEEDS
2 WHOLE CLOVES
2 TABLESPOONS WHITE MUSTARD SEEDS
1 TEASPOON WHITE PEPPERCORNS
2 TABLESPOONS TURMERIC
1 BAY LEAF
¼ TEASPOON DRIED HOT PEPPER FLAKES
¼ TEASPOON DRIED GARLIC OR GARLIC POWDER

Put the coriander seeds, cardamom seeds, cumin seeds, fenugreek seeds, cloves, mustard seeds and peppercorns in a small frying pan and heat gently for 5 minutes, stirring constantly until the spices are very aromatic.

Remove from the heat and add all remaining ingredients.

Work the mixture to a powder in a spice mill, coffee grinder or mortar and pestle. Store in an airtight jar.

CHAMBÉRY AND SORREL SAUCE

300 ML/½ PINT FISH STOCK (PAGE 29)
75 ML/3 FL OZ DOUBLE CREAM
2 TABLESPOONS CHAMBÉRY DRY VERMOUTH
15 G/½ OZ FRESH SORREL LEAVES
40 G/1½ OZ UNSALTED BUTTER
1 TEASPOON FRESH LEMON JUICE
SALT

Place the fish stock, half the cream and the vermouth in a saucepan. Bring to the boil and boil rapidly until reduced to about 100 ml/3½ fl oz. Meanwhile, wash and remove the stalks from the sorrel, then slice the leaves very thinly.

Just before serving, add the remaining cream, butter and lemon juice to the reduced sauce and boil for about 1 minute, to reduce a little more. Stir in the shredded sorrel and serve at once.

This sauce is a particularly good accompaniment to various fish dishes.

BÉCHAMEL SAUCE

50 G/2 OZ BUTTER
50 G/2 OZ PLAIN WHITE FLOUR
500 ML/16 FL OZ MILK
SALT AND FRESHLY GROUND PEPPER

Makes 500 ml/16 fl oz
Melt the butter in a saucepan until foaming, then stir in the flour until a thick paste is formed. Pour in all the milk and whisk vigorously to prevent lumps from forming. Simmer gently until thickened and no flavour of raw flour can be tasted in the sauce. Season to taste.

SAUSAGE STUFFING

3 TABLESPOONS BUTTER
2 LARGE ONIONS, CHOPPED
225 G/8 OZ WHITE RICE
1 LITRE/1¾ PINTS HOT CHICKEN STOCK
900 G/2 LB SPICY ITALIAN SAUSAGES
6 WHOLE GARLIC CLOVES
2–4 TABLESPOONS OLIVE OIL
1 LARGE GREEN PEPPER, DICED
1 LARGE RED PEPPER, DICED
225 G/8 OZ MUSHROOMS, SLICED
SPLASH OF MADEIRA OR PORT
25–40 G/1–1½ OZ FRESH FLAT LEAF PARSLEY, CHOPPED
1–2 TABLESPOONS CHOPPED FRESH SAGE
2 TEASPOONS FRESH MARJORAM
50 G/2 OZ PINE NUTS, TOASTED
SALT AND FRESHLY GROUND PEPPER
675 G/1½ LB MOZZARELLA CHEESE, CUBED

Makes enough for a 6–6.4 kg/12–14 lb turkey, plus an extra side dish
Preheat the oven to 190°C/375°F/ Gas Mark 5. In a heavy-based casserole, melt the butter and sauté one of the onions until soft and translucent. Add the rice and continue to sauté until the rice is translucent. Stir in the hot chicken stock and bring to the boil.

Cover the casserole and place in the oven for about 20 minutes, or until the rice is just tender. Remove from the oven and leave to cool slightly.

Meanwhile, place the sausages and garlic in a saucepan with just enough cold water to cover. Bring to the boil, then reduce the heat and simmer for about 20 minutes or until the sausages are cooked. Drain, discarding the water and garlic. Slice the sausages and sauté in a frying pan with a little olive oil, until brown. Drain the sausages on paper towels, then transfer to a large bowl.

In the same frying pan, sauté the remaining onion until soft and translucent. Add the peppers and sauté until tender. Add to the bowl with the sausages.

In the same frying pan, adding more oil if necessary, sauté the mushrooms over high heat until they squeak. Drizzle the madeira or port over the mushrooms and boil for a few minutes, then add to the sausage mixture.

Chop the herbs together and mix into the rice, together with the pine nuts. Combine the herbed rice with the vegetable and sausage mixture. Mix well, taste and adjust the seasoning if required. Leave to cool to room temperature or chill in the refrigerator.

Just before stuffing the turkey, add the cubed mozzarella. Spoon into the turkey cavities, being careful not to overfill them.

Place the remaining stuffing in a casserole and bake at 180°C/ 350°F/Gas Mark 4 for 30–40 minutes (while the turkey is resting) or until hot through and brown on top.

PEANUT SAMBAL

1 ONION OR 6 SHALLOTS, GRATED
2 GARLIC CLOVES, CRUSHED
3 CANDLENUTS OR MACADAMIA NUTS, CRUSHED
2 STALKS OF LEMONGRASS, WHITE PART ONLY, FLATTENED
2 DRIED RED CHILLIES, SOAKED, DRAINED AND CHOPPED
4 TABLESPOONS PEANUT OIL
1 TEASPOON GROUND CORIANDER
1 TEASPOON GROUND TURMERIC
375 ML/12 FL OZ COCONUT MILK
1 TEASPOON TAMARIND SOAKED IN 3 TABLESPOONS WATER
1 TABLESPOON SUGAR
1 TEASPOON SALT
125 G/4 OZ PEANUTS, ROUGHLY CHOPPED

Pound or blend together the onion, garlic, candlenuts or macadamias, lemongrass and chillies to form a paste.

Heat the oil in a wok or saucepan over a low heat, and cook the prepared paste for a few minutes, until it smells fragrant.

Stir in the coriander and turmeric. Add the coconut milk and heat gently, stirring. Add the tamarind water, sugar, salt and peanuts and simmer for 2 minutes. Leave to cool to room temperature before serving.

This can be made in advance and frozen until such time as it is required.

SWEET CHILLI SAUCE

2 TABLESPOONS SUGAR
1 GARLIC CLOVE, CRUSHED
2 TABLESPOONS FISH SAUCE
2 TABLESPOONS FRESH LIME OR LEMON JUICE
1 SMALL FRESH RED CHILLI, SLICED
1 TABLESPOON WHITE WINE VINEGAR OR RICE VINEGAR
1 SLICE OF LIME OR LEMON

Dissolve the sugar in 2 tablespoons boiling water.

Stir in the crushed garlic, fish sauce, lime or lemon juice, chilli and vinegar. Cut the slice of lime or lemon into tiny little wedges and float these on top of the sauce. They will look attractive as well as adding flavour.

SPICY DIPPING SAUCE

1 TABLESPOON RICE WINE VINEGAR
1 TABLESPOON SUGAR
1½–3 TABLESPOONS CHILLI SAUCE
2 TEASPOONS FINELY CHOPPED GARLIC
1 TEASPOON WHITE PEPPER
3 TABLESPOONS WORCESTERSHIRE SAUCE
100 ML/3½ FL OZ FRESH ORANGE JUICE
½ TEASPOON SALT
3 SPRING ONIONS, FINELY SLICED

Place all the ingredients in a small bowl and whisk them together with a fork.

This should be quite a hot sauce, because only tiny amounts are used as a dip. But since chilli sauce varies quite widely in its 'heat', it is better not to put the whole quantity in at once – you can always add more, according to your own taste.

It can be stored in an airtight container in the refrigerator for up to 1 week.

CUCUMBER SAUCE

1 SMALL CUCUMBER (ABOUT 85 G/3 OZ), VERY FINELY DICED
1½ TABLESPOONS VERY FINELY CHOPPED SPRING ONION
1 SMALL RED CHILLI, SEEDED AND VERY FINELY CHOPPED
85 ML/3 FL OZ WHITE VINEGAR
85 ML/3 FL OZ WATER
65 G/2½ OZ SUGAR
2 GARLIC CLOVES, SLICED
2–3 SLICES OF FRESH GINGER
PINCH OF SALT

Place the cucumber, spring onion and chilli in a glass or stainless steel bowl. In a small saucepan, boil the remaining ingredients for 2–3 minutes. Remove from the heat and leave to cool to room temperature, then strain over the cucumber mixture, discarding the garlic and ginger.

The sauce will keep for 4–5 days in the refrigerator.

SPICED PEANUT SAUCE

5 TABLESPOONS CRUNCHY PEANUT BUTTER
85 ML/3 FL OZ COCONUT CREAM
125 ML/4 FL OZ WATER
½–1 TEASPOON CHILLI SAUCE OR CHILLI PASTE
1 TABLESPOON THAI FISH SAUCE OR LIGHT SOY SAUCE
½ TEASPOON THAI RED CURRY PASTE OR 1 TEASPOON MILD CURRY POWDER
¾ TEASPOON PALM SUGAR OR SOFT BROWN SUGAR
SALT AND PEPPER

Place all the ingredients in a small saucepan and stir over medium heat until thickened. Season to taste with salt and pepper.

RED CURRY PASTE

10 DRIED RED CHILLIES, SOAKED FOR 20 MINUTES
6 GARLIC CLOVES
1 LEMON GRASS STALK, CHOPPED
2 SPRING ONIONS (WHITE PARTS), CHOPPED
2 CORIANDER SPRIGS (STEMS AND ROOTS ONLY), CHOPPED
1 TABLESPOON CHOPPED GALANGAL OR FRESH GINGER
1 TEASPOON GRATED LIME ZEST
1 TEASPOON PEPPERCORNS
½ TEASPOON GROUND CUMIN
1 TEASPOON SALT
1 TEASPOON SHRIMP PASTE
2–3 TABLESPOONS VEGETABLE OR PEANUT OIL

Makes the equivalent of 8 teaspoons of commercial red curry paste
Grind all the ingredients together in a food processor, blender or spice grinder, to form a reasonably smooth paste.

If you wish to keep the paste for more than 3 days, fry in a nonstick pan for about 6 minutes over medium heat, stirring frequently. Cool and store in a covered glass jar.

TOMATO SAUCE

2 TABLESPOONS OLIVE OIL
1 LEEK, DICED
1.5 KG/3 LB VERY RIPE PLUM TOMATOES, OR
2 X 400 G/14 OZ CANS PLUM TOMATOES
1 TEASPOON SUGAR
1 TEASPOON SALT
½ TEASPOON FRESHLY GROUND BLACK PEPPER

Makes about 750 ml/1¼ pints
Heat a large frying pan, add the oil and leek and sauté for about 5 minutes or until the leek softens.

If using fresh tomatoes, dice them without peeling; if using canned tomatoes, crush them together with their juice. Add the tomatoes and juice to the frying pan, with the sugar, salt and pepper. Bring to the boil over high heat, stir well, then simmer over low heat, uncovered, for 30–45 minutes or until the sauce has reduced by half.

The sauce can be stored in the refrigerator for 1 week or frozen for up to 6 months.

BRAISED WHITE BEANS

225 G/8 OZ DRIED WHITE BEANS
500 ML/16 FL OZ WATER
1 BAY LEAF
⅛ TEASPOON FRESHLY GROUND BLACK PEPPER
1 CARROT, CUT IN HALF
1 LARGE ONION, QUARTERED
2 GARLIC CLOVES
A FEW SPRIGS OF PARSLEY AND THYME (OR ½ TEASPOON
   DRIED THYME), TIED IN A PIECE OF MUSLIN
1 TEASPOON SALT

Makes about 600 ml/1 pint
Wash the beans, then leave to soak for 6–8 hours or overnight.

Pour off the water and place the soaked beans in a saucepan with a tight-fitting lid. Add the measured water, bay leaf, pepper, carrot, onion, garlic and parsley and thyme in the muslin.

Cover the pan, bring to the boil over high heat, then simmer gently for 1 hour. Add the salt during the last 15 minutes of cooking time.

Remove the herbs and vegetables and serve the beans hot or at room temperature.

QUICK PUFF PASTRY

This pastry will rise about 30% less than classic puff pastry, but it is much easier to prepare.

500 G/1 LB 2 OZ FLOUR, PLUS EXTRA FOR TURNING
500 G/1 LB 2 OZ FIRM BUTTER, CUT INTO CUBES (TAKE OUT
   OF THE REFRIGERATOR 1 HOUR BEFORE USING)
1 TEASPOON SALT
250 ML/8 FL OZ ICED WATER

Makes 1.2 kg/2¾ lb
Put the flour on to the work surface or into a bowl, and make a well in the centre. Add the butter and salt to the well. Work the ingredients together using the fingertips of your right hand, gradually drawing in the flour with your left hand.

When the mixture resembles breadcrumbs, pour in the iced water and gradually work it into the pastry, without kneading. When the pastry comes together to form a dough, but still contains small flakes of butter, roll it out on a lightly floured surface, rolling away from you, to form a 40 x 20 cm/16 x 8 inch rectangle.

Fold in the ends, as if folding a letter, to make three equal layers. Turn the pastry through 90 degrees and repeat the rolling process. These are the first two turns. Wrap the pastry in clingfilm and chill in the refrigerator for 30 minutes.

After 30 minutes, take it out of the refrigerator and roll out again, making two more turns. The pastry is now ready. Roll to the required shape, place on a dampened baking sheet and refrigerate for 20 minutes before use.

Alternatively the pastry can be wrapped in clingfilm and stored in the refrigerator.

CRÊPES

Use a small crêpe pan, 12 cm/5 inches in diameter

1 SLIGHTLY MOUNDED TABLESPOON FLOUR
PINCH OF SALT
1 EGG
85 ML/3 FL OZ MILK
1 TABLESPOON COGNAC
15 G/½ OZ UNSALTED BUTTER, MELTED IN THE CRÊPE PAN

Sift the flour and salt into a bowl, add the egg and whisk from the centre outwards, gradually adding most of the milk, until all the flour is absorbed.

Whisk in the brandy and melted butter. Add more milk if necessary to bring the batter to the consistency of double cream.

Wipe the crêpe pan with a paper towel to leave only a film of butter, and place it over medium to low heat. Remove the pan from the heat and rotate it as you pour in just enough batter from a small ladle to coat the bottom of the pan. The batter should sizzle on contact.

Return the pan to the heat. When the edges of the crêpe turn golden and curl up, slip a round-tipped knife beneath to flip it over. After a few seconds, slip the crêpe from the pan, using your fingertips.

Remove the pan from the heat for a few seconds between each crêpe to prevent it from becoming overheated, and give the batter a stir each time before ladling it out. The first side cooked is always the most evenly coloured and should be presented as the outside of a rolled crêpe. Stack the crêpes on a plate as they are finished.

A one-egg batter will produce more than enough crêpes for two. Cover the others with clingfilm and refrigerate for future use. If their congealed butter makes them stick together, warm the plate in a cool oven or over steam.

PASTRY CREAM

6 EGG YOLKS
125 G/4 OZ CASTER SUGAR
40 G/1½ OZ FLOUR
500 ML/16 FL OZ MILK
1 VANILLA POD, SPLIT
A LITTLE BUTTER OR ICING SUGAR

For coffee or chocolate pastry cream, omit the vanilla pod and use a little instant coffee or cocoa powder, to taste. If using cocoa powder, use a little less flour and a little extra sugar.

Makes about 750 g/1 lb 10 oz
In a large bowl, whisk the egg yolks with about one-third of the caster sugar until pale and thick (a light ribbon consistency).

Sift the flour over the mixture and mix in thoroughly.

Bring the milk to the boil with the remaining sugar and the vanilla pod. As soon as it begins to bubble, pour one-third into the egg mixture, stirring all the time.

Pour back into the saucepan and bring to the boil over a very low heat, stirring all the time. Allow to bubble for 2 minutes, then pour the pastry cream into a bowl. To prevent a skin from forming, dot with a few flakes of butter or dust lightly with icing sugar.

Pastry cream can be stored in the refrigerator for 36 hours.

CHOUX PASTE

This pastry will rise about 30% less than classic puff pastry, but it is much easier to prepare.

125 ML/4 FL OZ WATER
125 ML/4 FL OZ MILK
100 G/3½ OZ BUTTER, FINELY DICED
½ TEASPOON FINE SALT
¼ TEASPOON SUGAR
150 G/5 OZ FLOUR, SIFTED
4 EGGS
EGGWASH (1 EGG YOLK MIXED WITH 2 TEASPOONS MILK AND A PINCH OF SALT) – OPTIONAL

Makes 22–25 small choux puffs or éclairs
Put the water, milk, butter, salt and sugar into a saucepan and boil over a high heat for 1 minute. Make sure that the mixture is well combined and then remove from the heat. Add the flour at once, stirring with a wooden spoon to make a smooth paste.

Return the pan to the heat and stir for 1 minute. Be careful not to let the paste dry too much or it will crack during the cooking process.

Transfer the paste to a bowl and beat in the eggs, one at a time. Beat the paste until very smooth.

If the pastry is not to be used straight away, spread a little eggwash over the surface of the paste to prevent a crust from forming.

Prepared choux paste can be stored in an airtight container in the refrigerator for up to 3 days, or in the freezer for up to 1 week.

VELVET BUTTERCREAM

25 G/1 OZ CORNFLOUR
225 G/8 OZ CASTER SUGAR
375 ML/12 FL OZ HOT MILK
325 G/12 OZ UNSALTED BUTTER, AT ROOM TEMPERATURE
1½ TEASPOONS VANILLA ESSENCE
2 TABLESPOONS GRAND MARNIER OR COINTREAU

For a 22 cm/9 inch layer cake
In a saucepan, blend the cornflour with 85 g/3 oz of the sugar and 2 tablespoons of the hot milk. Mix until smooth. Stir in the remaining milk.

Bring to the boil over low heat, stirring constantly with a whisk. Cook for 1 minute. Pour through a fine sieve and leave to cool to tepid.

Using an electric mixer, cream the butter for 1 minute. Add the remaining sugar, 1 tablespoon at a time, and beat until the mixture lightens in colour. Reduce the speed and add the tepid sauce, 1 tablespoon at a time. Mix in the vanilla and Grand Marnier.

RASPBERRY VELVET BUTTERCREAM

325 G/12 OZ FROZEN RASPBERRIES, PARTIALLY THAWED
85 G/3 OZ SUGAR
VELVET BUTTERCREAM (OMIT GRAND MARNIER)
2 TABLESPOONS CREME DE FRAMBOISE (RASPBERRY LIQUEUR)

For a 22 cm/9 inch layer cake
Place the raspberries and sugar in a saucepan. Bring to the boil and cook, uncovered, until very thick, about 12–15 minutes. Press the raspberries through a fine sieve to remove the seeds. Leave to cool before using.

Using an electric mixer and working on low speed, add the raspberry purée to the buttercream. Flavour with a little raspberry liqueur.

FUDGE-NUT CANDY ICING

125 G/4 OZ + 2 TABLESPOONS UNSALTED BUTTER
175 G/6 OZ GOOD-QUALITY PLAIN CHOCOLATE, CHOPPED
175 G/6 OZ DARK BROWN SUGAR
2 TABLESPOONS LIGHT CORN SYRUP (LIQUID GLUCOSE)
¼ TEASPOON SALT
2 TEASPOONS INSTANT ESPRESSO COFFEE POWDER
125 ML/4 FL OZ BOILING WATER
300 G/11 OZ ICING SUGAR, SIFTED
1½ TEASPOONS VANILLA ESSENCE
1 TEASPOON LEMON JUICE
125 G/4 OZ TOASTED WALNUTS, ROUGHLY CHOPPED

For a 22 cm/9 inch layer cake
Place 125 g/4 oz butter, the chocolate, brown sugar, corn syrup (liquid glucose) and salt in a large saucepan. Dissolve the coffee powder in the water and add to the saucepan. Slowly bring to the boil, then simmer for 3 minutes, stirring occasionally.

Remove from the heat and whisk in the icing sugar in three additions. Stir in the vanilla and lemon juice. Add the remaining butter and beat until smooth and shiny. Stir in the walnuts. Set the pan in a bowl of ice-cold water; stir until thickened, but still warm. If the icing becomes too stiff to spread, reheat.

MELTING CHOCOLATE

It is important to melt chocolate evenly so that the resulting texture is smooth, without lumps. To help chocolate melt evenly, chop the chocolate roughly into about 1 cm/1/2 inch pieces. Put the chopped chocolate in a clean, dry double boiler or a bowl placed over a saucepan of hot, not boiling, water. Stir the chocolate often, using a dry spoon, until it is melted and smooth.

Alternatively, chocolate can be melted in a microwave oven. Place the chopped chocolate in a small, clean, dry bowl and heat at 100%. At 30-second intervals, remove the bowl from the oven and gently stir the chocolate with a clean, dry spoon. (Timings vary depending on the quantity of chocolate used and the power of the oven.)

CHOCOLATE SHAVINGS

Place a 50 g/2 oz block of good-quality plain chocolate in a bowl in a microwave oven. Microwave for 10 seconds on defrost.

Turn the chocolate over and microwave for a further 10 seconds. Put the chocolate on a cutting board. Using a sharp 20 cm/8 inch knife, cut the chocolate into thin shavings.

index